SHOPPING WITH MAMA

Write 'Til The End

Marion OMalley

This book is dedicated to my mother,
Wilhelmena Katherine Fuller Webb,
and to my father, Henry Bond Webb (aka Mack),
whose steadfast examples of the writing-life inspired me to report on
the universe and give my thoughts life on paper.

CONTENTS

Preface

Sharing tales of those we've lost is how we keep from really losing them. —Mitch Albom

Now, I am alone without you, juggling hundreds of pieces of writing: yours and mine, and thousands upon thousands of memories. Would you have appreciated my choices in these stories? Would you have been irate with me for all eternity for telling *my* truth, or forgiven me for revealing your demons, showing you sometimes in a less-than-flattering light? Am I misrepresenting you? Yet, aren't we all a fascinating mixture of good and bad, strength and weakness? In the end, don't we all invent our memories?

I think you would have wanted me to share these memories. I am writing about you just as you always asked me to and just as I promised I would. This is my version of events, my version of you in the last decade of your very long and vibrant life.

I am spurred on by Iyanla Vanzant's words: *"When you stand and share your story in an empowering way, your story will heal you, and your story will heal somebody else."*

I love you, Mama. Come on down and "haunt" me. Any way you want to do it, rattle my earthly chain. I miss you.
Marion

Introduction

No genuine book has a first page. It is begotten God knows where.
—Boris Pasternak

The older Mama got, the more she told me she wanted me to write about her. She wanted to leave a legacy. Plus, she didn't want to leave the party. Any way she could, she wanted to stick around.

Mama wrote and published her last book when she was ninety-two. She had a fifth book in mind when she finally slipped away on May 23, 2012, at age ninety-seven.

Writing mattered in our house. It was a noble thing, an adventure: to live by your wits, by the powers of your observation, then put it in print to tell a story. Both my parents wrote for a living; my father was a newspaperman, and my mother a novelist, biographer, and historian. Revealing the way you saw life had value. Writing was considered a brave act.

Whether investigative journalism—my father rode around in the back of cop cars in the middle of the night for a story—history, biography, or a novel, I always heard from Mama: "Go write about it, Marion. Write it down."

ABC's counted. Stringing letters into words and sentences counted more. I got my first diary, complete with lock and key, in the fifth grade.

Because of Mama's encouragement, I accumulated boxes and boxes full of notebooks and napkins and scraps of paper with dribblings and dashed-off tidbits about what was going on during every phase of my own life. I even had that first diary.

"There's *gold* in those boxes, Marion," Mama would say over and over. "Wait five or ten years. Get a little distance from it. Then pull it out. Pure gold." Her prospector eyes gleamed.

Mama could turn a phrase.

"I'm whickery as a nanny shad," she said over and over again. This phrase became famous in our family.

For those of you who don't know, a nanny shad swims upstream to lay her eggs and is therefore exhausted and may not know exactly where she is at any given moment—i.e., "whickery." Many years later, my son, her grandson, Tom Krueger, wrote a song with that name for her birthday.

"Whickery as a Nanny Shad."

I saw my physician, the other day
'Cause I had a suspicion, I had a malaise
I said "Please, dear Doctor, don't pull out the rug."
He said, "Don't worry, honey; all you need is a hug.

It ain't epizootics
Or the East Asian rag
You're just whickery
Like a nanny shad."[1]

Whickery or not, Mama could make history come alive for her readers. All those "who did what, when, and where in the past" things fascinated her, and in her hands, they became fascinating for others, too, because she focused on the people involved. With a novelist's eye, she was a fool for detail.

Mama's first book was about a Southern woman about to be named "Woman of the Year," but who is also having an affair with her husband's brother. The title, *The Curious Wine*, she'd taken from an Emily Dickinson poem:

> *I had been hungry all the years*
> *My noon had come, to dine;*
> *I, trembling, drew the table near*
> *And touched the curious wine.*

---

[1] See complete lyrics in "Afterword" at the book's end.

I badgered her about that old chestnut—writing what you know: Did she or didn't she? She always said, "None of your business, Marion."

Surely not with only Uncle Tom or Uncle Jim to choose from, I concluded.

Her second book began when her writing teacher, Manley Wade Wellman, told her there was no good book written about the man who lived down the street from her, Julian Shakespeare Carr, on whose mighty lap she sat when she was a tiny girl, as he spun his yarns in a commanding voice.

Mama turned that book, *Jule Carr: General Without an Army,* into an account of this idiosyncratic founder of the city of Durham, North Carolina, and the man after whom the nearby town of Carrboro is named. We are increasingly aware that our history, like us, is unique, complex, and incomplete, rarely unbiased, as recently Jule Carr has also been revealed as the personified affirmation of our sad history of white supremacy here in central North Carolina. But Mama knew him as a neighborhood girl, and chronicles his life as a notable white person of her time and station.

Her book of reflections on times past in Durham—she spent nearly a century there—*The Way We Were: Remembering Durham,* started as a compilation of bimonthly articles written for the local newspaper, *The Herald Sun*. My father, Mack Webb, had been the editor there, though not at the time Mama published. Short and informative, the articles are full of not only Durham history, but also of my mother. Many people still turn to this book when they want to get a taste of how Durham was in its formative years, and how it changed in the twentieth century.

Mama's final book, though lighter and perhaps not as prestigious, is my personal favorite: a series of random essays and stories called *Out of My Mind*—a title with a bit of intentional ambiguity, I imagine, as she pulled the stories out of her mind and, being in her tenth decade, thought she might well be losing some of her mental powers. "I've always been good at titles," she would say, just stating fact.

The book in your hands comes closest to that one. It's not a history or biography in any way, as the act of remembering inevitably involves neglecting and forgetting, too. I do not write about Mama primarily as the writer or the historian or the author, though because those things are as much a part of her as is her skin, they do show up. I write about Wilhelmena Katherine Fuller Webb from the perspective of a daughter of seventy years through my close-up, tainted, critical, admiring eyes. This is a book about us growing old together. And maybe growing up. It's a book about the main thing we shared: our love of writing.

§

For the last decade of her life, Mama in her nineties and I in my sixties, I went *Shopping with Mama* every Thursday afternoon. Soon endless doctor appointments became the norm. I evolved into Mama's caregiver and counselor as she and I both came to terms with the end of her life.

I would record the details of our day, maybe write them on sticky notes, sometimes right under her nose, then rush home to create a Word document while the memories were fresh. Our mutual love of words, as well as the natural tension between us—Mama with her Victorian mores and I, a child of the sixties—would be well worth preserving, I knew. Later, I would plumb them for meaning.

The details of our Thursdays would inevitably include generous servings of her unparalleled homemade vegetable soup and pimento cheese sandwiches on prairie bread, and, if I was very good, one of her famous Black Forest brownies for which she forever refused to give me the recipe. Our dates included Mama putting pink plastic rollers in her short silver hair, and dabbing on Oil of Olay face cream and Channel No. 5 or Shalimar in front of the movie star lights around her bathroom mirror as she readied herself for our outside venture. I would sit in her rose-colored lift-chair in the bedroom and wait, silently switching Fox News to MSNBC while she talked about her friends, some damn thing she had heard about the "fool guv'ment" on TV, or, more likely, a current family member's dilemma she was fretting over.

Finally decked out in her latest Talbots' outfit—Mama was a styler—she would go into the hall, put on her black leather coat and a furry scarf, select a cane from the umbrella urn, and turn off André Previn's "Like Love" or Oscar Peterson, whom Mama called Oscar Pee-

Pee-Man, part of the eclectic mix of jazz forever tinkling in the background of our lives. Then we would step out together into the cold—"Careful, careful now, Marion"—so she wouldn't fall, because everyone knew falls were what undid old people, as one finally, at age ninety-seven, undid her.

§

After she died, I "inherited" boxes of her stuff from the upstairs storage room: documents and invitations, ancient tourist club programs, dirty jokes and drafts of her writing, course notes, plus decades' worth of old letters written to her with spindly ink pens on vellum or onionskin. An historian by nature, Mama kept everything. For over a year after Mama's death I plowed through these papers, learning more about the woman who had birthed and raised me than I ever would have known without this period of research and mourning.

Though missing from my life, even in her absence, she was there. She was there in a way she was never there when old wounds and hurts and stories we told ourselves about each other were no longer in the air. Now it was only the words that connected us.

At face value, we couldn't have been more different. I was Mama's second daughter, a professional woman and barely disguised hippie who had built a house from scratch with her husband, started the Center for Peace Education in Carrboro, North Carolina and traveled the United States for twenty-five years, teaching people diversity and social-emotional learning skills.

Mama was a reputable Southern woman, a country-clubber and a consummate party girl. She was a yellow-dog Democrat turned Republican, one who believed war would always be with us and mine was a fool's errand. But more than anything, she would plead for me to "fix my hair" so that I, too, could be a reputable woman, or at least *look* like one. Appearances mattered, and in Mama's eyes, mine fell short.

§

How does one resurrect the thing that can no longer be held, touched, seen, corresponded with, and, most of all, listened to? Can words serve as replacements? Can the journals I plumbed for her words stand in for the mother I both loved and rebelled against? What secrets did they reveal? I viewed her papers as a treasure trove. For certain, this was a different kind of "shopping."

As Mother always told me, writing is both a deeply frustrating and deeply satisfying act. But in many ways, more than the actual people and places and things in our lives, writing kept us together, both as individuals and as a complicated mother-daughter duo.

Shopping with Mama: Write 'til the End is my homage to my mother, Wilhelmina Katherine Fuller Webb, whose life spanned a century in the South. It is my testimony, too, that the perspective and distance that writing can provide in anyone's life can save that life and preserve at least a contrail of that which has forever been lost. In this case, my mama.

Mama was a force. And, as she always said, wagging her finger at me when I forgot or rejected it, she was also my very best friend.

Chapter One

The Eye Appointment

Writing is seeing. It is paying attention. —Kate DiCamillo

She'd reminded me of it so many times I thought I'd go insane, snap at her like a dog if I didn't watch myself. How many times had I heard her say it? I would fail her. How many more times would there be?

Today what Mama worried about was that I wouldn't be on time, that I couldn't get up early enough to get her to Duke's Eye Clinic.

"By no later than 9:00, Marion!" she wailed, when here I was a working woman who'd been rising at dawn for the last thirty years.

Yes, now I was working a little less, controlling my destiny, piddling more, my life-long ambition. But Mama always thought of me as a teenager, and then a ragtag hippie "going with the flow" in my handmade peasant dresses, my two fat-cheeked babies in tow.

Her voice sounded tiny, and I said, "We'll be on time, Mama, don't you worry." For a minute or two she would relax. After a bowl of soup or a glass of wine together, some carefree conversation, she'd forget for an hour or so. But lately this eye appointment was always on her mind.

"Will I be able to see again? Is this Dr. Kim gonna tell me I have to learn to live with my fading eyesight? Am I going to go blind?"

Right next to that set of worries was: Will my prone-to-tardiness daughter be here for me in the way I need her to? So, to be certain, we arranged a slumber party at her house the night before.

§

Mama went to umpteen doctors. Each time it was like she was going to see the President of the United States or a monarch of a foreign country, someone who could exert a big effect on her life with a stethoscope or a blood pressure cuff. This person of infinite power would deliver a clear, cold analysis that could fill her with relief or send her spinning. She hated doctors, especially ones who were careless with old folks, foreign-born, "making all that money ordering up tests nobody really needed," arrogant, cavalier, or just plain young.

"Pip-squeaks" she called them behind their backs.

The night before the dreaded eye appointment, I got to her house about six. She opened the door, her hair in curlers, the smell of something hot and pungent coming from the kitchen.

"Oooh, don't you look nice, Marion!" she exclaimed, letting me into her inner sanctum. Brubeck tinkled from the radio. "I love that jacket, Marion. You look really nice. And your haircut! When did you get that?"

My own doctor's appointment had been that morning, the nine-month follow-up for my broken hip—inflicted when I flew over the handlebars of my bike and fractured my femoral head—but Mama didn't mention it.

"Sarah did it," I said, patting my hair and referencing my friend and neighbor in our Environmental Neighborhood who'd said she was "sick and tired of sitting across from me in the hot tub with my hair hanging down in my eyes." She had come at me with her scissors on a haircutting jihad the day before.

"God bless Say-rah," Mama said. "You tell Say-rah I truly thank her. You should always keep your hair that way, Marion." She looked me up and down. "You look better than I've seen you look in—well, ever!"

I doubted that. I was almost sixty.

"Lord, we both look like we're going to see our lovers when we go see the doctor," she said laughing.

We settled down at the kitchen table.

"I need to get my leg up," she announced. I put the pillow for her foot on the chair between us, still waiting for her to ask about my ailing hip.

"Now Marion, I've got a little slaw, and since you're on that Atkins, I made some turkey hash. You do eat meat these days, don't you?" I nodded. "I bought you some expensive curried tuna fish from Foster's too, and I thought I'd make a salad."

"I'll make the salad," I offered.

"And then we'll have a little treat afterwards." She hiked up her eyebrows.

Chocolate. I smiled. Maybe one of her world-famous brownies.

I was glad to be having a spend-the-night with my mama after so long being a grown-up in my own house. I thought of her that way now: "my mama," with a tenderness I'd never felt quite so intensely before. Like I was her baby, but she was my baby, too.

"What do you want to do? Watch CNN?" she prodded me, ever the newshound. "I'll get supper together. You go on and watch TV. Rest, baby."

Who asks you to do that when you come home at night but your very own mama?

"I think I *will* go up and put my pajamas on," I conceded. It was only 6:30, but I craved lounging in my soft flannel jammies, padding around in fuzzy yellow socks, and feeling all loose and comfortable in my mama's house.

"You just go on." She shooed me out of the kitchen.

I dragged my bags and file boxes to the upstairs bedroom, far more stuff than anyone would ever have time to look at, not to mention tackle overnight. This absurd jumble of papers and folders "just in case" I had a free moment, some tiny interlude in which I could somehow get some work done, was my security blanket and I knew it.

What I'd really be doing was talking with my mama, watching TV, reading a little in the *Tibetan Book of the Dead* I'd brought, and going to sleep pretty early too. Something about being at Mama's house made me feel my tiredness more acutely. I could give into it here.

I looked in the room where my son Tom had slept every Friday night on his "dates" with Mama before he got married, had kids of his own, and couldn't come anymore. Both beds were skinny twins with white eyelet comforters and ruffled hems brushing deep-pile carpets.

I chose the bed on the right and arranged my bags around the edges of the room; then I peeled off my clothes, ripping off the "Do Not Remove" tags on my new pajama bottoms. I looked at myself in the mirror in my new duds. Old but cute. My haircut *was* good. I slipped my feet into the yellow fuzzies and padded downstairs to tear up lettuce and chop carrots.

All through dinner, I propped my head in my hands and listened to Mama talk about this, then that: about my sister and me, about my children, about all the women in her bridge club, about the gay undertaker in her church group who had recently taken a shine to her and took her out to fancy lunches and other forays into the "new" Durham.

"Law, Marion, you should see what they've done to the Catholic Church!" she cried, delighted.

She talked about the people who had just died and the ones who were dying, about what was happening to Lib Mallard, my godmother, and Lib Lanning, who was at The Forest at Duke, Durham's swankiest old folks' home. And again, as always, how she *never* wanted to go to a nursing home, though tonight, for once, she didn't cry out, "Promise me, Marion!" like she usually did.

I thought about how it must be for her to rattle around in this house alone at night. Then I thought about my husband, Arthur, how one of us would die one of these days, and if it were he, how hard it would be to get used to being alone at night. I thought about the pleasures of my husband's body spooned against mine.

I prayed a silent prayer that tonight Mama would get some sleep, that tomorrow she could stay as much as possible in the present through this damned eye appointment and whatever happened. I saw her that night as brave and funny and mine, my mama, all too human, frail and failing, bit by bit, like the rest of us.

We didn't leave the dinner table 'til after nine. I wearily climbed the stairs and heard her opening and shutting doors from down below as I brushed my teeth and tried to relax into her pristine environs, my effects making the guest room look like Ma and Pa Kettle's. I flipped on cable and did the requisite run-through of channels I never got to see at home. But as soon as I turned back to the bed, I saw it.

"Oh God!"

The new pen I'd bought at Target and had been using to take the occasional note of Mama's always-colorful speech had leaked out a big black tarantula-like spot on the bedspread.

I ran to it, my mind racing, quickly realizing that even though I'd been leaking pens on people's furniture (mine especially) for years, I still didn't have the faintest idea how to get the ink stains out. I grabbed the bedspread and ran down the stairs, trying to remember to hold on to the railing and slow down.

"Mama!" I shouted.

"What?" Her voice came muffled from her bedroom.

"I got ink on your bedspread." I tried to sound calm but my heart was racing.

"Oh Lord, oh Lord. I'm coming, I'm coming."

Mama looked at the mess and winced. By now the fraying black spot had grown to the size of a beaten biscuit. Holding on to the walls, she pushed past me into the laundry room. "Lemme get my book." She reached for *Heloise* and handed it to me. "Look up ink."

Back under her 200-watt bulb we were directed to two different methods: One involving hairspray and blotting, the other soaking with alcohol just before washing.

She handed me her Spray Net can. No wonder I couldn't do anything about my ink-stained clothes. I would never have Spray Net in my arsenal.

"Go upstairs and try it!" she directed, flapping her hands.

I bolted up the stairs and did as she said. I sprayed. It bled. I blotted. It dimmed. I sprayed. It bled. I blotted. It faded. But the big ugly spot endured. It looked like live black coral, wriggling at the edges, smack-dab in the middle of the bedspread. It was ruined.

"How's it coming?" Mama hollered periodically, standing at the bottom of the stairs holding tight to the newel-post.

I hollered back, "I'll pay for it, Mama, I'll pay for it. We'll go to Linens-N-Things. I'll take you there."

Sheepishly I carried the comforter, and now the sheets as well, which the hairspray method had also stained, down the stairs. "Let's try the alcohol, Ma. May as well, and throw it all in the wash."

She harrumphed. We found the alcohol and dumped on a liberal dose. Then my ninety-pound mama snatched the twenty-pound spread out of my hands and stuffed it into her washing machine.

"This isn't going to work, this isn't going to work," she sighed.

There was nothing more to do but go to bed. I noticed it was now my knee that hurt as I walked up the stairs, favoring it rather than my hip. I wondered what I'd done to it when I ran downstairs with the mess I'd made.

Some things don't change. Mama was right to worry about me—about me getting her there on time, about my habits. Kerfuffles. Accidents. Disarray. Disorder.

"Shit," I said, sliding into the musty envelope of a bed that hadn't been slept in for months. I listened to the washing machine churning downstairs and flipped off the light. To hell with the Tibetan Book of the Dead.

§

"Mar-i-on!" Mama hollered it once, then twice. I pulled out my earplugs. "Get up!" she commanded.

I went downstairs, ate her classic breakfast—Weetabix with blueberries—and drank the coffee she had brewed. Then I sat in the dimly lit living room and read Christmas cards still arranged around a brass serving tray filled with holly leaves on her large round coffee table.

I heard her call out from her bedroom every now and then, "I'm coming, I'm coming. Taking my bobby pins out. Just a minute."

Mama emerged in a beige wool pantsuit with a fuchsia scarf knotted around her neck, and pulled on her leather gloves. "It's cold out there, isn't it?"

I nodded.

"Let's go," she said, steely eyed, shrugging on her coat.

She followed me outside into the cold, grim faced and muttering, "Marching to the gallows."

"You're a good girl, Marion. You don't know how much I appreciate this," she said as we wound our way through the majestic trees of Duke Forest, passing the Veteran's Hospital and, sooner than expected, turned in to the Eye Center where we parked in a handicapped space.

Before my feet hit the pavement, Mama was out of the car and taking tiny steps toward the entrance. By now my knee was really hurting. I shrugged it off and followed her, limping, into the one-story glass-and-concrete building. The blind leading the lame.

It was hopping in the Eye Center at 9:00 a.m., dozens of people plastered to the wall in three or four separate waiting rooms. The receptionist ushered us into one of them and promised that a girl with a coffee cart would be coming through in a minute to take our orders. High-class service, I thought. The City of Medicine, indeed!

But it was tight in there. We found the last two seats together and sat down. Across from us, two women stared. One big—maybe 350 pounds, sat on one hip, her leg stretched into the aisle. The other, a smaller blonde, turned out to be her sister.

We fiddled with our pocketbooks and talked about the art on the walls and the sculpture in the waiting room. Public art in places where you were trapped was a blessing. I thought of Martha Stewart making crafts in prison. New opportunities everywhere if you were looking.

"What do you think that is?" Mama pointed her cane at a huge wooden piece on the table behind us. I said I saw it as a lopsided heart. She saw a huge upheld hand saying "Stop."

"Now that's the difference between you and me," she said, expelling a sigh and lowering her pointer.

The women across from us were still staring. The big one struck up a conversation. She told us all about her condition, then her complete life history. She eyed me and winked—I was closer to her age — then looked over at Mama and said, "Now she is just gorgeous!"

Mama knitted her eyebrows together and stared at the woman. I could see her knuckles turning white as she gripped her pocketbook. I smiled like it was me who had been given a great present and said, "Isn't she?"

Mama harrumphed and said so loud that everybody could hear, "Now that's why you're in the Eye Clinic!"

Before the coffee cart came, we were led into an examining room. A perky nurse asked Mama to read the eye chart. She did pretty well with her left eye, reading all the way down to the third line, but I could see her struggling when it came time for the right eye.

Back in the waiting room, the big woman still hadn't moved. She picked up with her conversation right where she'd left off.

"Elegant!" she said, nodding toward Mama. "She's just elegant." And it was true. Mama was elegant.

When Mama went off to the bathroom, the woman (from West Virginia, I was now informed) turned to me and repeated, with everyone listening, "Just gorgeous! And elegant! I bet your daddy near 'bout worshiped her."

"Well . . . ." I thought about how to say it. "He loved her, all right. But I wouldn't say worship."

I heard other old people in the room chuckle.

"He was from the old school, though. Real polite," I added. My accent took on an exaggerated Southern twang.

"Well, I been married forty years and I love my husband," West Virginia began for those assembled, "but I went back to my hometown last year, didn't I?" She turned to her sister for confirmation. "And I saw the other man who asked me to marry him, the one I turned down, always thought would never amount to nothin', thought he was probably drinking in the bars somewhere, wouldn't have nothing at all. Well, he had the biggest car lot in town, huge ole thing, miles and miles, name in lights, big as life. Everything!"

A nurse came and told me Dr. Kim was ready for Mama. I fished her out of the bathroom, and we were placed in an examining room. An interim Asian doctor—not Dr. Kim—came in to measure her eyes. Mama queried him about just what he was doing, then gave him an unsolicited history about how her "real" eye doctor, Dr. McCracken, had referred her here.

Finally, the great man himself entered: a smooth brown baby with spiked black hair and a big chest, glasses, clear skin, and huge square teeth: Dr. Kim. He looked no more than thirty years old, but I figured he was older since he seemed to be head of everything. An entourage had followed him to the door and peered in to look at Mama. He answered their various entreaties over his shoulder and then closed the door in their faces.

"Well, Mrs. Webb, what have we here? I'm Dr. Kim."

Mama looked at him with "duh" written all over her face. She gave a weak smile.

He flipped little round spy glasses up and down over her eyes, shone in his light, then leaned back and said, "Well, Mrs. Webb, you have Fuchs' corneal dystrophy."

"I know that," she said, her mouth set.

"You're not seeing much in that right eye."

Mama looked offended.

The door opened.

"Excuse me, Dr. Kim," the nurse said, "but Dr. Johannsen is on the phone." She shrugged, and Dr. Kim excused himself.

"How old do you think he is, Mama?" I asked to fill the void.

"I don't give a damn!"

"What's the matter, Mama?"

"I don't like how he was looking at you. That's what they do to old people. They never look at us. They talk to you, like you're the only one who can understand anything!" The man hadn't said more than two sentences, but Mama was already incensed. Afraid too. "And he isn't telling me anything I don't already know!"

"Mama, be nice."

"You just wait!" She pointed her gun finger at me

Dr. Kim returned and picked up where he'd left off. "Mrs. Webb, you have Fuchs' dystrophy and cataracts, especially in the right eye. You're basically reading out of the left eye now."

"I know that!"

"And so, we have two choices."

"What are they?"

"Well, you can have the cataracts removed in your right eye now—it's a day op—and you will have a fifty-fifty chance that your eye will get better just with that."

"Or what? What could go wrong?"

"Since you have the Fuchs' dystrophy, your eye might swell up and you might see worse in that eye."

"Worse!"

"Yes, ma'am. And then you'd have to have the corneal transplant."

"Oh, Lord! And then what?"

Dr. Kim sat down.

"Then you'd have a ninety percent chance of seeing better, but the recuperation can be a long one."

"How long?"

"It could take as much as a year. A month to a year is what we tell people. But, Mrs. Webb, you'd still have your left eye to be seeing out of. *Or* you could just go ahead and have one operation and get the whole thing done at one time. Save yourself a second trip to the hospital."

"Now you listen, Dr. Kim, I'm almost ninety years old!" Mother looked like she was talking to the class dunce.

"Yes, ma'am." Dr. Kim smiled at her, then looked at me.

"Let me see if I hear what you're saying," I said, picking up the ball. "You're saying that since her left eye is good, you would start on the right one, and start with the simple cataract operation."

"Yes, that's an option," he nodded, taking on a more serious expression and rotating his stool to face me. "Unless your mother doesn't want to possibly have two operations. Then she could just get it done all at once: the cataracts and the corneal implant."

"I know what he's saying, Marion," Mother snapped. "Dr. Kim, you're not telling me anything Dr. McCracken hasn't already told me." Then she repeated just what he had told her.

"But they wanted you to come and get a second opinion, Mama. Remember?" I was trying to rescue Dr. Kim from Mama's deliberate obtuseness. He looked nonplussed, but hardly needed rescuing.

"I know that, Marion," Mama spat. "Dr. Kim, do you know Ike Manning?"

"Of course, I know him," Dr. Kim's voice took on reverential tones. "He's a fine man." They discussed Dr. Manning for several minutes.

"Well, I knew him when he was a baby," Mama went on, doing her best to put Dr. Kim in his place. "Knew his parents, too. I went out to his house just this Christmastime, watched him with his grandchildren. It was so darlin' seeing him with his grandchildren."

"Yes, yes. Dr. Manning, a fine man. A fine man," muttered Dr. Kim.

The two of them sat staring at each other, Dr. Kim revolving a little on his stool, Mother with her feet not quite touching the floor, staring him down from her patient's chair. I sat this one out on the sideline, and that was clearly where she wanted me to stay.

"Let me ask you something, Dr. Kim."

"Yes, ma'am."

"If I was your mother, what would you say to me?"

He didn't hesitate. "I'd ask you how bad your sight was; how much you needed to see."

"Well, Dr. Kim, I'm a writer, and I love to read, and I can read those large-print books, but I can hardly see anything in the newspaper these days."

What about driving, Mama? I wondered silently, but dared not ask.

But I definitely needed to get as much information as possible. "If Mama *did* want to do the operation," I asked, "who would do it—you, or Dr. McCracken?"

"I would," he said without hesitation. "Corneal implants are my specialty." He shot me a headlight smile. He was the star.

Dr. Kim rolled his chair up to Mama and placed his hand on her knee. He looked at her intently, full of understanding, and patted her once or twice. "You just take your time and decide, Mrs. Webb. It's completely up to you." Dr. Kim had been in this tiny little examining room for longer than his allotted ten minutes.

"Well, I'm glad you admitted it. I do have a third choice, Dr. Kim. And that's to do nothing."

"That's right, Mrs. Webb. Just remember, though, that if you do want to do it later, your left eye might not be as good then, either."

"It's too cold to do anything now and besides, I've got to get past my ninetieth birthday." Mama was shaking her head. She wore a false smile.

"I understand completely," Dr. Kim agreed. He stood to leave.

"Dr. Kim," I blurted before he disappeared around the doorjamb. "How old are you?"

"Thirty-eight."

Then he was gone.

I helped Mama out to the car. All the while she grumbled. "He won't do it unless I say he can do it. Didn't tell me a thing Dr. McCracken hadn't already told me."

As I buckled my seatbelt, watching Mama fumbling with hers, she added, "You know I hate it when they come up and touch you like that."

I started the car but said nothing.

"And you know something else I hate?" she asked, narrowing her eyes and holding on fast to her pocketbook.

"No, what?"

"I hate it when people in the waiting room just start talking to you like that woman did."

"But Ma, she said you were gorgeous. And elegant. Gorgeous and elegant all in one day. And Dr. Kim was just trying to connect with you."

"I don't care," she said with finality.

"Think about their intent, Mama. They were both trying to be nice. Their intent has to count, doesn't it?"

She thought about that for a minute, then said, "I still hate it."

§

Mama bought us a reward lunch at Southern Seasons. She fussed about the heat, so we moved; and then the cold, but we stayed put, too embarrassed to move again. She commented about the pigtail our largely bald-headed waiter had and how he wasn't even looking at us as she flapped her fingers and tried to flag him over for more hot tea. She complained about how Chapel Hill was changing so fast she didn't recognize things anymore, about the fool government and how everything was already in the hand basket. She tried to complain about both my sister's and my husbands, but I raised my hand in the "stop" sign, and she desisted.

"Okay," she said, petulant. "I just won't ever say anything about anything to you anymore."

I knew that wasn't true. But I stayed quiet, nose buried in my lamb stew, letting her ramble.

Finally, Mama leaned over and said to me, "You know, Marion, I can remember when I used to take Mama out like this, and she couldn't find a thing she liked. I've turned into her exactly. And I apologize."

"Well, you haven't found too many things you've liked today, that's for sure," I said. Still, my tone was sympathetic. She looked up at me, surprised.

"Well, what *have* you liked today?" I asked her.

Mama thought a minute.

"I've liked you," she said triumphantly. I saw the twinkle of a thought come into her eyes.

I smiled at her.

"I've liked you. I really have. And guess what! There's something else I've liked, too." She paused for effect and clinked her teacup with her spoon.

"What?"

Her whole face lit up.

"The ink came out of the bedspread!"

Chapter Two

Indoor Girl

I've always been charmed by houses, and descriptions of them are prominent in my novels. So prominent, in fact, that my editor once pointed out to me that all of my early novels had houses on the covers.
—Anita Shreve

Mama was strictly an indoor girl. Born in Atlanta near her Grandpa Bacon's house, her family moved to Durham, North Carolina, following one of several financial disasters, and lived in a number of downtown homes when she was a child. Her proud father, Ralph Bell Fuller, dubbed "the Skipper," suffered periodic money woes.

This was all before Skipper and Mater moved into the downtown Main Street "mansion." Built by Mama's Uncle Tom Southgate between 1885 and 1903, 313 Main Street was Mama's primary childhood home. An indoor girl's dream.

The house bustled with visitors, some who stayed for months: the Huskes, the Kennedys, the Longs, and always Uncle Tom Southgate.

A Victorian gingerbread with scrimshaw and Turkish corners, 313 was in remarkable shape, inside and out, and displayed enduring good taste for the time. There was an entrance hall with an unusual green-burlap wall covering and heavy Mission leather furniture. The grand hall also featured an Edison phonograph that turned 46 1/4 double-sided platters right there for all to see.

Embossed green-and-gold wallpaper hung in the library to the left, where oversized rocking chairs held the aroma of Uncle Jim's opulent cigars. They faced each other in front of a slim-pillared mahogany fireplace topped with a delft-blue tile mantle. I remembered that library as a graceful dream.

A Napoleon table supported the globe lamp that stood high on a brass column in front of floor-to-ceiling bookcases holding the huge calf-bound Century Dictionary (twelve volumes), along with a number of books about Napoleon, whom Uncle Tom admired. As a girl, I often fingered through a huge book of *Famous Orations*, mostly uncut.

My childhood memories in that house supplied some of these details, but much of the rest I took from Mama's correspondence with her oldest brother, Ralph. The two had written back and forth about 313 Main all their lives, and I found their letters in one of those boxes after she died.

"It was only years later I realized how soundly the house was constructed," wrote my uncle. "Under the clapboards the diagonal sheathing was 2 x 12 pitch pine! In all the years we lived there, I don't recall a single leak in the slate roof."

I remembered 313's front lawn spreading thirty feet from the porch to the sidewalk. The walkway was figured bricks laid in a herringbone pattern. Outside the gate when Mama was a girl, Main Street was mud. But inside the yard, there was a wooden lawn swing, five-o'clocks along the walk, and ferns in jardinières hanging on the front porch, which was long and wide with a railing all around for the gentlemen's feet. The "verandah," as it was called, was the backdrop for regular Sunday afternoon gatherings, as well as the means of egress for unexpected company who came up often and sidled back off the porch when another adventure beckoned.

Mama wrote her brother back: "Remember, Ralph, in the back yard, there was a sizable truck garden with corn, tomatoes, snap beans, butter beans, okra, collards and a chicken house. There were roses on the serving room side and a pomegranate bush on the other, slanting cellar doors and a rain barrel."

Uncle Ralph answered: "Yes, Mena. And Rose? We all have had gastronomic adventures in our later life, but have you ever eaten such really good food as Rose cooked for us every day—breakfast, dinner, and supper? The Mater used to make excellent smothered chicken and rice pudding, and in other ways was quite a good cook. But no Jew-boy ever smacked his lips over the memory of his mother's Kreplach as I do at the thought of Rose's veal chops. How could this untutored genius, without benefit of garlic, basil, vermouth, or anything but good meat and onions produce a dish that Brillat-Savari would have smeared a little bit of on himself."

Rose planned and cooked all the meals that were then served by Sadie, her partner and coworker, who also lived at the house with the family even before Mama moved in.

I remember Mama rhapsodizing once, "In addition to beaten biscuits, Marion, there was Sally Lunn, a rich, slightly sweet yeast bread brought to the colonies from England that subsequently became a favorite in the South, and roast chicken, roast beef, tenderloin, sweetbreads, veal cutlets and chops, birds in season, crispy fried fish when somebody had caught a mess." Her eyes misted over. "Plus, home-baked bread, Parker House rolls, muffins, pancakes, waffles, not to mention angel and devil's food cake, sweet potato pudding, ambrosia."

Just the word "ambrosia" sounded like heaven to me. I asked her to repeat herself so I could write it down.

Mama never had any doubts about the dependability of her parents or her family. She likely took for granted the excellence of her social position and gave it little thought. She had no reason to worry about money or to fully understand her father's struggles. Her Uncle Tom was rich and prominent, and her father would have been, too, had he not been so proud that he wouldn't go to work for his brother. Instead, he insisted on making it on his own in the insurance business, Mama told me much later in her life, still miffed by his poor decision.

She loved her schooling in the building that bore her Fuller name, had no complaints about the political or educational system, was attractive as she grew into a woman, and had never been hungry a day in her life. Not for food anyway.

"Remember Uncle Jim's 'cabin' out near University Station," Uncle Ralph wrote her, "where we used to occasionally drive out in the summertime, and his fabulous Thomas Flyer? It was a seven-passenger touring car with carbide lamps and leather straps to stay the windshield, driven by the chauffeur, Billy Long Morton, which he pronounced Motun. Motun had it easy while our family was 'in the country.' Do you recall that he named his first boy Thomas Fuller 'Motun'"?

The description of Uncle Jim's cabin was like no country living I'd ever known: two stories with peeled pine logs chinked with white plaster, four bedrooms with polished pine floors, a wide verandah on three sides, and two cigar-store Indians flanking the front door. There was a separate kitchen and a "cool house" built over a spring in the back, and Canna lilies all over the yard.

"The place was wild with turkeys and guinea chickens," Uncle Ralph continued. "Two maidservants and a yard man tended that place."

Maybe this was being in the wild to Mama. I vividly remembered her stories about the "wild" parties she and Daddy went to at this house when she was all but grown. But, in general, Mama had no real reason to prefer the out-of-doors. Her indoor digs were fine enough, and her life was lived largely in her imagination anyway.

I have only a few memories, and one or two pictures, of my mama outdoors, mainly at Nags Head at the Raney-Webb beach cottage, where we went for two weeks every August. She was standing on the porch in a bathing suit with a pleated skirt and a broad-band straw hat, shading her eyes, and looking out at the ocean.

But there was one very important day she spent outdoors. She married outside on August 4, 1935, one of the hottest days that year, she told me—104 degrees. Mama wore a long dress and a sidesaddle veil, and my father looked a bit portly in his white linen suit. They shared marriage vows that would last more than fifty years, and they must have been ecstatic for more reasons than one when they finally took their clothes off later that night.

Still, Mama was never more than two steps from the kitchen. I don't ever remember her wanting to be outdoors in the greenery with the bugs, the gnats, and the no-see-ums. She was used to high living in nice houses with valuable, inherited furniture. She possessed what they now would call a great sense of *feng shui*, giving close attention with a fine, natural eye to her inside decor. Other than her familiar daily haunts, Mama never hankered for travel, either.

She was an indoor girl.

Chapter Three

Outdoor Girl

Nothing coaxes jumbled thoughts into coherent sentences like sitting
under a shade tree on a pleasant day. With a slight breeze blowing,
birds chirping melodies, wee bugs scurrying around me and
a fully charged laptop or yellow legal pad at hand,
I know I'll produce my best work. —Carol Kaufman

I, on the other hand, am an outdoor girl. I was raised in a nice section of the suburbs just across the railroad tracks from Hayti (which we pronounced with a long "i," like Hay-tie), the black section of Durham. This particular spot, on the edge of two entirely different worlds, shaped me from the get-go.

In my twenties, I eagerly joined the civil rights cause, as well as the emerging back-to-nature movement that arose in the 60's. My first husband and I gravitated to living in the country. Soon afterward, we built our own house out of other people's old houses, recycling slate for our terrace from the Morehead farmhouse where the Blue Cross Blue Shield building now stands, and metal rocking chairs from the old Watts Hospital. The beams for our roof came from an 1860's pioneer home along the Yadkin River that we painstakingly lowered to the ground, numbered, and then lifted with a "come-along" up onto a flatbed truck before driving it back to the Triangle.

Cajoling a horde of other back-to-nature types to help us with offers of kegs of beer and good music, along with whatever other inebriants we had on hand, we raised those beams, one by one.

Nothing is particularly level or plumb in our house, but somehow it suits me just fine. I've lived here for thirty-five years, now with my second husband, and I love it: the privacy, the hot tub, the cats, the nibbling deer wandering around ten acres of trees that transform with the seasons and remind me of the constancy of change.

I admit that niceties like air conditioning and some of the finer pieces of furniture I inherited from my mother have made it quite a bit better. There's Mama's oversized mahogany dining room table, and six matching chairs with white satin bottoms that we'll surely have to cover before the grandkids make mincemeat out of them, plus odd and assorted pieces of silver and candlesticks, as well as Daddy's mother, Nana's gorgeous oil paintings of magnolias and sea oats and seagulls flying over the Atlantic, all in ornate gold frames. With decks all around, I now live in what looks like a hippy boat with Elizabethan furniture inside. The old and the new together have quite a pleasant effect on me, and I feel the thread between Mama and me tightening.

Nevertheless, I was always really my father's child: an outdoor girl.

§

My father, Mack Webb, also grew up in a "fine family"—meaning privileged—up the road in Hillsborough. Though it was once the capital of the Confederacy, Hillsborough was considered a hick town by the worldly urban denizens of Durham.

As a boy, Daddy drove his pony wagon to school, hunted and trapped in the mountains around his house (hills, really, thus Hillsborough), played baseball and football, and snuck around imitating Indians all day in the woods. Other than his lifelong passion for writing newspapers (which he did by hand, five columns wide, beginning at age seven or eight), most of Daddy's favorite activities happened out of doors.

Being a man, and thus not responsible for the cooking and the housework, he tended to us instead, taking my sister and me on half-day walks far beyond the reach of our neighborhood and inspiring our interest in collecting all things natural.

Daddy often found arrowheads poking out beneath the leaves, and glittering pieces of rose quartz powdered in red clay. He told us endless tales about Indians (not cowboys.) He respected the Indians and wrote stories about the native people who lived in Central North Carolina before the so-called "Lost Colony," which Daddy insisted was never lost at all. His stories about this made it into national magazines in the early years of his writing life. He believed what has now been proven, that the "Lost Colony" of white settlers had simply intermarried into the native population.

Once Daddy and I found a huge sea turtle at the beach, that we put in an aluminum pail on the back porch of our Aunt's cottage and fed lettuce. I cried like a baby the last day of our vacation when we had to release that turtle back into the sea.

On the weekends, he put on old pants, a Perry Como sweater— a V-necked button-up affair— and he mowed and raked, drawing up piles of leaves for us to jump in. He planted the japonica bushes and the willow tree, built the backyard terrace—letting me help; and then for breaks, when he didn't sit down outside with a drink in his hand, he would just as likely take us for another walk down the dirt road along the railroad tracks where we could see the "clay eaters"—black people digging clay out of the banks (for medicinal purposes, I'd later discover), or to watch the mules at a farm hidden back in the trees.

Once out of the house, we piled into the Plymouth (a wild black-and-yellow model with silver stars on the interior roof that Daddy had driven off the lot, shocking Mama) and took leisurely rides where we stopped to go walking down unfamiliar paths to see old mills or the trapping areas of his youth. We'd end up in towns we'd never heard of, buying "Co-colas" in small green bottles at roadside stores, moving slow.

Outside, the rules didn't apply. Spontaneity was the name of the game, and I loved it. We were aimless and free.

Though I was small and skinny, my physical prowess revealed itself in my prized status as fastest runner in all of my elementary grades. I was even faster than the boys. I was a fierce and determined little girl who could hit a mean softball and break through anybody's arms, however big, in Red Rover, Red Rover. Outside, I was finally free to be the tomboy I truly was—to hell with all that girl stuff. In addition, I earned the admiration and attention of the person who was most important to me in all the world, the handsomest man alive, my father.

Even now, living far away from everything in our hand-built house, my current husband, Art, and I still choose to go camping on our vacations, get further off the grid every time we can. Hotel rooms, even fancy ones, don't hold much appeal.

When I am inside, I find I spend far too much time moving things from one room to another, which people invariably do when they have a lot of things in a house with too many rooms. I never seem to be able to get things uncluttered, and keep them that way.

I don't have a maid or a cook. My tastes run more to fresh, uncooked vegetables from our garden or a farmer's market anyway. The culinary prowess extraordinaire my mother experienced through her cook, Rose—and I through her—have bypassed me. Interestingly, these skills have become the province of my two sons. I can cook, but it rarely beckons me. And the fascination for keeping house skipped me altogether. I call my upstairs back bedroom, where I also write, "Shipping and Receiving." I know I would write a lot better with less stuff in there.

Currently following the tiny house movement, I want nothing more than to dramatically reduce my footprint—build a darling mobile enclosure that we can pull around the country and park wherever we please. There, I fancy, I can write, and my husband can paint. People will come up to look at our darling tiny house—barely a house at all—and buy Art's masterpieces.

When everything I need is packed into a backpack, the entire householder thing gets much simpler. There is time for activities I'd much rather be doing: bike rides and walks and naps, back rubs and swimming, playing with my grandchildren, rubbing the cats, good long nights of sleep, sex, and writing—time for my mind and my heart and my soul.

This particular disparity between my mother and me in no way captures all the ways we are different. We are a contrasted pair. There are layers and layers of social and political, even moral, differences that may separate us. But somehow, I think this indoor/outdoor thing is pivotal.

Mama never understood why I wanted to go to Ecuador and build yet another house, or why I like camping and want to travel so much.

"Why don't ya'll just go to Wilmin'ton?" she would ask over and over, bewildered. "You can get all the adventures you can handle down there. Plus, relaxation. You never relax, Marion! Why not go to The Blockade Runner or rent somebody else's big beautiful beach cottage? You don't have to build the damn house!"

Maybe that day will come. When my legs give out. When I can no longer lift the backpack. When I don't like driving, though given my childhood road trips with my father, I can't really see this happening anytime soon. Moving through space to someplace you know not where is deep inside of me, even in my DNA.

Now, upstairs in Shipping and Receiving (which I currently have renamed "The Staging Area" for my next outdoor adventure), I paw through Mama's things and find cards from me that she saved throughout the years. On the back of one of them she scribbled:

From my daughter, Marion. I love Marion, the burr
beneath my saddle, the eternal rebel who now
makes me laugh. Reckon I cried a river over her too.
I went through a helluva lot being Marion's mom.
But it was worth it.

Back at you, Mama, I think. Right back at you. Indoors or out, it's been fun riding shotgun!

Chapter Four

Depressed

It was Antonin Artaud who wrote on one of his drawings, 'Never real and always true', and that is how depression feels. You know that it is not real, that you are someone else, and yet you know that it is absolutely true.
— Andrew Solomon

Mama realized she had been paying $24 a month for the last five years for nothing, and that the "goddamned cell phone was broken!" It was time for action: a trip across town to Northgate Mall. Would I please take her? "The phone doesn't hold a charge for twenty minutes, Marion!"

The morning we were to go, Mama called and left a message: She could barely get out of bed. She didn't know if she could go out anywhere. But if I wanted to come to visit anyway, that would be fine. I could hear the faintest trace of "I don't want to be an imposition, but, in fact, I do hope you come" in her voice.

I called to assure her I would be there by one o'clock as planned, and that we'd just play it by ear.

§

Mama lives in a two-story condominium in a curvy, tree-lined neighborhood near a golf course. When she opened the door, she seemed smaller than just two weeks ago. Her hair had been cut in back and ringlets of frost-colored curls framed her face. I thought of Thumbelina as I gave her a hug. Not one to sink into people's hugs, a cheek-peck more her style, this day she accepted it gratefully. Then she straightened.

"Have you eaten?" Mama picked up the bowl of soup she'd been eating, her unparalleled homemade vegetable soup, and peered over the spoon. Birdlike: a sandpiper at the beach or a killdee.

"Nope, but if we go out, I can get something at the Food Court."

"Food Court. Now, Marion, I thought we were just going to return the phone," she said indignantly. "I can't go walking all over that mall to some Food Court. Not the way I'm feeling."

"Oh, it'll be quick," I assured her, realizing that I was, in fact, hungry, nothing in my stomach since breakfast at seven. "It's right down from the phone store." I moved toward the refrigerator, trying to distract her.

"I'm not feeling worth a damn. My knee is killing me. It took an hour to get up and going this morning. Now, Marion, don't you go raiding the refrigerator. I need that food." She hit at me with her hand. "Though actually I haven't been able to eat much lately. I'm feeling whickery."

"Which knee?" I asked, bending over to look at her leg, but keeping the refrigerator open. Both of her legs looked skewed sideways to me.

"My good one." She lifted up her right one, holding on to the counter.

"That's too bad. Have you tried to take a walk today?" I stood back up with a handful of cashews and a hunk of cheese hidden in my hand, feeling eleven rather than sixty.

Mama looked at me like I was stone-cold deaf and stupid, to boot.

"I C-A-N-'T walk on it, Marion." She enunciated her words pointedly. "It's going bad."

"Do you think you'll need a new knee on that leg too?" I asked, trying to sound "can-do," but realizing immediately that I must seem cavalier to her.

"I couldn't survive another operation, Marion. I just couldn't survive it."

"Yes, you could," I tried to reassure her. "You're tough."

Mama'd certainly suffered with the earlier knee operation, but she had come out fine, even throwing a jazz party with my cousin's three-piece band in the corner of her living room afterward and dancing a step or two. She was feisty, a survivor.

"Not half as tough as you think I am." She set down her soup bowl sharply on the counter. The spoon rattled. "I'm depressed," she announced.

No shit, Sherlock, I thought, but said in what I hoped was a soothing tone, "I'm sorry, Mama," and shifted into listening. No advice. Advice was the last thing any depressed person needed. I knew that firsthand. Last week I had blubbered like a baby over the possibility that my youngest son might end up living in Europe with his then–true love, Natalie, a Nederlander. Corey pronounced her name "Naughtily," easily shedding his Southern drawl for her crisp European syllables. Letting go was a bitch. I'd hated it when somebody gave me advice when I was sad.

"What do you want to do, Mama?" I asked. "Stay here? We don't have to go. Whatever you want's fine with me." I sat down at the kitchen table.

"I guess I want to go on and get this phone thing taken care of," she mumbled. "Give me a little bit, will you, while I go get ready? Is it too cold for just a jacket and a scarf?"

Mama hobbled back into her bedroom, saying over and over, "I'm sorry. I'm sorry. I know I shouldn't be behaving this way. I'm gonna get over myself in a minute. Forgive me, Marion."

"It's okay, Mama," I hollered back brightly. "Be any way you want to be. I'm in a good place today. I can handle it." I went back to my scavenging. Half an hour later, Mama emerged. She looked like a woodpecker in a red blazer with a black collar and a white wool scarf. Her black pocketbook was draped over one arm, her cane over the other.

"Where's my cane?" she asked, frustration flooding her face.

I retrieved it from her arm and put it in her hand. "Here. Come on. Let's go." I took her hand. It was already two o'clock.

"Slow down, Marion," she snapped before I'd even taken a step toward the door.

"And I'm going to drive," she announced. "I need to see if I can still do it."

She inched fifteen-miles-an-hour through Hope Valley, riding the brake, slamming her foot down every fifty feet or so, driving with the halt-jerk of a bumper car to the main road.

She bit her lip and darted her head from side to side, trying to see out of the windows at each intersection. But as far as I could tell, she wasn't dangerous, so I settled back on the seat. "Deep breathe," I told myself.

After a few miles, she grew more confident, and though her driving style continued to be acceleratus-interruptus across town, she began to talk about anything and everything, sprinkled with remarks about her aches and pains, her sorry attitude, and her depression.

She managed to get in a few of her favorite themes: my sister's and my wholly inadequate husbands who could never be good enough for us except, of course, my first husband whom I'd stupidly divorced; the tragedy of men's inner lives or the lack thereof, except, of course, my son Tom's—her grandson, the crown prince, who could do no wrong. She talked about the failing economy, the sorry state of the world, and the dearth of reliable cleaning ladies, someone who wouldn't bump the Hoover on the edges of her furniture.

Then she asked me to drop off some purple slacks at the cleaners and to please tell the woman they were from Mena.

"She calls me Mena," Mama explained as we jerked up to the Rockwood Laundromat and turned off the motor. Made sense. That was her name. "I've got the place pinned where the spot is.".

I did as I was told, feeling unexpectedly thankful I could get out of the car and walk the few steps across the pavement.

"These are Mena's," I said to a short woman in an Arabic headdress who came whooshing through the curtain smelling of dry-cleaning fluid.

"Last name?"

"Webb."

"Oh." The woman lit up. "Mrs. Webb? Is she all right?"

"Yes, she's just in the car," I said. "She's driving." I was proud of her. "She's fine. Just a little depressed."

"Depressed? Oh no. You tell Miss Mena not to be depressed. Nothing could be wrong with Miss Mena!"

The woman revealed a Wife-of-Bath gap-toothed smile, folding up Mama's purple pants and writing out the ticket.

"Not with Miss Mena," she said again. "She's alive!" She was almost shouting.

I examined the folds in her headdress.

"She's not alive to be depressed!" The woman repeated everything twice as if I was the one foreign to English, not she. "You tell her that."

I assured her I'd relay the message. I planned to impart the unadulterated pleasure she took in "Miss Mena" the minute I got back in the car.

When I did, Mama smiled. "She's a sweet girl," she said. The woman was at least fifty, but anyone younger than Mama was a girl. "She's from the Middle East somewhere."

"Turkey?" I asked.

"No, I don't think so."

"Greece?"

"No, not Greece. What's over there? Oh, I don't know!" she said as if disgusted with herself. "I forget. I forget everything." Her mouth turned down into a half moon as she bumped up Duke Street, saying under her breath, "Pitiful. Pitiful. Pitiful."

We got across town to the mall, where the traffic was horrific. Mama gripped the steering wheel, looking terrified. "Help me, Marion," she ordered. I guided her in and out of the proper lanes to the sanctuary of the handicapped parking garage beside Belk's department store.

"This is the only thing good about getting old," Mama grumbled, her face now blotched with anxiety. "The damned handicapped spaces." She clicked her tongue and began inching into the space in front of her, parking slowly, but every bit as good as I could have done. All the while she moaned, "Oh God. Oh God." Then she began to belittle her driving skills, announcing the rapidity of her diminished capacity.

"Stop it, Mama," I admonished. "You did just fine. Besides, that's what old people do all the time, and it makes me mad!"

"What?" she asked, pulling up the hand brake and letting her head fall back on the headrest. All the blood had drained out of her face.

"Put themselves down. Say they can't do anything anymore, that they're inept, stupid, useless. Apologize all the time."

"I didn't say that, Marion! I know I'm not useless. I'm a damned sight better than most people, and I know it. I'm not apologizing. It hurts my hands, that's all, and my back. Let's just rest a minute. You wait. You'll see. It takes courage to be old."

I reached for her hand and began to rub it.

"We may as well go into Belk's now that we're here," she said listlessly. "Get John a birthday present." Then she added, "I can't wait to watch you doing this when you get old."

"Yeah, but will you be laughing at me, or cheering me on, Mama?"

She didn't answer.

§

Once inside Belk's, in a matter of minutes she bought a birthday shirt for her son-in-law. There were only five all-cotton dress shirts for her to fiddle with, and given John's proclivities, only two would do, so the choice was easy. At the register the fiftyish man with the dark pompadour and black square glasses offered to wrap it for her.

Mama beamed. "This must be my lucky day," she crooned. Damned if she wasn't flirting.

To me, she turned and whispered, "Why would anyone want a dress shirt for his birthday?" She rolled her eyes. "B-O-R-I-N-G!" She turned back to the sales clerk. "Why, you make the nicest bows!" she sang. "Who would've thought a man would be wrapping my birthday present? You just don't know how much this helps me, sir. Saves my fingers."

He turned and continued to curl the ribbon as she swished her fingers through the air. Implying he was swishy.

"This was too easy, Marion. I didn't think it would be this easy. I can't thank you enough, sir."

The clerk turned back and, with a flourish, presented it to her. "For you, madam." Then he stuck it in a Belk's bag.

Mama batted her baby blues and bowed. "Thank you, sir," she said softly, looking up at him like he was Sir Lancelot. Court behavior. Past lifetimes, I thought.

§

When we got to the car after Belk's, Mama asked me to take over for her. "I don't feel like driving," she announced.

Instead of heading straight for Verizon, I quite spontaneously moved the car across the lot and parked in front of Talbots.

"Why are you stopping here, Marion?" Mama asked. "For god's sake, Marion. I don't want to go to Talbots!"

"Why not? I thought Talbots was your favorite store?"

"That's why I don't want to go in. I can't afford Talbots right now. I'm not going in there!"

"Look," I lied, "I need to get something myself. I go with you all the time. You can sit in the car or go in with me and sit in the chair. You don't even have to look."

"Yes, I will have to look, and I'm not going, Marion!"

I really didn't have anything to buy, especially not at Talbots, but I suspected a little retail therapy might raise her mood. After a few sallies, I finally convinced her.

She jerked her leather gloves on, slung the cane over her arm, and disembarked. "Okay." She sounded resigned. "I'm ready to brave it."

I reached to steady her, but she shook me off. "Let go of me!"

I stepped out ahead.

"And don't you go walking off ahead of me either, Marion. That's rude."

I stifled the impulse to tell her just who, in fact, was being rude, remembering how much I, too, hate talking to my husband's back when we take a walk and his long-legged strides have him out four or five steps ahead of me. Immediately, I forgave her.

When we stepped up to the store, Mama was confronted by a giant red sign: "Talbots BIG SALE, everything 30-60% off!"

She stopped and staggered.

"Oh, God!" she said, taking my hand. "We gotta get outa here! Come on, Marion. I gotta walk fast! Gotta get out of here!"

Still, holding onto me now, she did not change direction but entered the store. She walked slower than usual through the aisles, her face childlike, as she brushed past the 100 percent natural fibers on either side of her. She parted the scarves on the jewelry counter. "O-o-o-o-h," she whispered, her mouth a little O, her face roseate.

Mama's "in rapport," I thought. She looks beautiful.

Mama had always loved things. Fine things. Expensive things, especially when they were on sale. Or if they were passed on to her from some Arthurian ancestor from the British Isles. "I believe in going first class!" she often testified. "It's first class for me all the way." That also meant she didn't travel to many places outside of Durham.

I cheered her on as she fingered a scarf. "Mama, you look so pretty. You're having fun in here. I'm not in a hurry. We've got plenty of time."

"No, Marion! I am not going to shop." Her voice was firm. She picked up the pace from snail to faster-snail. "I do need a vest though."

Mama had a walk-in closet chock full of stylish clothes. She always looked like she'd just stepped out of a bandbox. Last fall she'd bought a leather coat and threatened to buy matching leather pants just to shock the neighbors on her afternoon walks. "Except it would take me all week to get in them," she'd sighed.

I thought about the Dalai Lama calendar I had given her, opened on the table beside her recliner when I'd picked her up today: FRIDAY, JANUARY 17: "You cannot buy peace of mind in a shop."

Yet in some important way, she did need a vest today. She needed something that would pleasure her.

I flagged over the trim, country-club-looking saleslady with the brown, plastered-helmet cut and too-red lips and asked, "Can you help my mama?"

"I don't need any help." Mama tried to wave her away, but then added sweetly, "Do you have any vests in my size?" The woman's smile was as firmly in place as every hair on her head.

"Why, of course."

Twenty minutes later, Mama called me over to the racks along the wall. She had two vests folded over her arm.

"Hang these back up for me, will you Marion? I don't want to try these on now. We'd better be getting to the Verizon store. And then to the grocery."

I took the hangers. She planted herself between me and the rack, and began clucking her tongue. "I bet you don't even have the grocery list I gave you, do you, Marion?" She shook her head.

I showed it to her and turned on a smile. "Right here, Mama."

It's just her movie, I told myself. Nothing to do with me.

We wasted another twenty minutes in Talbots. I'd determined in advance not to buy anything, because I was broke after Tax Day; but in Talbots, with my orange cotton Indian pants and Earth Trekker shoes, I looked even more like a hippie than I had in the parking lot. I spelled "O-u-t o-f p-l-a-c-e."

I threw on a black and brown Italian wool poncho that'd been reduced from $90 to $30 and stood in front of the mirror admiring my new look, waiting for Mama.

She was still walking through the petites, touching things and mumbling, "I need a top. I need some wool gloves. I need a green jacket."

While trying to think if I had a little loose change in any of my bank accounts, Mama looked over.

"You're not going to buy that, are you?" she asked and made a face.

Shit. I thought I looked good.

"You look just like Pocahontas," Mama announced, loud enough for everyone to hear. "And besides, you're gonna be in a shawl soon enough, Marion. I'd leave shawls alone for now if I were you. While you can."

We left and headed for Verizon, nothing in our hands.

Mama was upbeat, but now I was a little bit depressed.

Chapter Five

Verizon

Our mothers remain the strangest, craziest people we have ever met.
—Marguerite Duras

We stepped out of Talbots into the interior of the mall. Mama stood for a minute, blinking. The lights were bright. Mama's mouth was quivering. "This hurts my eyes!" she cried. "I shoulda brought my sunglasses in here." She looked like a chicken at the plucking plant. "Too damn bright."

But then suddenly, she stepped out ahead. Lewis and Clark. "Let's go." We began walking to the Verizon store.

"Where is the damn store, Marion?" she demanded. "I thought you said it was right across from Talbots." Further proof that she couldn't believe anything I said ever again.

"Right there, Mama." I pointed. She stopped and squinted.

The bill-paying line in Verizon was a sure thirty-minute wait, so I steered Mama over to customer sales.

"We need to find Condolita," Mama said. "Condolita's the black girl who sold me the phone." She said this to me as if I hadn't been with her for that purchase, too—who knew how long ago? Mama always had to announce it when it was a black person. No amount of trying to get her to stop had worked.

"Maybe she doesn't even work here anymore," I told her just as I spied Condolita stuck behind the desk in front of a mass of bill payers. It was easy to remember her name, because of the current National Security Advisor, Condolisa Rice.

"Let's find someone else, Mama. Condolita's busy."

Mama ignored me and turned to another associate. "Is Condolita here?" She radiated innocence, looking up at a girl who was joking with two male salesclerks about her age, her hair a skullcap of tiny black knots.

"Condolita? She's over there," she pointed.

"She's busy, Mama. Let's let her help us," I urged.

"No, it's okay," the new one said. "I'll go and see if Condolita can come over."

The girl smiled at Mama. She had brown teeth like she'd been smoking every day since middle school. "I'll be right back, honey," she said to my eighty-nine-year-old mother and threaded through the crowd toward Condolita, her bottom the size of a lifeboat.

Mama drummed her gloved fingers on the counter and squinted at two guys who no more knew she was two feet away and looking at them, than they knew they would someday get old and die. No one over twenty-five years old was on their radar, certainly not some little old white woman. They, too, were following Salesgirl #2's rear end.

"Condolita's busy," she told Mama when she returned. "We work on commission here, so I had to get her permission to help you. She told me to take good care of you. What do you need, honey?"

Normally, Mama wouldn't have put up with someone a quarter her age calling her "honey" for half a second. But she was warming up to this girl.

"What's *your* name?"

"Stephanie." Stephanie seemed not to notice Mama's imperious tone. In truth, her face was aimed at Mama, but she was paying attention to the two guys behind her.

"Well, Stephanie," Mama began, "I need a new cell phone." She motioned to me to hurry up and put her old one up on the counter.

"Lord, you do!" Stephanie exclaimed. "That one's five or six years old. What kind do you want, honey?"

"One that works."

"What's wrong with this one?"

"It won't stay on," Mama said.

"Loses its charge," I added, trying to give Stephanie the correct lingo.

"Well, no wonder."

By then we had all moved over to the revolving rack of tiny phones, some no bigger than a credit card with buttons the size of baby fingernails. I spun it around and saw only three models that were even big enough for Mama to handle.

"These are the ones you want, Mama," I showed her, pointing. "They're $29.99, $39.99, and $149.99."

"What?" Mama asked sharply. "How do *you* know, Marion? What about all of these?" She turned to Stephanie.

I twirled the rack again. "They're too small."

Mama edged closer and squinted.

"They're too small," Stephanie repeated. Mama believed Stephanie.

"What're their advantages and disadvantages?" I asked, pointing to the cheaper models, trying to both facilitate and hurry the transaction.

Mama looked resistant.

"Well, this one might be best." Stephanie picked up the $39.99 model. "It's got a green button for go and a red one for stop. Real simple." She pointed the buttons out to Mama, who was mouthing "Green for go."

"You mean green for talk?" Mama asked.

"Yes, sweetheart, green for talk and red for stop talking." She turned to me. "I bet it's hard to get your mama to stop talking. And this here is 'Clear,' and you've got Caller ID on the screen and three-way calling.

"Caller ID?"

"Yeah, like if your, your husband here," Stephanie pointed to me, "I mean your daughter." She laughed out loud. "Look at me. What am I saying? Schwew! It's been a long day. Been here since seven this morning." Still holding the phone, she rested both of her hands on her hips. "I mean your daughter. What's your name, honey?"

"Marion."

"If Marion here called you up, you could tell it was her." She pointed out the two-line feature on the phone's tiny screen. "And it's got text."

"Why do I need all that? I don't need all that," Mama said flatly, smacking her lips shut just as I was imagining leaving her an "*I love you*" or a "*Hang in there*" text on her screen.

But Stephanie walked her through the ease of this particular Nokia and then asked Mama to fill out some forms so she could activate Mama's new phone.

"I'm not going to tell you when I was born," Mama declaimed. "What do you need to know that for?"

Stephanie shrugged and smiled.

"I'm older than God," Mama said to Stephanie in a hoarse whisper, as if confiding a highly classified secret.

"Well, I don't need the year, but I do need the day," Stephanie replied as Mother wrote down April 26th in her loopy hand.

"Why, that's my wedding anniversary!" Stephanie exclaimed. "April 26th!"

"How many years?" I asked, trying to get in on the conversation.

"Two."

"Just two?" Mama clucked. "Well! I was married over fifty years to her father."

"Any advice?" Stephanie asked.

"Just hang in there, dearie," Mama shrugged. "Good luck. Oh, I do have one piece of advice," she added.

"What?" We both turned to her, waiting.

"Don't try to change him," she said. We leaned back, nodding at the good sense of her logic. It was a chestnut. Everyone said that.

"Cause they're all the same, anyway," she said. "And I mean in every way!"

Mama raised her eyebrows and gave us an "And you know what I mean" look, as I imagined Stephanie and I seeing white and black body parts. I turned away, embarrassed.

"What's your last name?" Mama asked Stephanie.

"LeSane."

"LeSane? Don't you mean Insane?" Mama asked, twinkling. "Stephanie Insane." She was teasing her.

Stephanie grinned, still filling out the form. "That's what my husband says too."

Stephanie left to ring up Mama's purchase.

"It'll just take a minute more," she called over to my mom. "Then let me bag you up."

Mama whooped. "That's the last thing anybody's gonna do to me!"

Stephanie Insane squealed and yelled for her colleagues. "Ya'll gotta come over here," she shouted. "This lady's funneee! Mena's her name," she told them as they drew near us.

"I said, 'Lemme bag you up,' and she says, 'That's the las' thing anybody's gonna do to me—bag me up.' Lis'en at her!"

The others chuckled politely and looked quizzically back and forth between Mama and Stephanie Insane.

"Don't you all laugh," Mama said to those boys. She was holding court, having fun. "Last thing anybody's gonna do to all of you, too!"

"Your mama's sure a funny one," Stephanie crowed. "Sign right here, honey," she pointed a scarab nail at a line on the form.

"Law," Mama said, "How many more signatures you gonna need?"

"Las' one."

"Whatever." Mama sighed.

Stephanie raised her eyes at me and cocked her head towards Mama, silently mouthing "Whatever" like Mama was a bona fide trip. "Lis'en at her," she chuckled.

§

When we left Verizon, Mama looked much better than she had when she walked in.

"She's got good manners, Stephanie. Condolita did too."

True. Both of them had taken time with my mama, had treated her kindly, without the condescending over-care reserved for the elderly, which Mother would have surely registered and soundly repudiated. They'd talked turkey. They'd laughed. Not at her, but with her. They'd hung with my mama. Just us chickens here.

"Black people generally have more respect for older people," I explained. "In my opinion, they're a lot more comfortable with their elders than white people are. Especially the women, the griots."

"Hmmph," Mama said. Then tapping across the tile floor, she asked, "What's that mean?"

"Storyteller." I was glad to be of use, to have some expertise myself. "You know what they say? When an old person dies, it's like losing a whole library."

"Got that right!" Mama snapped, inching her way back across the mall. "I hate malls."

In the parking lot, Mama turned to me and said, "That's another reason I'm depressed."

"Why?" I asked, opening her car door.

"Because I couldn't write about the black people in my book. I lived right down the street from all those folks at N.C. Mutual, all those people doing the impossible, everything stacked against them, and I didn't even know they existed!" She hung her head. "Nobody but the maids. I didn't have any memories of any of them, and the book I was writing was my memories. You drive, Marion."

She got in and poked her packages in around her feet. "I can't help it when and where I was born!"

"No, you can't." I got behind the steering wheel.

"But I feel cheated anyway," she pouted. "Cheated! And don't you go too fast, Marion. I'm sorry. I know I shouldn't be acting this way. You're a wonderful girl. I don't know what I'd *do* without you. Got to put on a happy face. That's what your sister tells me. People like to take care of 'sweet little ole ladies,' and I'd better watch out or people won't take care of me."

I eased onto Gregson Street.

"We'll take care of you, Mama."

"But I don't feel sweet! And what would you and Carol think if I suddenly turned sweet anyway?"

"No worry there, Mama."

She swatted me with her gloves.

"And don't you go telling me 'Everything's gonna be great' either! Carol's always telling me 'everything's gonna be great in heaven,' but who wants to wait that long?"

"Okay, I won't tell you everything's gonna be great."

Everything would get better. And then it would get worse. And then better again and then worse. That was the nature of things.

"And it may not be *that* long, either," Mama added.

I took the short route to Mama's house. The sun was setting, the sky streaked golden and gray behind Lakewood Shopping Center.

"Everybody I really liked is dead," Mama announced, looking at the display of color. The sun on her face made her look young and tender.

"Like who?"

"Like Fanny Patton and Polly VanArsdale. The people I really liked and had fun with."

"Isn't there anybody left you really like?"

"Not really. Not from the old gang." Her hands lay limply on her lap. "Some of the new ones maybe. The young ones."

Mama had more friends than anyone I knew. I never understood how she kept up with them all. She had a genius for friendship. I could see how she made them too. Stephanie Insane had loved her, and Condolita, and the present-wrapping man and the dry-cleaning maven. Mama was a charmer.

I thought of Ruth, her old friend.

"What's going on with Ruth?" I asked, just then passing the Lakewood Cemetery where some of Mama's relatives lay, maybe even my great-grandfather, whose grave I'd never gone in to see.

"She had to go to Hillcrest to recuperate from her hip operation, and she can't get a single room. She doesn't even have a curtain in her room." Mama shook her head and shuddered.

This was Mama's greatest fear: the dreaded Nursing Home, some pathetic little brick, one-story prison camp.

"Well, I know it's unpleasant, but it might be good for her in some ways, no?" I said.

"How do you mean?"

"Well, you know, cosmically, karmically. She's used to getting her own way all the time." I was thinking about Mama, not Ruth. "It'll just be for a little while, won't it?"

"Yeah. And you can say that again," Mama spat. "All any of my friends care about is stuff. Monogrammed tablecloths and cut crystal."

"Huh?" This was my mama talking?

We rode in silence.

"I hate this street," she suddenly piped up. "For God's sakes, Marion, why did you go this way?"

I looked around. Men were in the street, some just getting home from work, others having been there all day on their porches or in their postage-stamp yards in metal chairs: unemployment land. Kids and dogs ran back and forth across the road.

"Colored town," Mama said. "I hate this street."

"How can you say that?" I asked indignantly, my heart picking up speed. I swerved gently around a tricycle and a ball rolling into our path. "A minute ago, you were all remorseful about not getting to know more black people, all complimentary and sad, all lovey-dovey."

"I wasn't lovey-dovey, Marion. That's you! You'd drive ten miles out of your way just to go through colored town."

I did like black people. It was true. But this was just the straightest line between two points.

"Quickest way to get you home." I lightened my tone to let her know she couldn't get to me, but I could feel my temperature rising, my patience leaving like a train out of the terminal.

"It hasn't got anything to do with it being colored town, anyway," she said smoothing her jacket. "I hate this street because it's hilly."

"Oh, you hate hilly streets now," I mocked. For all of our lives, we had lived on the top of a hill on Carolina Circle. For twenty years Mother had captained copious carpools up and down that hill.

"Yes," she said matter-of-factly, "I hate hilly streets."

We needed to change the subject.

"Maybe we ought to go out and see Fanny, Mama," I said, speaking of Fanny Patton, one of Mama's favorite "girls." "I'll go with you. I always liked Fanny."

"Where we gonna go, Marion?" Mama looked up from underneath her yellow-gray bangs. "I told you. Fanny's dead, Marion."

My hands tightened on the wheel.

"That would be pretty far out there then, wouldn't it?" I tried to joke. I couldn't keep track of who was dead and who wasn't.

Mama sighed and closed her eyes. "You will come in for a little while when we get home, won't you, baby?"

"Sure, Mama." I reached for her hand.

Chapter Six
Love and Writing

Writing is my love. If you love something, you find a lot of time for it.
—A. P. J. Abdul Kalam

Mama never felt adequately loved. She told me this often.

Her exhausted, perpetually busy mother, Caro Bacon Fuller, tried for a natural abortion with castor oil, followed by bumping down the stairs on her bottom. She had had her fill of babies. She made a parlor story out of it within earshot of Mama. Its retelling became a standard party piece that got lots of sympathetic laughter.

Her father, Ralph Bell Fuller, was a stern and distant head of household. Mama called him Pater, though everyone else called him Skipper. When Mama's arrival was announced, Pater had tuberculosis. He most certainly was not enthusiastic about having another child. Mama was guilty just for being born.

As the fourth child in a busy Victorian household in 1915, Mama grew up feeling neglected and unseen. No one had time for her except her maid and cook, Rose Bumpass, whose full brown bosom she fondly remembered burying her face in for comfort and solace.

As a little girl, Mama retreated into her imagination, escaping to the cool, dark space under the front steps where she made "pin" shows for passersby. For as little as a penny (or a pin)—metal of any kind had some value in those days—people could come up into the yard and see the terrarium six-year-old Mena had made. Digging a hole in the smooth dirt under the porch, arranging in it twigs and buttons and acorn caps, filling it with tiny pebbles, scraps of cloth, a shard of quartz, a broken mirror laid down for a lake, a piece of glass on top—voilà!

Her most frequent escape was to slide through a break in the west-side hedge to go to the Durham Public Library, conveniently located next door. There she found not only sanctuary, but all kinds of friends engaged in thrilling adventures between the covers of the umpteen-thousand books inside. Her love for the printed word was seeded and sealed.

They say you inadvertently marry your parents even if you try not to, and maybe that's true, because Mama never felt she got as much love from my father as she gave him, either.

A dark, handsome, Clark Kent–like figure, Mama's husband—she told me to my great shock—never actually said the words "I love you" until the very last year of his life.

"On his deathbed," she said. (I found out later that wasn't true.)

My sweet daddy, an introvert and conflict avoider if there ever was one, would sometimes say to her threateningly, when she was nagging or complaining ("just trying to start a conversation," she would've said), "I guess you just don't want me around here, Mena."

For Mama, living in an era where divorce or not being married (a spinster, for God's sakes) was tantamount to being a pariah, that was all he had to say. She backed off and behaved.

To my great delight as a child of the sixties, Mama finally claimed to be a feminist in her eighties. She confided that, truthfully, she didn't think Mack would have survived a day without her; that as much as she had been programmed to think he was the pillar she leaned on, her rock, it was really the other way around. He relied on her wholly.

In the final weeks of Mama's life, she surprised me again by saying that she actually didn't think she'd loved my father as much as he had her. So, who really knows?

But Mama definitely thought she never received the love she dreamed of and deserved all of her life.

§

In truth, Mama was a woman loved by many, including her children, who naturally held more complicated views. Her grandchildren adored her. Many people admired her and liked being in her presence. After her death, the boxes and boxes of cards she saved from people, known and unknown to me, attested to this.

There I found piles of cards from me to Mama, too, tied up in a red ribbon, often starting with the testimony: "Mama, I love you so much. And admire you. And enjoy being with you." I said that frequently, not only because it was true, but because I knew she needed to hear it. Sometimes when I told her so in person, she would pause, peer over her glasses, and ask, "Do you really?"

§

What Mama loved is as interesting as the love she wanted back.

She clearly loved words and stories and parties and music. And men. She was the essential party girl. She could play the piano by ear. Errol Garner and Dave Brubeck tinkled in the background, the sound track to my childhood.

She valued coming from a "good family"—meaning prominent. When I asked her what "prominent" meant, she would say, "People who did something, contributed, Marion!"

She had no real insight about class, other than that she was from the higher order. She talked about this often, as well as about money and what it could do for you. She rued the fact that she didn't have as much money as she wanted to the end of her days, wagging her finger at me and admonishing that I had better get it together, because in the final analysis, it was all about money.

Her favorite thing, though, was writing. And after that, reading. The loss of her eyesight was the major blow of her old age, more tragic than losing her hearing or her mobility. She could never get used to books on tapes, and was absolutely apocalyptic about the loss of the book. She sometimes wished she had learned computers before it was too late. "But they are no substitute," she would add. "Life without books will be hell."

Against my father's reluctance to have children, she lobbied hard for her babies, me and my sister. But children ended up not being her thing.

Oh, she drove us everywhere, meticulously sewed our costumes for school plays, made fantastic lunches in shoe boxes for long road trips in our old Plymouth, sandwiches with the crusts cut off and ladyfinger desserts. She was a great cook and knew what we loved. She "did" for us.

But spending time with kids was not her desire. She left that to our father, who luckily liked little people better than he did grown-ups, and listened better than any man I have ever known.

On Sunday afternoons Daddy got us out of Mama's hair, taking us on rides out into the country, back to his old childhood haunts in and around Hillsborough. We played the left-right game, taking turns at the intersections to see where we would end up, while Mama got a break, rested or read, or, in later years, more likely wrote.

Daddy told us stories about the "olden days." He patted our knees and said we were the prettiest things on earth, and that we could grow up to be anything we wanted to be.

Hearing this, Mama would've harrumphed and explained that she was not there with us only because she was always in the kitchen doing the things a woman was meant to be doing.

But that was only partially true.

I remember Daddy begging Mama to get out of the kitchen. All he needed, he would tell her, was a salt sandwich (which he actually ate: mayonnaise between two pieces of Merita white bread with salt.) But Mama was thorough and fastidious and tied to her duties. Having me and Carol on her knee and reading us books, letting us babble on and on, that was his job, not hers. The kitchen was her kingdom.

Even had she had a maid and money like she always wanted, she wouldn't have lingered longer with us. She was a woman ahead of her time: Someone who wanted to be out in the world and aspired to be an intellectual. She was interested in other adults and *their* doings. Not children. Not after the first "hello," a few "oohs" and "ahhs," and a cookie. Then it was "Ya'll run play."

She longed to be a scholar, to receive some acclaim, and to leave a legacy far beyond that of being a mother. Or a wife.

Mama worked a part-time job in a travel agency when we were teenagers, rare for women of her station at that time. She wanted to contribute. She wanted to make some of her own money, too, and always advised me to be sure to have some of mine.

§

All of our damage comes from somewhere. Do any of us completely outgrow whatever happened in our earliest years? Like many kids who feel less than loved, she grew up prone to anxiety, low self-esteem, and depression, masked by a show of superiority. Even as a locally celebrated author, she never fully got past that early, left-out period of her life.

Her family, she felt—my Dad, my sister, or me—never did enough for her, in spite of the fact that she probably received more attention and support than anyone I know. She often complained we weren't calling enough, or that we were traveling too widely and leaving her alone. When we were around, most of the time we found her otherwise occupied, unavailable. Mama was the approach-avoid two-step personified.

The effects of her early less-than-favored status were certainly not all bad. She defensively developed a suite of survival skills and the ability to charm and disarm, a bright wit with natural charisma, perceptiveness, and selective empathy. Mama had a desire to shine that served her well. She was an extrovert who had the presence of mind and discipline to sit down and write four fine books.

But the pain of being ignored growing up had lasting negative effects too, which, of course, affected my sister and me in multiple ways all of our lives. She was more than a bit megalomaniacal, insisting upon being the star in any room she occupied, actually glowering on the rare occasion this didn't happen and another luminary took center stage. Then Mama would inevitably find some way to stomp her metaphorical foot.

Accounting for what happened in our childhoods and who and what our parents were—how they succeeded and failed us—is the work we all do in the process of becoming whole, grown-up people. And I am still growing up in my seventies.

Sometimes I think I have Mama's essence, and then it slips away from me as easily as a dream. I do not pretend to know her at the core. Every person is a miracle and a mystery, a collection of selves.

I confess as I read through all the *stuff* left after a life is done, I have grown to know her far better than I ever would have without time for reflection and research.

In the end, when Mama was almost blind and I could record or write down her words under her nose, Mama would pause, somehow knowing I was writing, and smile. "Be kind, Marion. Be kind," she would say. But never once did she tell me to stop writing.

Mama was way too colorful a soul to polish the patina with sheen and blandishments. I believe she would've wanted me to tell *my* truth.

But above all things, Mama wanted me to follow in her footsteps. She wanted me to write. She had given up on every other form of duplication.

In this way, we were alike: Whatever happened in our lives, we both enjoyed nothing more than seeing characters, creating characters, making up stories, and telling them—creating alternate lives and describing and elaborating on the lives around us.

"Now you can write at last, Marion," she told me in her very last days. "And for God's sakes, do it!"

Fortunately, there is almost nothing I would rather do.

Chapter Seven

The Brownies

Things that were hard to bear are sweet to remember.
—Seneca

"Let's just make Thursday a 'whatever' day," Mama told me the week before. "I'll just see how I feel. There are a lot of little things I might need to do."

"Like what?" I pushed a little.

"Well, I know I need to go get Tom a Christmas present."

It was February.

"No, you don't, Mama. You did that with me, remember? The apron, the Carolina mitts. Remember, he said he wanted something Carolina blue."

Silence hung on the other end of the phone. "Well, maybe . . . Let's just see though."

§

When I arrived at her condo, Mama was dressed and listening to jazz. Little bowls of leftovers were set out around the counter. We were eating at home.

"Do you want some soup?" she asked.

"Sure."

"I was afraid you wouldn't want to stay."

"I want to stay. I love soup. And it's cheaper than going out. I'm all for it." I took off my coat, hung it in the hall closet, and plopped down at the kitchen table.

"Me, too," Mama said. "I couldn't live without soup. Make it once or twice a week."

We proceeded to discuss the glories of soup, her soup, my soup.

"There was a book the other day at the bridge club just about soup." Her back was to me and I could hear the sound of her slicing celery against her thumb. She had the knack of doing it this way without cutting herself. I stared at her hands in wonder, little crookety fingers. Mama still filed her nails.

"I never would've thought you could put spinach in a soup though," she added. "You know what else is good in it? Sweet potatoes." She unwrapped one of the little dishes on the counter and plopped the last two spoonfuls of some past dinner into the pot. "You know Kate's having an operation."

She was referring to a childhood playmate of mine. I hadn't really seen Kate since I was ten years old. Maybe once or twice at some cotillion we were both roped into as teenagers. Kate was now a buxom redhead who'd married well, and was living the "respectable" life near DC.

Somehow, Mama always felt compelled to report to me about Kate. Her bridge club partner and very old friend, Tina, a tight-lipped little lady if I ever saw one, was Kate's mama.

"Yeah, Kate's having a 'tuck up'—you know, to prop up her bladder and all the other stuff." Mama stirred the pot. "Course Tina's so ladylike, she keeps saying she doesn't know what kind of operation Kate's having. 'I don't know,' Tina keeps saying. 'The doctors are just going to do something, I don't know'—as if she wouldn't know what kind of operation her own daughter was having. But you know Tina. She wouldn't mention a bladder for all the tea in China. I hope you like celery, Marion."

"I love celery," I answered. "Good for your joints."

"I worry about celery," Mama said.

"Why?"

"You know they say it's soaked in all that poison water."

"What?" I heard my voice rise.

"Yeah, really." She gave me the eye. "You know that water they spray over the vegetables to keep them fresh. Well, it just sits there in those pipes. They never clean 'em and then they spray all that gunk all over your vegetables. Celery really soaks up water. Heck, it's practically all water."

I was amazed. Mama knew so many things about her health. She was a fool for Dr. Weil.

"So are we," I said.

"Yeah, but we don't lie around in that grocery store spray. My trying to live healthy may be a good thing, but I tell you, it takes all of my time. And I don't have too much time left."

She threw a new copy of GNC's nutrition magazine on the table. "Just read that article on supplements. The guv'ment's gotten in on it, now that America is so obese and all." She rolled her eyes. "They're saying they're going to start regulating supplements. Can you believe that? So, we'll have to go to doctors to get them; won't be able to get what we want. Damn doctors. I do everything I can, take that bilberry for my eyes, eat blueberries. Ain't gotten a damn bit of that from the doctors. They don't even believe in it."

She shook her head and tasted the soup.

"There isn't a doctor on this earth who really wants anybody to get *well*," she went on. "Richest group on the face of the earth, and that's all they're in it for."

I'd heard all this before, but I didn't interrupt to tell her about hedge fund managers.

She turned to look at me: "And don't you go saying they decided to go into it because of public service, either, Marion, because they wanted to help the human race." Mama walked slowly to the refrigerator and peered in. "Because I don't believe a word of it!" She said each word slowly and distinctly into the vegetable drawer, then stood with a bottle in her hand.

"They just want to give out drugs. There're all those kickbacks they get, you know. The drug companies. They wine 'em and dine 'em, give them the best football tickets. Makes me sick!"

Mama walked back to the stove and peered into the pot. "Okay, now, you cook, you hear me? Whew! I think I need to put in a little Bloody Mary mix." She poured and tasted. "Now this is good."

She turned off the burner, spooned the soup into two bowls, and settled in beside me.

She tipped her glass to me. "Anyway," she said, water glass in mid-air, "I'm glad I'm here to bitch about it!"

"Me too!" We saluted each other.

We talked about who was sick, who had Alzheimer's, who she heard from last week, and Nat Gregory's second wife who recently died.

I'd met Nat's wife once, a wispy, ultra-feminine blonde who talked in a whisper and walked on tippy-toes. "She was a trip," I said, focusing on the huge amounts of celery floating in my bowl.

"So is he."

"Really?" I'd always seen Nat Gregory as a good-looking, suave, dark-haired man who danced like Gene Kelly at the country club—twirled his wife around, and looked at her like he really loved her, too, which Mama said he did.

"Oh, yeah. Nat. He was always jumping up and down. Acting silly. 'Joy Boy' is what Daddy called him. Silly. Have you ever known any silly men, Marion?"

I immediately thought of my husband, but held my tongue. Besides, I liked silly.

"But Nat's good-natured and that's worth a million bucks!" she added. "Sometimes the two go together."

"Yeah. Arthur's good-natured." I did say that.

"If you have one person in a couple like that, it's good. One can be a tonic for the other. But," she raised her spoon and pointed it, "two people like that get married and your children will be"—she made the cuckoo-twirl with the spoon beside her ear.

"Maybe better than depression though," I said.

She stood shakily and turned to retrieve a napkin from the counter. Then she dropped her knife.

"Shit," she said and slowly lowered to retrieve it. Her fingers barely grazed the wood floor.

Mama righted herself. "You know, Marion, I've said 'shit' nine times today already. And it's not even one o'clock."

She spread butter on her prairie bread, and we turned to other topics: my broken-down car, what I'm going to do about it, the wonders of having money, Tom and his upcoming marriage, my sister, Mama's boring friends, the wonders of having money.

"What do you mean 'boring'?" I asked about her friends.

"They're just so predictable. I always know exactly what they're going to talk about. All my interesting friends are dead." This was becoming a weekly theme. "Now, I do have some interesting new friends, though. Did I tell you about . . .?" Mama proceeded to tell me about five or ten folks I'd never heard of who've called her or come by in the past two weeks. Miss Congeniality.

She stood to get some Jell-O.

"Am I predictable, Marion?"

I hesitated a little too long.

"Now, Marion, I am, aren't I?" she whimpered. "Don't tell me that I'm predictable."

"I didn't say that!"

I looked around her into the refrigerator. There was a tin of brownies stuck back on the second shelf, but Mother hadn't offered me one. Instead, she was spooning me the Jell-O.

I immediately dove into woolgathering about why Mother never offered me her brownies, pissed. She saved the best for company, and for Tom, the crown prince. I did not qualify as company, and certainly not royalty.

I resolved to get a brownie while she primped. Steal it. Can't keep me away from those brownies no matter how hard you try, I thought. Daughter's prerogative. I looked at her, smiling and listening with one ear.

While I rinsed the dishes, Mama retreated to her bedroom. I headed for the brownie tin and opened it. Wrapped carefully in two layers of wax paper, it was stuffed full. I carefully lifted one out and rearranged the others, sat at the table, and took the smallest nibble. Mother's brownies were the perfect combination of fudge and cake, the very best brownie I'd ever had.

I thought about the conversation with Gen Tilopa last night at my Buddhist group. Tilopa clearly had a thing for chocolate. When we were talking about things one should and shouldn't eat according to Buddha, Tilopa acknowledged he loved chocolate. And coffee. "Coffee is a poison," he said, "but it's not an intoxicant, according to my teacher."

Whatever that meant . . .

"Isn't an intoxicant anything that takes you away from yourself?" my daughter asked me later. "Changes your chemistry. Coffee sure does that."

Gen Tilopa had waxed on into a long rap about the perils of a huge Toblerone and the importance of not eating too much of these "poisons." It wasn't the chocolate, but the attachment to the chocolate that was the problem. In life, we would find our pleasures ephemeral, and when we got what we desired, we'd also find it was really not as good as we thought it would be.

I took another little bite. And then another. Delicious.

Mother was taking her good ol' time in the bathroom. This was working out fine.

After finishing the first brownie, I hesitated for only a minute before I sneaked another one. In the interest of science. Just to test Gen Tilopa's theory.

He was right. The second one wasn't quite as good. But it was still good. The pleasures of this life may be fleeting, I told myself. But they damn well aren't nonexistent. There's suffering, yes. But there's also Mama's brownies.

Now, I mused, maybe three *would* be too many.

Chapter Eight

Biopsy

There is nothing to writing.
All you do is sit down at a typewriter and bleed.
—Ernest Hemingway

Mama sounded brighter on the phone today—more upbeat—even concerned about me a bit, but still making sure I would be on time tomorrow for her appointment with the man who was to deliver her destiny with the biopsy he would perform on her breast.

I was happy to see that, even for a moment, she could lift up out of herself and her ultimate demise. I vowed silently to be there for her in these so-called "end-times," and also to savor, like crème caramel, any moments she still had left to be *my* mama rather than me just being hers.

Here I was, over sixty years old, and I still needed to be babied by her.

§

I was five minutes late and driving far too fast, taking the back roads, hugging the curves, trying not to tailgate.

When I get to her house, Mama was on the pot. She hollered for me to go ahead and start her car.

I slung my huge green bag of overdue work projects into the backseat and tried to start her BMW. It ground but didn't turn over, so I sat back and waited, tried to decompress, doing the "Hum So" breathing that I'd learned in my Buddhist class and watching a few leaves flutter to the concrete.

Ten minutes later, Mama came out.

I could have slowed down, I thought to myself, still saying "Hum So" in my mind. I reached across the seat to open the door for her. She slid in and arranged herself, commenting on the disreputable disarray in her backseat which looked absolutely pristine to me: only one small bag of paper trash and her Yellow Cab sun visor hat on the floor.

She gave me instructions for starting the car, and I watched her hold her breath as it refused to turn over. By the third time, it did. We both relaxed.

Out of deference to her, as well as any cop car that might be lurking around, I drove the requisite 35 miles-an-hour through her neighborhood, but I did try to make the lights so we would get there on time, supposedly her biggest concern.

"Now, Marion, you're going to have to slow down. It's thirty-five here."

She was using an even voice, clearly trying to control herself. "Hurry-up and wait" was the trumpet call of this phase of her life. I slowed down.

Satisfied that I had heard her and was at least trying, Mama chatted on, and I responded appropriately. She interspersed her tales with: "Now, Marion, there are policemen on that corner." "Now, Marion, they really drive crazy over here."

Once, when I changed lanes to avoid some particularly nasty pothole, she commanded, "Stay in this lane!"

I did as she said and took not-a-little pleasure in the grimace on her face when I rattled through the hole. "Whatever it takes," I said to myself, continuing my "Hum So" breathing.

"I had a wonderful time on that corner," she asserted as we crossed Duke and Lakewood where an elderly high-rise now stood.

"What happened there?" I asked.

"Oh, the Lyons lived there, and we had a lot of parties and played games on the lawn as children. They were the richest people in town," she remembered. "And her mother was real permissive."

"That's a good combo." I imagined my mama doing things on that rolling grass lawn a mile from downtown Durham.

"You know what our guardian angels need to do?" Mama asked abruptly.

"No, what?"

"Learn to drive!"

I laughed. I was determined to laugh. Hum So. So Hum. So Ha. So what?

As we rolled over the railroad tracks near Morgan Imports, Mama continued reminiscing about people who lived along Duke Street. Appreciating what a fantastic storyteller she was, I settled back against the headrest to listen. The Hum So was working.

She ruefully pointed out that she couldn't see the street signs now, or the colors of the lights. "If I could just see, everything would be better!"

"How bad is it?" I asked her.

"When I get up in the morning and go in the bathroom to look at my face, I can't really see the features anymore."

That was bad.

After the sign to Durham County Regional Hospital, we turned the corner on Carver Street, where stood a small gray-and-black historical marker extolling Ben and James Duke as famous tobacconists and hydroelectricists.

"Hydroelectric," I said. "I didn't know the Duke boys were into hydroelectrics." But then, I remembered Duke Power.

"Oh, yeah. They started hydroelectrics in North Carolina," Mama piped up. "The oil, the water, tobacco—they got hold of all those kind of things." She sighed.

We turned to one of her favorite topics: money and how expensive everything was.

"When did you take Social Security, Mama?" I asked. This was on my mind as I neared the sixty-two-year-old mark in an age of Social Security stability scares.

"Sixty-two," she said. "I took Daddy's, because his was the highest. I never made much money, just working every now and then, and only part-time at Circle Travel. I remember it being $200-and-some dollars at first. It goes up a little every year—'cost of living,'" she smirked, "and now, twenty-seven years later, I get almost $1,100 a month. Not much, but more than I would have initially gotten by several hundred dollars."

I took mental notes.

"But you know, Marion, every time it goes up, the insurance goes up the exact same amount," her voice raised. "Makes me so mad! To the exact penny! They're so blatant. Those crooks in Washington. Goons in the White House. Everything's in a terrible mess."

I was pleased to see she knew this, and that it bothered her, Bush and Cheney being this year's goons.

"Well, it's you who decided not to vote," I chided as we got out of the car in front of the surgical center, a huge white building that looked like the Taj Mahal sitting by a man-made lake.

"Can't hide money!" Mama snapped.

We walked up the walk, both in black. I wore red shoes, though, to throw a little hitch in the gloom.

Inside the foyer two huge Chinese statues were surrounded by ficus and rubber tree plants.

"Humph. If I had it, I'd flaunt it too," Mama said. She pushed through the glass doors.

"What would you buy, Mama?" I asked, humoring her.

"A chauffeur."

She would not get my goat today.

"Would you buy a new car too?" I asked, protecting my "goat."

"I guess I'd have to."

Mama's car was still Carol and John's old BMW, in good shape, certainly better than my ratty old Volvo, but smaller and stiffer.

"You mean a chauffeur wouldn't drive this one around?" I asked.

"Nope."

I led Mama up to the receptionist's window and sat down on a fake-leather settee to spread out my work and wait for her.

Mama pulled out all her cards at the desk, the insurance card, the drug card, the long-term care card, Medicare—. I heard the women behind the glass calling her "Honey." They crooned softly back and forth. I pulled out my checkbook to pay some bills.

Mama finally returned to the sofa, her cane in one hand, a clipboard in the other. "You gotta help me with this," she whimpered. "I can't read a thing."

The forms were especially pale and small. I read out the lines to her: "Name, D.O.B., phone number, work number."

Her pen hovered over each blank and swirled in a little circle in the air before she put it to paper.

"I'll swear," she said every now and then.

When we get to her emergency contacts, she seemed stumped.

"Just put me down," I suggested.

Her pen revolved over the paper like a hypnotist's pendulum. I heard her breathing hard.

Finally, she said, "I guess I'll put you and Carol."

"Great," I said, eager to see how she was going to fit both of our names in her loop-de-loop handwriting in the teeny, tiny space they'd provided.

"Two of the most unreliable people—" she stopped short, catching herself.

"Now, Mother," I began. I sounded just like she did with the "Now, Marions," I'd hated all across town.

Mama peered over her glasses, looking like a little girl caught with her hand in the offering plate.

"I mean hard to locate," she corrected herself quickly. "You're reliable once somebody can locate you."

She didn't understand a daughter who had work and play that took her elsewhere. Why I was not there to serve her anytime she needed it? she was always thinking. Like a slave girl. Or maybe like daughters used to be?

"Drug allergies. Oh Lord!"

We stopped to figure out how to spell penicillin. It had been twenty minutes since she started this damn form.

She turned the page.

"Oh God, red. I can't read color," she wailed. "I gotta do this again? I just did that."

The nurse came and called Mama into the examining room.

"Thank God," she snapped, closing her pocketbook and standing up, putting the clipboard under her arm. "Do I just bring this?" she asked, now meek and compliant.

"Yes, ma'am." The nurse with brown Vienna-sausage hair rolls under her cap smiled sweetly as Mama wobbled toward the door.

Mama was in there a long time, so I got a lot of checks written. I even began to figure out the yearly budget for a project I was coordinating in Tennessee. I started a rough draft letter to the chief financial officer and heard the door open behind me. Mama teetered out. She looked pleased.

"Let's go, Marion."

I gathered my stuff and held the door for her. We retraced our steps back past the two huge Chinese statues, which once again Mama stopped to inspect.

"What'd they say, Mama? And what do you want to do next?" I asked.

"Lunch."

"Okay, if you're paying. I'm broke. 'No lunches out' is my September motto."

"Of course, Marion," she said dryly. "It's the least I can do."

We tried to think of an alternative option, but settled, as always, on Whole Foods.

On the way over, Mama talked about the physician, whom she described as an 'old country doctor.' She clearly liked him. His wife—the one in the sausage rolls—was his assistant. He said the actual biopsy would take place Monday week in the morning at 8 o'clock. She would meet the anesthesiologist tomorrow.

I offered to drive her there.

"It'll be awfully early," she warned, meaning, "You'll never be on time."

I ignored her.

She told me that the doctor said at her age there's a 90 percent chance it would be nothing, but whatever it was, they would take it out.

Our talk turned to old age, skin, and tummy tucks.

"You get wrinkles even down there, you know, Marion," Mama confided, then tittered.

A parking place opened up right in front of the store. The day was cold, but sunny. A dapper black man held the door for Mama as she slowly climbed the steps, resting on each one and looking around, blinking like an owl caught in the sunlight.

I thought of Mama raised on racism and wondered what she was thinking of this man's kindness. She seemed grateful and flashed him one of her sweetest smiles. I was happy that I was here to watch her have her thinking complicated, her heart opened.

Once inside, she whispered, "High yellow's what we use to call that color."

I winced and watched the man whistle as he went out to his car. I saw helping out a little ole lady was one of the pleasures of his life. I felt grateful to be helping her out too, no matter what shit she said.

I swirled around the store noshing on all the free samples they offered, then, half full, made my decision: It would be a salad.

Mama tapped skeptically around the salad bar.

"I usually won't eat from a salad bar, you know, Marion."

No, I didn't know that, but it made sense. Germs are verboten when you're ninety-plus.

The sneeze hood was a big one, though, so I keep dishing up. Mama gingerly lifted a tray and began to pick at the greens. "Okay, I'll try it," she said, sounding resigned, even though there were a thousand other choices. A risk taker. "What is this, Marion? Spinach? What is this? Romaine?"

She got about a third of the amount I had piled on, and we went to the register where I ordered us iced coffees and grabbed a booth while Mama paid.

When she settled down at the table, she looked around the cafeteria as if she were at the Met, then asked me to help her pry off the top of her salad box.

"I could look at people all day long," she sighed.

The coffee thankfully counteracted the nap my body was crying out for, and we chatted inconsequentially about this and that. Mama fumed about having to ask someone else to help her meet the anesthesiologist tomorrow morning, as I'd realized I had my own doctor's appointment then. I urged her to consider giving up a little of her precious independence. "You're so lucky," I reminded her. "You have so many people around who *want* to help you and who are available to do it."

She decided to call Tom, my first-born.

At about 4:00 PM, I drove Mama back across town. It had been a successful five-hour junket and, though nothing could be certain yet, the chances that Mama's lump would not be cancer were good. I thanked all the gods everywhere as I assisted her out of her car, refusing her offer for afternoon tea because I needed to run an errand before the stores closed.

Though Hurricane Ivan had been threatening to hit us all day long, the sun peeked through the branches. For now, at least, it seemed to be skirting the Triangle.

§

Two days later when talking on the phone to Tom, I asked him if he'd taken her to the hospital Friday morning.

"Hell, no," he answered. "She never even asked me. She drove herself there in a hurricane!"

He was almost shouting. "We've got to do something about her. What are we going to do about her, Mama?" he asked me. "She can't see worth a damn."

It was the $64,000 question.

I sighed, but I halfway admired my mama's clumsy attempts not to *need* her children, not to have to inconvenience anyone. I was also frightened that she would go to such lengths, drive through the interminable gray drizzle just so she wouldn't have to ask for help. She could easily take someone out if she was to crash.

"We've got to get together and *do* something about Grams," I heard my son saying definitively on the other end of the phone.

Out loud I agreed, but inside I thought: Easy for you to say, my thirty-something son who is so far from the world of dependence that old age foists on everyone who doesn't keel over dead with a heart attack first. One way or the other, giving up that "I can do it myself" stance would sneak up on each of us, an affliction understood only by the afflicted.

I thought about my future, about my kooch getting wrinkled, and about Mama, ninety years old, starting out on a junket no less intimidating than Lewis and Clark's, squinting and gripping the steering wheel, resolutely driving herself to the hospital to meet her anesthesiologist and her destiny, in the outer bands of a hurricane.

Chapter Nine

Country Club

A good writer is always a people watcher.
—Judy Blume

My sister, Carol, arranged it at Jimmie Southgate's funeral. We were to meet for a luncheon at the country club with Mama and all her oldest friends. I'd been wanting to see Mary Lucy Cobb, in particular, for decades. If not now, when? These ladies were all past ninety.

My car had finally given up the ghost. The day of the luncheon I was test-driving a "new-used" lime-green Beetle, downshifting around the curves on my way to the Hope Valley Country Club. I felt like the green M&M, my favorite, smug and cute. I passed the steep embankment where my high school friends had had that awful wreck when I was blessedly laid out at home with mononucleosis. I passed the house where Mama grew up before the Depression hit and her father lost his shirt. I wondered who lived in the Kenan house now, and what had happened to my old friend, Anne Edwards. On the inside of the serpentine road, yellow, close-cropped winter grass surrounded brilliant greens on the golf course. Flags flapped.

I rounded the final curve. The club rose like a Hollywood estate. I pulled into the circle in front, finding a space between a bank of black BMWs, Lincolns, and Infinitis, my chartreuse Bug making its own kind of statement.

I pushed through giant front doors into a quiet entryway. Long, carpeted halls stretched past the kitchen and the sunlit dining room where tables covered in white linen stood at the ready. On the right were the familiar downstairs powder rooms. I remembered teasing my hair and lining my eyes in *kohl* in those rooms.

To the left, the club's vast parlor was now almost bare, with ancient wood flooring, a few Victorian sofas arranged in front of the fireplaces at either end, two lamps softly glowing, the furniture all some dark, expensive wood.

I tiptoed into the dining room where I'd had my wedding dinner with my first husband. This was the room where I'd also taken dancing lessons from Mrs. Bagby in junior high, one of Mama's last desperate attempts to teach me how to be ladylike. Here I'd also watched Mama's friends dancing and eating cucumber and purple onion sandwiches with the crusts cut off, piling too much food on small china plates from cut glass bowls mounded with fresh shrimp, crab dip, and cheese straws.

I hadn't been inside this club in over thirty years. Our luncheon was to be in the bar, I knew, but I stood for a moment looking at the dance floor, remembering. I was alone. I didn't pass a soul or hear a sound until I neared the end of the hall and heard muffled voices, a laugh, ice tinkling in a glass. It was like walking into a dream, my former life.

The spacious bar was banked with windows overlooking the golf course and the pool. I saw my dark-haired sister coming toward me. Behind her, silhouetted in the sunlight, Mama sat upright, a grimace on her face. Carol buzzed my cheek and walked me back to her.

As I leaned in for my kiss, Mama hissed, "Don't touch me. My neck's hurting God-awful. If it weren't for these pain pills, I wouldn't be here."

I quickly retreated. Mama sat frozen in place, pretty in her green suit, but unmoving, a paper doll.

"What's the matter, Mama?" I asked. Her neck had been bothering her off and on for weeks.

"It's seized up on me," she whispered, looking panicked. "I don't know how I'm going to get through this lunch."

I turned to my sister and blurted: "Mama needs a driver, Carol. She can't drive that car anymore. You and John need to help her get one, because no one else can do it."

Carol raised her eyebrows. She looked at Mama, who normally would have protested, but now sat, unblinking, not saying a word.

Mama was indebted to my sister and brother-in-law for so much. She lived in a condominium they owned, paying half the rent she would have paid otherwise. They had given her their old BMW for a thousand bucks.

But Mama secretly hated that car. It had no power steering. The doors were impossible to open, and it was a tight squeeze on a good day. She had trouble getting in and out. With her neck, she could hardly turn the steering wheel without hurting herself, not to mention look back over her shoulder to see if she could back out. A month before, my son Tom, told me Mama had started a honking-fest when she found herself going the wrong way on a one-way street.

"I got turned around," she'd said with a shrug. "Durham isn't at all like it used to be!"

No, and neither was Mama.

But she wouldn't tell my sister that. "Beggars can't be choosers," Mama had pounded into our childhood brains.

She needed to drive to the grocery story three times a week. Fresh vegetables were a must for her, which meant four green beans at a time, a golf ball–sized tomato, a handful of spinach. She also needed to go to the library and to the bottomless pit of doctors she saw.

"I can't do it!" she'd wailed to me one day. "I'm just interrupting everybody else's life! I may as well die."

Just last Thursday, she hadn't gotten out of bed until noon. It was unmade when I arrived for lunch. Unheard of. Pain was on top now, and she was depressed, had been for weeks.

"Mama, is that true?" Carol asked, leaning over. Sometimes Carol was offended when she didn't hear the news directly from Mama's mouth.

Mama's nod was almost imperceptible, but it was there.

"Well," Carol turned to me and smiled, ever generous, "we'll just have to get you a driver."

"Right now?" Mama breathed.

"No, not now. Now, I'm going out to look for Mary Lucy," Carol said and smiled. "They're bringing her over here in the Carol Woods van. She's in a wheelchair now, Marion. Did you know?" And she walked out of the bar.

Mama watched Carol's retreat, then looked up at me. "I'm trying to live in the minute, Marion, positive thinking and all that." She knew my mantra. "But if I can just get through this lunch, I'll be happy."

I was amazed that there had been no protest about the car. Maybe Mama was finally coming to terms. She saw she needed help.

I sat down and scanned the room.

"Who's that?" I asked, nodding to a woman who had just nodded to Mama.

"It's—" Mama hesitated. "I swear I get ready to say somebody's name and it just skittles outta my mind."

"Join the club," I replied.

"Marion, you don't know what you're talking about."

"Yes, I do. I've always been this way. Especially with names. Marilyn and I were saying last week that maybe we had one good brain between us."

"You just wait," she threatened.

I turned and looked out the windows, remembering the days at the pool as a child, me with no worries and no awareness, day after day perfecting my dive, showing off by almost grazing my nose on the side of the pool as I flipped up my legs and swooshed straight down through the water, swimming through Daddy's legs, sitting under the aqua surface holding a tea party with my imaginary friends, seeing how long I could hold my breath.

For a skinny girl who couldn't keep up her knee socks, this was my place. I was a good swimmer. I could shine at the pool. Even though I was shaped like a number #2 lead pencil until I was fourteen, bee stings for breasts, I had skills.

Then finally my boobs popped out. I flashed back to that summer, recalling the Lanz bathing suit Mama bought me, black with white squiggles—or was it white with black squiggles? And a square neck that made my breasts bunch up like an English milkmaid's. That summer I felt cute, even—at long last—sexy. The boys were paying attention, too. We began the mating dance around this pool.

"Starlu," Mama said suddenly.

"Huh?"

"Starlu Satterfield. That's that girl's name."

There. She had found it. I turned and looked again at the sixty-year-old woman Mama was calling a girl.

Back then, I'd always seemed to play second fiddle to some of the more sophisticated girls. Still, I saw it was going to happen, and I could wait. One of these boys would someday prefer a girl with some skills, a girl with some spunk. To hell with the rules that said you had to bat your eyes and act like everything they ever said was brilliant, touch their barely muscling arms, shouting "Got you last!" and winking before diving in.

Not for me. I bounced up and down on the high dive before I sliced through the water as pretty as you please and came up gleaming all over to do it again.

I remembered one night when some boy, maybe Charlie White, put some kind of pill in everybody's drink that made your pee turn fuchsia, so we could see who had secretly peed in the pool. We watched the expression on that stuck-up blonde-who-had-the-convertible as she slowly pivoted in a billowing bloom of pink, everybody around the pool hee-hawing at her mercilessly. Charlie's father was a doctor. I wondered whatever happened to Charlie. He was cute. And I had been in on the joke.

At that moment, a second party of two entered, interrupting my ruminations.

"Well, hello, Marion," one of them said sweetly to me, and stuck out her hand.

"Hellooo," I smiled at her. "Good to see you!" My standard line when I had no idea who somebody was.

I went through the same routine with the other lady I didn't know before they both settled down and began their chatter.

I leaned over and whispered to Mama, "So who are they?"

"Marion, that's Jeanne Taylor," she chided. Jeanne had lived across the street from us my whole growing up. "And Marcia Muller. Don't you remember? She went to St. Mary's with you."

"No, I don't remember." One had gray hair, the other dyed black. Both had double chins.

"Marcia Muller was Miss North Carolina once. Don't you remember?"

A vague ghost crossed my mind. This out-of-a-bottle raven-haired matron had once been an untouchable, cherry-lipped beauty who lived down the hall from me in my college dorm, a girl so beautiful and mighty, few of us even spoke to her. Now she was talking to me as if we were dearest friends. I liked how old age evened everything out. I wondered if I looked as comparatively cute as I thought I did. Surely, I didn't look as old as these two. I felt for my chin and stroked it back into place.

Carol reentered the bar with one of Mama's friends and her daughter, a thirty-something in a pink cashmere suit. They settled around the table amid pleasantries. Mama turned on her smile.

Mama's friend was shaped like a circus tent in black—Darth Vader with purple lipstick. It had been years since I had seen this woman. I never would have recognized her on the street. The last time, she had been a tiny bird of a girl. Must have eaten like a bird too, I thought unkindly, ten times her weight at every meal.

I felt her discomfort as she arranged herself in the chair and sucked in my own stomach. Mama batted small talk back and forth. Their attention turned to the daughter, who began to coo about her babies and her husband, who traveled for Chili's, whatever that meant. The talk devolved into babysitter troubles.

This pair was followed by Tina Land, walking through the bar upright and smiling. She settled down next to me, patting my arm. Tina looked like she always had, corkscrew curls perched atop her head, scalp showing, square gold earrings pulling down long lobes, everything in place. As she talked, I thought of my father scurrying back into the bedroom in his underwear, cursing, when Tina would arrive unannounced on our doorstep with a birthday card and push the doorbell. Tina's claim to fame was that she never forgot anyone's birthday in town. She had a special calendar for it, she told me later.

But my father would snarl and say, "She just does it to embarrass the rest of us."

Our black cocker spaniel, Topsy, would inevitably roll over on his back and expose himself when anyone came up on the porch. "Roll out his lipstick," Daddy called it. Though normally embarrassed by Topsy's welcoming routine, Daddy liked it when he did it for Tina.

All this went through my mind in half a second as the woman across from me talked about her daughter's successful marriage, meaning ease and money. Behind Tina, I saw my godmother, Lib, walking toward us slowly, with a cane.

Lib, at ninety-three, was the oldest in the group. Though stooped, to me she looked like she always did, broad faced and smiling, leaning forward to pat my hand, her goddaughter, whatever that meant. We never saw each other, never communicated. Would this have really been the woman who took care of me if my parents died in a plane crash? Didn't godmother mean someone in a sparkly crinoline with a wand and magic powers? Or maybe just an extra Christmas present, something my parents couldn't afford? The Mallards had money, so it was usually some silver for my so-called wedding chest. But all that stopped abruptly when I hit puberty.

I probably hadn't been too sterling a godchild either. Lib was a happy sort, but she and I'd never had much in common. She was into monogrammed tea towels and crystal goblets and propriety at about the same time I was letting everything rip, including my clothes and my manners, my material existence receding in importance to the women's movement that saved me from all this.

She talked about her sons. One ran a boating outfit and was "always at the beach," she said proudly. The other was a money manager somewhere. "And all those darlin' grandchildren," she sighed.

My grandbaby-hungry insides tightened. When in God's name would my own children produce? What were they thinking? That their lives were their own?

Just then, everyone turned to look at Mary Lucy being wheeled into the room by sweet Carol, who had been doing her duty at the door while we were all catching up. When they got to the table, we stood to make room.

"Sit, sit," Mary Lucy admonished, waving her hand. "Don't get up 'caus'a me."

One of her shoulders was a good ten inches lower than the other one.

"I want to sit at the table," she said, looking at me. I rushed over to the wheelchair and began to park it, locking the brakes.

"I can do it, I can do it," she chided as I tried to lift her.

I watched as she slowly hoisted herself up with arms trembling, and then sank into the chair. It took ten minutes to inch her up to the table, but when she was there, she sighed and smiled at all of us.

"Now don't you let me interrupt," Mary Lucy said kindly. "Go on back to what you were talking about."

Mary Lucy still had the thickest Southern drawl of them all. I thought back to summers at Nags Head. Her family was always in the cottage beside ours, we children playing in the pebbly sand while our parents had highballs up on the porch, their soft laughter and stories rising in the wind above our heads.

I asked Mary Lucy all the perfunctory questions, remembering, as she answered, her indomitable curiosity and good humor on those beach trips.

"Everything's just wonderful,'" she used to croon and crooned now, trying to peer at the menu at the same time.

"Can I just have a half a sandwich?" she asked the waitress over her shoulder. "How big is that? Show me with your fingers. Could you give me just half a portion?"

Everyone else ordered the soft-shell crab, except Mama and me. We asked for the salad bar. As I got up to fill our plates, she whispered, still immobile, "Not too much, Marion. Not too much." Wasting food was a sin and disgrace.

We ate and reminisced, me with my eye on Mary Lucy, whose physical changes were drastic, but whose spirit seemed the same. I was acutely aware this could easily be the last time I saw any of these women. We chatted companionably through dessert.

After the luncheon I offered to drive Mama home, because Carol again needed to wait for Mary Lucy's assisted-living van. I really wanted Mama to see my punch-buggy, and I wanted a little more time with her, too.

The luncheon had been a success, defined as: We all got there and carried on. Though when I'd kissed Lib good-bye, she'd confided, "You know I didn't hear a word anybody said."

"Well, you smiled in all the right places," I assured her.

§

On the way home, I drove gingerly. Mama even mentioned how well the car handled.

"The pill hit me about halfway through," she told me. "Otherwise I wouldn't have made it. Isn't Mary Lucy pitiful?"

I nodded that she was, though not entirely thinking so. Mary Lucy was happy, and though Mama and her friends had always derided it, "Mary Lucy's just silly." I liked it. She reminded me of how I wanted to be. I loved silly.

We eased silently around the curves in Hope Valley. Then Mama poked my arm.

"Marion, I had the most wonderful dream last night and it's after breakfast so I can tell it."

I looked at her.

"You know, it's bad luck if you tell a dream before breakfast."

I nodded, unsure.

"But I gotta tell you. I'm fighting to keep my spirits up, and it's what kept me going during that lunch. You were in it, and Kirsten. She looked like a ragamuffin, the way she did when she was little." Mama slipped in that dig. "We were with a lot of strangers in a two-story house. And Mack was gone." She sounded disconsolate.

"And I kept thinking, 'I don't know why I don't hear from Mack. He went off and he said he'd be right back, but it's been two weeks, so something terrible must have happened.' And then I would think, 'He's gone to that other woman,' but you kept saying, 'No, Mama, he'll be back.' And then I looked out the window, and there, coming, was Mack, with that jaunty walk of his. I screamed and ran out and hugged him and he kissed me. It was the most wonderful kiss."

She was silent for a minute, remembering. We eased by a gaggle of men in a golf cart on the shoulder of the road. I thought about dream kisses and how amazing they could be.

"He said, 'Mena, I've got the most wonderful news.' His hat was back on his head, and he had his arm over his eyes to block the sun. 'It's really good news. Just wait 'til tomorrow and you can read it in the papers.'

"And I said, 'No, Mack, don't do this to me. Tell me!' And he said, 'Okay. Well, we have gotten a bunch of money to do something really important on an international scale.' He was excited, Marion."

I thought of Daddy's dual life as a newspaperman and a CIA agent.

"I feel like it's a message, Marion. Maybe something wonderful is going to happen!"

I looked at her. Her face was expectant, hopeful for the first time in weeks.

"I tell you something, Marion," she said, still staring forward, "*old* love is great love. I can remember when your daddy was sick, he would say to me," her eyes misted over, "'If it weren't for you, Mena, I'd'a been dead a long time ago,' and I would say, 'Me too.' And he would say, 'Yeah, but I really mean it.'"

This was their love song.

We had arrived at her condo and sat in the car talking about Daddy.

"Remember that thing he used to say?" she asked.

"What thing?"

Taffy is a thief.
Taffy went to my house and stole a piece of beef.
I went to Taffy's house but Taffy wasn't home.
Cause Taffy went to my house to steal the marrow bone."

I pulled the post-it notes out of my pocketbook and started scribbling. I had never heard this in my life. She repeated it, laughing.

"It's amazing what turns a person on." Mama's memory for verse was amazing too. "Your daddy was no angel," she said, "But he was funny. And believe me, Marion, that goes a *long* way."

We got out of the car.

"And you know what?" she said before she tried to unlock the door with her leather-gloved fingers. "He's an angel now. He never would have wanted it, but he's an angel now. My neck's tightening up. I'd better get inside. Drat," she added as she dropped her cane. I bent to retrieve it.

"Now, don't you go telling Arthur about that dream," she warned, finger wagging. "He won't understand it. Besides, it's my dream."

"I won't, Mama," I assured her, not understanding why this was important.

"Go on now. I'm gonna be all right," she said. "I appreciate everything you do for me, baby. I'm gonna be all right. Guess what Carol told me just before we left the club."

"What?"

"She thinks she may have found me a driver. The husband of the lady at the front desk. He's just retired, and the lady said if she brought it up right, he might go for it."

"Hey, that's great, Mama." I hugged her. She smelled of Shalimar.

"Yep," she said, standing in the glass doorway, wiggling her fingers at me like she always did when I left her, blowing me a kiss.

She opened the front door a crack as I cranked up the engine.

"Remember, Marion," she hollered.

"What?"

She looked like a different person now, infused with light and some happiness my father had brought her in a dream.

"Something good is going to happen. On an international scale!" She glanced over to her neighbor's condo, a spitting distance away, to see if anyone had heard her make this outrageous pronouncement.

I nodded, grinning.

"I believe it," she cheered me on. "And you better believe it, too!"

"Let Daddy be right," I whispered. Then I scratched off into the sunlight.

Chapter Ten

Mama and Men

What a strange thing man is; and what a stranger thing woman.
—Lord Byron

On a writing retreat after Mama died, I found two things in a shoe box: a worn, brown *Herald-Sun* envelope, fat and rubber-banded with the words "Love Notes" scrawled across it in red magic marker, and a single yellowed article from *Cosmopolitan* magazine, circa 1937, called "Adultery for Adults." I read it with my morning coffee.

The Case for Creative Adultery, the book from which the article was excerpted, began by describing not only the corporeal pleasures associated with what was called "horizontal enrichment," but how it would do everything from saving the world to keeping your shoes shined.

Some friend had sent the article to Mama, writing across the top that she knew Mama would like it, and that she was getting the unabridged version. So, I knew it wasn't something Mama picked up for research on her own first book: *The Curious Wine*. Mama had struggled mightily with that book. The editors in New York who'd reviewed it wanted her to put more sex in it., and this was hard on Mama. It became a family joke.

I'd asked her many times how she got the idea for the book and if she'd ever had an affair. Inevitably she would answer, "That's for me to know and you to find out, Marion," in a sing-songy tone. Mama loved being mysterious.

As a teenager, when boys and sex were about all I could reasonably be expected to think about, Mama had assured me—probably in answer to some other inappropriate inquiry of mine—that she and Daddy had never had any trouble in *that* department.

"It's damned hard to write about, though, Marion," she said, blue Ice-O-Derm all over her face, trudging back into her bedroom in her nylon pajamas, while Daddy smirked and shrugged his shoulders.

Mama and Daddy kissed in front of us. They dated. They taught me the value of parents who went out on the town and had friends and lives outside of us. I remember many a night when they came home happy and smiling, probably tipsy after some engagement at the country club or a friend's house. These events were frequent: parties and dances, even costume balls.

She was rewarded with a largely happy marriage, a sexy marriage. Other than talk, a currency Mama wanted from my father but which he was not in possession of, they were content together.

Still, talk was Mama's trade. She liked a good repartee. I remember her flirting with my first father-in-law, a great conversationalist, who not only flirted back but conversed with her enthusiastically. Mama was coquettish to the end of her days.

But this: "Adultery for Adults"? Just the Table of Contents was provocative:

- *What to Wear*
- *How to Begin*
- *Where to Go and How Often*
- *Things to Say if Cornered*
- *Combinations and How They Work*
- *Occupational Hazards*
- *Dangerous Partners or Types to Watch Out For*
- *A Word to the Working Wife*
- *Do's and Don'ts*
- *Ending the Affair*
- *Combinations and How They Work*

Mama?

I would have given my eyeteeth to know why she saved that article, why she had it in the first place. But I would never know. I couldn't ask her now. And she wouldn't have shot straight anyway. Mama'd told me so many contradictory things about her beaus and love life before Daddy, it was a tangled web.

She was a virgin when they married, I knew that. I heard about Daddy buying her that yellow nightgown from Saks Fifth Avenue, and the rest of her New York City honeymoon cystitis story so many times, I could write it verbatim. It was high-value tragicomedy.

That morning, I put down the article and threw up my hands. Then I unbanded the Love Notes envelope. On long, flesh-colored typewriter paper that unfurled to my knees, so thick it felt like shammy cloth, were dozens of notes from my father, Mack, to my mother: self-deprecating, funny doggerel he'd written and folded a check into for her birthday or Valentine's or at Christmastime. Daddy's love notes.

He may not have said it through his lips as Mama'd declared, but my father certainly professed his love for her in writing, at least on the requisite days, and I was convinced that no matter how she may have vexed him, or he her, theirs was a love story.

He wrote:

"Alas, pity the plight of I
Who just can't talk, much as I try.
But that is that, and I'm your fate:
A lug who won't communicate."

May half of your troubles continue not to happen.
And may the other half keep on being mostly me."

There he drew a heart with a chagrinned face, an arrow piercing its head.

Inside was a note in Mama's handwriting:

"Daddy wrote me this on August 7, 1984, three days after our 48th anniversary, and less than a week after his surgery to remove a tumor in his throat and his palate. He couldn't talk, but he had by no means lost his ability to communicate. He was full of beer that I had given him through a tube in his nose, as well as love. He wanted that beer, and I gave it to him. When it went down, he said, 'Wonderful!'"

Daddy's note, in a shaky hand, read:

Mena, you men-a lot to me.
I'm sorry August four was not marked for you

By sounding of horns and crashing of cymbals.
It would have been, had I not lost my nimbles.

Your mistake of 48 years ago gives me
happiness and life,
While all I've given in return is trouble and strife.
Admittedly yours has been at times
accompanied with frowns,
But better than my increasingly unintelligible grunts
and grumbles, that now have to be written down.
You need acclaim, not a damned clown.
Now YOU even admit there's no way for me to tell you
How much I love you,
But I'm not going to stop trying.
As a hint, I'll tell you it's considerable
And the only other thing that's considerable
Is the trouble I provide.
I'm sorry I messed up this anni-VERSITY.
But unless you give the word
I hope to be around for the 50th.
Try to have a good day, Mena. ILY
(Meaning "I Love You"—underlined five times)

It was signed: D-Bumps. In each of his notes, Daddy called himself names: Daddy-Bumps, DB, Ebert (Mama's secret lover), only occasionally what everyone else called him: Mack, but never his given name, Henry.

I closed the box and sat back with a second cup, to muse on my mother and father's love life. The way they were together inspired me to want the same thing. (My husband would have said it 'ruined me forever.') Romance was valued in the Fuller-Webb household.

My parents were openly affectionate. They teased each other good-humoredly and went out on dates. We knew over time the things they didn't like about each other. But their promise was to never fight in front of us, and they didn't. We saw Mama in tears every so often. That was just her nature, we thought, as we gathered around to console her. Daddy was circumspect.

As they grew older, they doted on each other. They would say "Your mama just . . ." or "Your daddy just . . ." when trying to explain the other to us if we didn't understand. They were faithful supporters and protectors of each other.   .

§

In Mama's last days, when she talked about seeing Daddy again in heaven—how he would probably have his hat cocked back on his head and would say when he saw her, "Well, hello Miss Peevy," he liked to call her that—she would also ruminate on this question:

"I wonder if your father ever had an affair."

"Daddy?" I would cry. "Upright and upstanding Daddy? Impossible!"

"Well, you know he was the person who hired the first woman at the paper. *And* the first black, Marion," she added to prove her point that they were way ahead of me.

Then she would tell me again about Ann Colavito, a young reporter I remembered with a big bosom and curly brown hair, from somewhere in the Northeast, who she knew was in love with Daddy, even if he didn't love her.

Always, Mama would shake her head and smile magnanimously after telling me this story and say, "I don't care whether he did or didn't, really. Whatever your daddy did was just fine with me."

A product of her era, and no fool about who held the reins and the purse strings. Mama was decidedly heterosexual, preferring men to women in every way all her life. She played up to men, flattered them. But often she tossed off disparagements behind their backs, as well. Once I heard her say: "Look at that man blubbering over there. That makes me so happy. Men are big horses' asses."

Still, being girls, my sister and I were always at a distinct disadvantage with her. We might extol the secret of life itself, but Mama would invariably look at us askance. The very same "secret" out of some man's mouth, and she would be batting her eyelashes. I would go so far as to say that after my father, my son, Tom, was Mama's favorite person. The rest of us were jealous of the influence she allowed them.

Mama had many "boyfriends till the end of her days," men who came courting with flowers, chocolates, and wine: Henry Satterfield, for example, though Mama said he did that to a lot of ladies, and it didn't "mean-a thing."

Another was a "big Hollywood producer" (Mama always said it that way) of the Cagney and Lacey show, the husband of Sharon Gless, or Lacey (the blonde). His name was Barney Rosenzweig. Mama met him in her writing class at UNC in days long past.

Barney stayed true to Mama. He would often come to North Carolina on his way up or down to Palm Beach and take her for a ride.

"Guess who came by today!" she would beam. "Barney Rosenzwieg. And we went to ride in his Bentley!"

Once, near the very end of her life, when I drove over to visit Mama at Hillcrest where she'd finally landed, she was bent over in intimate conversation with a white-haired man in front of the fake fireplace in the parlor, which she usually didn't deign to visit because she really didn't want to be around all those "old" people.

As I approached, she introduced me, then waved me off. "Marion, you'll just have to come back some other time," she said. "Barney's here."

Chapter Eleven

The Humanities Center

Above all, watch with glittering eyes the whole world around you because the greatest secrets are always hidden in the most unlikely places. Those who don't believe in magic will never find it.
—Roald Dahl

Today Mama decided she wanted me to take her to the Humanities Center where her painter friend from The Three Arts Club had a show.

"I've never been to the Humanities Center, Marion. Do you even know where Alexander Drive is?"

I did. I listened to her complain that it must be halfway to Rawleigh, as we piled in the car and headed east.

On the way, I drove past my daughter's place of work, a shiny glass building in Research Triangle Park. Mama marveled that her very own granddaughter could work in a place so fine; then she complained about the sunshine reflected in the windows and worried aloud about her next eye appointment coming up in January.

This was an ongoing worry for Mama, for whom reading and writing was every bit as important as breathing, but she was still refusing surgery. So, after Christmas I was to take her to get another specialist's opinion.

§

As we turned west onto Alexander Drive, the setting sun made her cry out again. She fumbled frantically for her sunglasses, as if they were an oxygen tank.

"I can't see Marion! I can't see!"

If we were going west into the sun, I reasoned, we were headed the wrong way, so I turned abruptly at the National Toxicology Center where a guard the size of a linebacker rushed out like we were planning to bomb the place.

"The Humanity Center," he smiled, fumbling through the papers on his clipboard, "Oh, it's about four miles that way," he pointed. "In the other direction."

Mama didn't notice the annoyed line of cars on our tail or the concerned look on the guard's face at my audacious four-point turn. She was just glad to be getting away from the sun in her face.

"You know, these days, there are only certain times of day I can even go out!" she keened.

"Mama, you need to quit driving. Period." There: I said it. In spite of the happy talk, Carol had yet to secure her a driver. "Except to the library and the grocery store, which you could drive to with your eyes closed," I added sympathetically.

Just last week, Mama'd confided that she'd had another incident going the wrong way down a one-way street, and we all knew she had trouble telling the color of the traffic light.

"But what would I do?" she begged of me. "I can't keep bothering Carol."

"I would drive you twice a week." I was already on for a regular Thursday afternoon gig. "And Carol would help out, you know that. Kirsten's off at noon on Fridays. Tom comes over every Friday night. And with all those friends of yours, you wouldn't have any trouble." Mama had thousands of pals, all eager to be in her company, the grand old dame of Durham.

I'd better get busy making some more friends and being nicer to the few I have, I thought, feeling impotent, then guilty. What a crappy reason to make friends.

We finally arrived at the Humanities Center, then wove through thick pine woods off the interstate to a low-lying concrete building, all angles and glass, hidden deep in the trees. No wonder neither of us had ever been there before.

The handicapped spot was a good walk away from the front entrance. We got out, and I slowed my pace, hovering to help my ever-independent Mama if she requested it. She struggled with her leather gloves and shooed me away. Mama hated to have someone guide her elbow, hated to be touched at all. She felt demeaned unless she specifically asked for help. Invaded.

The walk through the largely empty gallery took about twenty minutes, but it seemed much longer. Mama and I eyed her friend's paintings, moving backward and forward, shading our eyes: all smeared Italian landscapes in blues and greens, Lake Como, various countryside duomos and villas.

The Center's resident scholars glided quietly past us to stacks of clothbound reference books that lined the inner walls. In one corner stood the largest Christmas tree I'd ever seen, a giant blue spruce brushing the ceiling, decorated with one-of-a-kind handmade ornaments. We stood before it, relishing its scent, transfixed with mouths agape, even Mama, a self-declared Christmas cynic.

On the way out, the sun cast a rose and purple sky from behind the trees. The air was cold. Mama grabbed my arm.

"I'm glad we did that, Marion."

"Me too, Mama."

This was the first time in ages we had gone anywhere other than shopping or to the doctor's office. A new venture. Successful, too.

"I'm glad I didn't have to go here with the artist and ooh and ah and pretend like I liked the pictures more than I did. Interesting though," she added, not one for unnecessary cruelty. "I liked her colors, but who would ever think up that way to paint something? I think she may not be able to see any better than I do."

I laughed.

We started up the car and eased down the long winding drive.

At the stop sign, Mama grabbed my arm.

"Promise me something, Marion."

"What?"

"I know it's not going to happen while I'm alive, or at least it doesn't seem like it is." She paused, and with the chill and the sun going down, I could feel the ghost of life's last act hovering between us.

I looked at her in her black seal coat and leather gloves, tiny and shrinking, her eyes foggy, her mouth pursed. Then she broke into a smile and squeezed my wrist. "Promise me you dedicate your first book to me."

"Oh, I will, Mama," I assured her, touched by her request, and her certainty that there would be a first book.

"And I'll know if you did or not too, Marion," she admonished me, cocking that finger. "I'll be watching. I'll be up there soon, you know, and I'll be looking straight down."

Chapter Twelve

Widow

What kind of wife would I be if I left your father simply because he was dead?
—Jess Walter

Mack Webb's dying left a black hole in Mama's life.

Daddy had a long, debilitating illness, and Mama was courageous and steadfast in bearing up under the complicated and tiring procedures that go with a terminal illness, and finally the death at home, of one's lifelong partner. She stayed focused and busy.

I remember feeling critical of her for that. I wished she would sit down and talk to Daddy, hold his hand, help him relax. But that was not her nature. She was busy: busy taking care of him, cooking for him, feeding him, emptying his bedpan. Then he died.

Decades later, after she had died, I found her handwritten testimony to hospice, who had given her support afterwards, among her papers:

Halfway through my first group meeting, I thought: I can't come here again. I can't talk to strangers about my pain. But I did go again, and now I thank God every day for the strangers who have become friends through suffering. They are people to whom I listen, and who listen to me. We disclose some of the most poignant experiences of our lives, and thus we mitigate our common grief.

Hospice did not just accompany the dying to the door. It saved lives. Mama's, for one.

Grieving takes a long time. There are so many losses in a loss.

As it had been during Daddy's dying, the only remedy for her afterwards was staying busy. True to her vision, she continued to work for over ten years on her book about that outrageous little man who called himself a general: Julian S. Carr. Her writing kept her sane. Daddy never saw that book finished. He had actively supported her writing habit all their lives, but he lived only to see one out of her four books in print.

With Daddy gone, Mama wrote and wrote. She was often depressed during those years, but she later told me that she felt the depression was utilitarian, because it closed down her system when she needed a rest from the world and a new way of approaching her life. Her body and mind were telling her something: she could simplify and change her priorities. Now, she could become a full-fledged writer.

She took a course at Duke on grieving, saving the reading list for the course in one of those boxes. It was daunting, filled with the current books for the time: *Necessary Losses; When Bad Things Happen to Good People; The Dance of Anger.* It included academic and philosophical books: Glasser's *Control Theory*; Reick's *Listening with the Third Ear*; Rollo May's *My Quest for Beauty*; plus, *The Little Prince* and *A Whole New Life* and one with an intriguing title: *What Tom Sawyer Learned from Dying.*

There were also books on childhood: *Making Peace with Your Parents, Childhood and Society*, and one by Margaret Mead's daughter, Mary Catherine Baker, *Composing a Life*, along with a mound of worksheets that asked questions about how her own family had handled death. Mama had written in her notes:

> *Especially after a loss, it's important to adapt and change, and to redefine yourself. Loss breaks down defenses: It makes you re-value yourself, your life. The goal of grieving is not just acceptance, it is redefinition. You must promote a more compassionate way of viewing yourself: How you grew, rather than how you were held back from growing. We invent ourselves, and I can re-invent myself.*
>
> *My name is Wilhelmena Webb, but everybody calls me Mena. I've lived in Durham all my life and I am a writer. I started with fiction, but now I am more into local history. I'm working on my memoirs. I have two books*

published. My mission is to elicit feelings of sadness and
joy through stories.

At the bottom of that same box of papers, I found a small blue notebook. On the first page in her familiar scrawl was a note:

"His name was Mack. Almost from the beginning that's what it
was in spite of the fact that he was christened Henry Bond Webb."
And then a letter to herself:

Dear Mena,
    I know you miss him. I just don't know how much.
I only know you'll miss him for the rest of your life!
      He was one of the great ones.
                  Love, Mena

"Afterwards, there are times Mack feels oddly present," she'd added. *"Mack was very romantic, successful at it too. And I know one thing: if Mack had a, secret life, he was also very successful at that. He was like the "Old Owl Who Sat in the Oak," and if I was smarter, I would've known he was trying to tell me something."*

        'The Wise old owl sat in the oak.
        The more he saw, the less he spoke.
        The less he spoke, the more he heard.
        Why can't we all be like that wise old
        bird?"'

I shook my head in admiration at Mama's ongoing efforts to make peace with the forever-loss of her husband, sadly wondering how I would handle it if Art died before me.

Distressed, I was about to box all the stuff back up and move back to the living, when I found this small folded essay in the back of the notebook:

One Moment in Time
I've been asked to focus on one moment in time and write
about it. Why did I immediately think of the day Mack

died? Was it because the day was bright and sunny, like today? It was cold, like today too, because it was October instead of January—the first day of October, and the sky was bright blue, and the clouds, bright and puffy, like cotton, and the sun warm and welcome on your skin after the long hot summer when you couldn't walk out of the air-conditioning into the plain air without complaining.

It was a beautiful day, the day he died, and it was mid-afternoon, not a fit hour for death. People should take naps at two or three in the afternoon. People shouldn't die then.

Of course, he'd been dying for days and days, and I suspect, now that I think about it, he'd been in a coma for a long time. I'd never seen anyone die, and I'd never seen but two people dead. One was the father of one of my friends in the third grade, and the other was my Uncle Tom. I was no more than ten then, not even ten, and it didn't impress me. Both of these men were just very, very still. Too still to be sleeping, but not a bad still—it wasn't frightening.

So Mack hadn't yet become that still when the hospice nurse called me to come in. He was just lying there as he'd been lying for so long, with his eyes closed and his hands crossed on his chest, and his chest moving as he breathed, and his mouth slightly open. He would've hated it if he'd known all those women were watching him. He was vain. I suppose all handsome men are. Maybe all men, handsome or not.

But he looked better than the average dying person, I'll bet. And it was all so peaceful. There we were—Marion, Carol, and I—his three women, and the nurse who had become like a family member, and I was propped up on the twin bed next to his hospital bed, and the girls were there too, down at the foot, and we were talking and laughing. I can't believe it now, but we were, and it was good. We were talking about family things he'd done and said all through his life, and actually laughing.

The nurse said, "You know, hearing is always the last thing to go." That was reassuring. Instead of being ashamed about laughing, I was glad.

Mack had laughed so much during his long lifetime, and when he died, there we were with him, laughing.

Chapter Thirteen

Anger

She wished she had had the guts to go up to him and say hello.
Or possibly break his legs, she wasn't sure which.
—Stieg Larsson

On the way to Mama's just before Hope Valley Road, I impulsively
called my daughter who was home from work nursing two pulled
wisdom teeth. Our chat quickly turned from the perils of Percocet to
last night's Buddhism class, which we were both attending, but she
had missed.

Gen Tilopa's talk was on anger, and Kirsten and I were
continually "working on" our own anger, trying to understand it, if not
get rid of it, see what it was and was not good for.

"I have some fear that if I let go of my anger completely, I may
not continue to exist," I admitted.

"Maybe that's exactly the point," she said.

"I kept asking Tilopa about fight/flight and all that, our inborn
need to protect ourselves, dropped into every single one of us no
matter what our culture. It's what we do with our anger that's the
problem, isn't it? Not the anger itself? I kept asking him that."

I was a Buddhist "wannabe," teaching Anger Management
classes at Duke, so I needed to know this. I didn't want to lead others
astray.

"What did he say?" Kirsten asked. I heard the Novocain in her
voice.

"He kept talking about what the world might have been like
since 'beginningless time' if we'd had no anger. I reminded him that,
unfortunately, that was not how it all happened. I asked, 'What about
slavery? How would we have gotten out of it, or some of the other
oppressions without some anger?'"

"What did he say to that?"

"He blamed slavery on self-cherishing, and back and forth it went. I do want to diminish my little pile of anger, baby. I clearly see the problem of anger in the world." I sounded exasperated.

"Did you know you are always the one who asks him the first question in class?" Kirsten sighed. "I'm ambivalent too. But he's here, and we agreed it was important to investigate whatever arose before us, Ma," she reminded me.

§

When I pulled into my mother's tree-lined driveway later, I found a "Come on in" note scotch-taped to the door. Still talking with Kirsten, I let myself in and hollered, "Hey!" finding Mama in her bathroom pulling out her rollers. I trailed through the hushed rooms of her condo finishing my phone conversation. By the time I was through, Mama was dressed and ready to go.

"How are you?" I snapped the phone shut.

"Trying to rise above my present circumstances," Mama said. "Who were you talking to?"

"Kirsten."

"What about?"

"Anger."

She raised her eyebrows.

"Gen Tilopa talked about it last night. Kirsten couldn't go because of her tooth."

"Who's Tilopa?"

"You know, the Buddhist guy I took you to before Christmas. He asks about you."

"No, he does not!"

"Well, maybe not," I admitted, "but I told him you said to tell that good-looking Buddhist man Merry Christmas, and he sent you a Merry Christmas back."

She smiled. Her eyes looked milky and wondrous, like a child's.

"What did he say about anger?" She stopped dead still in the middle of the room. I told her the whole conversation in two minutes.

"Where're my keys?" she said under her breath, walking around to touch all the surfaces. "Oh, Lord, Marion, this is all I do nowadays."

I blathered on about anger as if she had actually asked me a question she wanted answered. Mama occasionally flashed doubtful looks in my direction as she pawed the furniture.

"What circumstances are you trying to rise above?" I finally asked after what was far too long an interval.

"Constant pain," she answered as if no time had passed.

"I'm sorry, Mama." I waited an interval. "Where?"

"All over." She shrugged. "I'm depressed."

We'd planned a lunch at Guglhupf, a great German deli nearby, and I was hungry. "Are you ready?"

"Yep." She turned slowly around the room mentally gathering up her possessions. "I swear, Marion, I just get seduced by books." She was still circling.

"At least you still get seduced by something," I teased. "That's good, isn't it? Books are good things to get seduced by. No?"

She harrumphed. "Maybe so, but I see a book and I sit down to look at it for a minute and then I'm gone. For hours maybe." She wrinkled her face. "Can't get a thing done."

"Maybe reading books is what you're supposed to get done," I offered.

"I'm just like my mama," she complained. "She used to walk around our house all the time saying, 'Hunt, hunt, hunt. Hunt, hunt, hunt. That's all I do,' she would say. 'Pick, pick, pick.' We called her Mrs. Hunt-Pick."

I laughed, pulled out my Post-it notes and began scribbling. This was better than a discourse on anger any day.

"You know you sorta get a kind of mean satisfaction outta knowing everybody's going to understand that one day," she said. "Everybody who lives long enough. Hunt, hunt, hunt. Pick, pick, pick. What are you writing, Marion? I can just see it now." Mama cocked her head and eyeballed me.

"Let's go," I said.

"Well, first I want to give you a compliment, Marion."

"What?" I raised my head. This was a twist.

"You've turned out to be a cooperative, responsible, helpful woman, which I always wanted you to be."

"Thanks."

"And which I never thought you would be," she added under her breath, shrugging a coat on over the coat she was already wearing.

"Give me a break," I shot. "And it's not cold outside, Mama. Besides, *I* always knew I would be."

"Well, good for you, but nobody else did," she countered, poking me on to the front door with her white vine-covered cane.

"There you go," I complained, stung by her words. "Always getting in your digs. You do that, you know. Take digs. Besides, what's important is that I knew it."

"That's just the nature of the beast, Marion," she said calmly. "And if there ever was a loyal mother, it's me."

I sincerely doubted that. I flashed on all the anger Mama and I had thrown at each other over the years.

She turned back to her fumbles. "Now I can't find my gloves. I hate that." She stirred around again in her pocketbook as if I hadn't spoken. "Damn it. I just had them and now I've lost them."

I rolled my eyes. This "getting out of the house" was proving tortuous. And Mama's compliment had been decidedly left-handed.

Mama finally pulled on her gloves.

"Just don't make me a creature of ridicule in your writing," she interjected.

"I won't." My notes and pens were safely tucked down deep in my coat pocket anyway.

A half-mile down the road, we arrived at Guglhupf and settled in at a table by the window near the stairs. Mama had her chicken sandwich and tea. I ordered a beet, arugula, and walnut/cream cheese on rye.

A tall brunette waitress in tight beige pants and a stiff collared shirt bounced up and down the steps at a fast clip with a tray on her shoulders.

"See that little girl? I am consumed with envy when I watch her." Mama's face was raised in wonder.

I continued to stuff the beet sandwich into my mouth. Mama hadn't taken a bite.

Another girl climbed the stairs.

"Look at that girl," Mama said. "She has caramel-colored skin." I looked back.

"Umm hmmm" is the only thing I could say with so much food in my mouth.

"You have to be black to have skin like that."

I turned again to look. "How's that?" I managed.

"You just do, Marion. I saw her. She's beautiful, but she is black."

"*And* she is black," I corrected.

"For God's sakes, Marion. That's what I meant!" Mama wrinkled her mouth and shook her head.

She continued to scrutinize everyone in the place—especially those climbing up and down the stairs—and take in all the details.

"I swear, I'm reverting back to childhood," she said finally, observing beige pants descending with a second tray. "Always having to hold on to something when I move now. Wouldn't that be wonderful, Marion? To be able to go up and down the stairs like that?"

I agreed. Already I had to accommodate my hip and knee on such climbs myself. My current effort was to get up and out of chairs without using my arms: something I read in *Prevention* magazine was a key to good musculature as you age. But I couldn't always manage it.

"Look at that one," she nodded toward a woman gathering silverware at the table behind me. "Fat ass," she said simply.

I winced. This particular woman had been smiling sweetly at Mama and me on and off for the last five minutes. And I had a beef tenderloin around my own middle. I felt personally offended.

"But she's nice, Mama. She's been smiling at us ever since we got here. And that's what matters!" I heard the righteous indignation in my voice.

Mama finally picked up her sandwich. "You have to be extra nice when you're shaped like that," she said, taking a bite.

I followed her gaze yet again to see two henna-haired ladies in reds and golds descending the stairs.

"Look at those two. They're best friends," Mama whispered. "I wonder what their secret longings are?" she added.

We watched as they exited the restaurant by the side door.

"You sure are a writer, Mama. We've got to get you a computer."

"Hmmph," she made a noise. "I did write a little yesterday. She patted her lips with a napkin, and then turned to her food again. "But

I'm just out of it, that's all. And this chicken is dry. Not worth the money."

"Wrote about what?"

"I'm not telling you."

"In general?"

"About Tom."

"What about him?"

"When I was first introduced to him," she said bluntly, trying to cut off the inquiry. "It's not good to talk away your writing, Marion."

"As a baby? That's great, Mama," I encouraged.

A busgirl stirred around in the dirty dish tray behind us. She was beautiful, but sullen.

"Look at that one." Mama cocked her head. "You know it's a hard time of life for people like that. People Corey's age," she added, referring to my youngest.

I contemplated what she was saying.

Suddenly she put down her sandwich and made a sour face. "Oh, Marion. I'm just losing it! I don't want to end up being a toothless wonder, a little ole lady with no teeth and a corsage."

"You don't have to have the corsage," I teased.

"Hell, I want the corsage," she retorted. "I ought to get something!"

We sighed together.

"I miss your daddy."

"You can still communicate with him, can't you?" I was relentlessly trying to turn this conversation into something more hopeful. She looked at me as if I was crazy.

"I don't know." She shook her head. "I don't know much about anything anymore."

"Welcome to the club."

"You don't know what you're talking about, Marion. I'm a charter member of that club. You're an initiate."

An initiate here, too.

"And besides, one thing more, Marion. You can't write if you don't have anger!"

"Huh?" Where was this coming from?

"You can't," she insisted. "If you haven't suffered, you cannot be any good at writing."

"Well, there's no worry there," I snapped. "Everyone suffers. Maybe you have to have known anger. But you don't have to *be* it."

"You've got to have some anger in you to even want to put anything down on the page," she pronounced. "I'm going to talk to that Buddhist about that," she said. "There're some things I want to ask him anyway."

"Okay. He's coming over tomorrow and I'm meeting with him here, as a matter of fact. Would you like to come too?"

"At Guglhupf? You are? Must be great to have your own personal guru."

"He's not my guru."

"Well, what is he then?"

I thought about that. "He's my learned friend. A teacher. He teaches me some things. But I don't agree with him about every single thing he says."

"Yes, you do!" she pronounces. "You and Carol. One on this side, one on the other."

Don't squeeze this lemon, I told myself. Let it pass.

"I still do want to talk with him though," she added.

We moved into eating and our own silent worlds.

§

The day before, I'd heard Alanis Morissette on a radio interview, saying, "Anger is a life force and it can move worlds."

When the commentator probed, she added, "If there were to be any quality for which I became a poster child, I'll take anger. Because as a woman, two of the main emotions that we are, quote-unquote, 'not allowed' to feel are anger and sadness. But anger is behind every activism and every act of service that I do," Morissette went on. "It's anger that fuels it. So, for me, to think that anger can go away is naive."

It was true. A woman's anger was the scariest thing to a man—anger denied or bottled, and most certainly anger expressed. And Alanis agreed with me. It was the form that anger took, what we did with it, and the degree to which we were responsible for it; that we didn't allow it to be too destructive, I told myself.

Still, sometimes, I acknowledged, anger did have its way.

"This sandwich is no good," Mama interrupted my thoughts. "They gave me white bread instead of sourdough."

"What's the difference between a Buddhist and a non-Buddhist?" I leaned in and noticed her disappointed mouth.

She shrugged.

"A non-Buddhist thinks there's a difference."

Mama didn't laugh. Time passed before either of us took up the gambit.

"Mack came to see it in the end," she said enigmatically.

"What?"

"He'd see me flying off the handle when I was writing, and he'd come over and pat me down. Watching me reinforced his belief that there was just one way to do everything."

"And that was?"

"To be calm." She was staring out the window now. "Equanimity. Just like that Buddhist guy. Your daddy always thought he knew more than anybody else." She sounded resentful.

She wasn't telling me anything I didn't know.

"You could always tell by his sniff, though," Mama added.

Daddy's sniff.

When anyone said anything he thought absurd, when my boyfriends came to get me and weren't wearing socks with their loafers, when one of them had a thought contrary to his conservative politics, there was the sniff. Most of them learned to "Yes sir" and "No sir" him. But if they didn't, Daddy would be perfectly polite, but we, who knew, got to hear the sniff.

"What exactly was it he saw in the end, Mama?"

"That my anger helped my writing." She pushed her sandwich around with a finger.

"He was really a good lover," she announced out of nowhere. My ears perked up. "I think he would have liked more from me in that department, but I didn't know any more, Marion!" She looked at me as if for absolution.

I was dumbstruck.

"But if I had known more, I probably never would've gotten up with your father anyway."

"How come?" Now I was truly perplexed. Daddy was eye candy. And genial.

"Oh, I just would've been off doing my thing, I guess. But it was so romantic with Mack. My mama taught me that from the cradle."

"What?"

"How wonderful romance was."

"How?" I thought about Granny living with stern old tubercular Skipper, not much romance in that union.

"She was always just thrilled to death when me and Carolyn had a boyfriend. 'Oooh, he's such a nice young man,' she would say. 'Youth is the time for love and romance!' I heard her say that so many times. And then when I met your daddy, it was like that 'across a crowded room' thing, 'cause we were up in New York at a party in someone's hotel suite, and he was across the room, and honey, you could feel the heat . . .." She paused, remembering.

"Too bad you have to fall out of it," she said after several minutes. "Pisses me off."

She turned again to the passing parade.

"I think that woman's pregnant. And here comes old faithful." She nodded towards beige pants making another run up the steps. "You know I'm always writing in my head. All the time. And you know what else? I still listen to old love songs: Satchmo and Gershwin and André Previn. For romance."

I reached for her hand. She smiled and wagged me forward. I waited for the secret she was about to reveal. "Now, Marion, why don't we just have some of that Sachertorte for a finale?" she whispered.

Chapter Fourteen

Plan B

A few writers gather. For an hour or two the isolation that all writers feel is replaced by relationship. A small miracle of community occurs.
—Eric Maisel

On Thursday, I was to pick Mama up after my writing group: go somewhere, do something.

At this particular session, we'd canned our usual reading and feedback format and scheduled a talk with Sharon, our most successful member, about how to write query letters, *Writer's Digest*, websites we couldn't afford to miss, how to get an agent, whether or not to use flashback in the first five pages, the advisability of taking a certain professor's writing course, someone who'd helped Alice Sebold publish her wildly popular book, *The Lovely Bones*, as well as other do's and don'ts and a lot of things that required me to be something I was always trained not to be—a self-promoter—that maybe only extroverts could do and that could easily fill up an entire lifetime.

Who would have time to write? I asked myself incredulously. It's hard enough to write and do my sit-ups in the same week.

Ashamedly, I failed to feel anything but a sluggish kind of jealousy for Sharon, rather than the joy I should be feeling; Sharon, who writes religiously from 8-1 every day after her two little children go off to school and her husband does whatever he does to bring home the bacon. Sharon, who was recently featured in the *Raleigh News & Observer* as an emerging writer, and has received several honorable mentions and a $250 check for a short story, plus has three completed, FedEx-ready novels to ship off in an envelope, awaiting those three little words: 'We'll take it!' Sharon, who gets a 33 percent "send me the first four chapters" response to her inquiries and has her own website.

I can't tell if I'm more jealous about the husband or the recognition, but then I decide it's really the self-discipline I'm envious of: the determination; her *knowing* that this is what she wants to do above all other things and then having the will to do it. I have always been short-shrifted in the self-discipline department. That's the real trouble.

§

Mama, too, had been highly self-disciplined all her life, finely creased and organized: her beds always crisply made, hair coifed, pristine white pile rugs in the living room, small servings of food that don't touch each other perched on antique, hand-painted china plates, crystal goblets and epergnes on the polished dining room table, centerpieces tastefully changed with each season's dictates.

And then there's Mama herself, who at age ninety-one, after years of dutiful Oil-of-Olaying, had softer skin than I did.

Plus—and this is the important thing—Mama had published three books: a novel, an historical biography, and just last year a popular period piece about Durham. She was thinking about a fourth.

§

I arrived at Mama's feeling depressed, trying to bolster my mood and telling myself things like, "Well, at least I love the *process* of writing," and "So what if my writing doesn't exactly fit into any given category, I am un-categorizable," and other such bluster.

I sighed and rang the bell. I just wasn't in their league. Do you have to be dedicated and driven to publish? I asked myself, and concluded, Yes, you do.

I resolved to pick Mama's brain, how she did it, what the tricks of the trade were from her point of view; I would report back next week at writing group.

As I waited for admittance into her condo, my mind turned glumly to my raggedy-ass novel (stuffed in the bottom drawer of a file cabinet) that had broken every single rule of what is never to be done in the first five pages and didn't have a chance in hell of seeing the light of day. How could I, who am not sure myself, crystallize just exactly what my 'un-categorizable' book was about, reduce it down to the required one-sentence summary? Impossible!

Mama answered the door neatly dressed in a ribbed black, brown, and white tufted sweater, black slacks, and gold earrings.

"I left the door open for you, was just calling to see where you were," she said instead of hello.

Naturally I'm late.

"Oh," I said, "I couldn't get it open."

We both feigned a try at pushing down the door latch, which I still could not do. Mama opened the door.

I am weak, weak, weak, plain and simple. And starving, too, I thought.

I peeked around the corner to see silverware and bowls laid atop place mats on the kitchen table. At least I would be fed. I plopped down in the chair awaiting Mama's instructions. Better not to rush these things.

"I just have some turkey soup," she said apologetically. "Not much. And slaw."

"That's great," I said, meaning it. I once planned to write a book called *Build Your Meal Around Slaw*. I love slaw. Where is that book?

I watched Mama inch her way across the room to peer in the pot, marveling at her ability to finagle yet another meal out of that four-fifths-empty refrigerator I'd already managed to sneak a peek into on the way to my chair. Nothing. Certainly nothing grabbable. Mama drives herself to the grocery store three times a week because, as she says, she likes her food fresh.

Realizing this was a perfectly good time and place to practice my breathing, since it would more than likely take her at least ten minutes to spoon the soup into the bowl, I picked up the newspaper on the table. It featured an article on the rising number of centenarians in town. I spied my old English teacher, Mrs. Phillips, in the color photograph, now a smiling, fluffy-haired lady I would've never recognized. Mrs. Phillips spent her 100th birthday delivering Meals on Wheels to others more infirm than she, I read. Damn! The discipline thing again. Who could imagine spending your birthday in such a selfless way? Not me. Not daydreaming, hedonistic, distracted me.

Other centenarians in the foldout were cutting roses, needlepointing chair seats, lifting weights. By then, Mama, who I fully expected and prayed would be a centenarian herself, and not too soon either, because then, by god, I'd be seventy-one, would probably have published two more books. She's talking about one now she fondly calls "Plan B," which I'm sure will be a best seller. I would read it. It sounds like the story of my life, not hers.

What happened to me? I wondered, leafing through the paper and glancing at another full-page story about thirty-somethings currently delaying marriage. I flashed on my own grandchildren-less state. Something must have gone awry.

I don't care what those centenarians say. Sixty-one feels old. Time is running out, and I should have started writing sooner. I shouldn't have tried to save the world and be a peacemaker. Who the hell was I kidding?

While I was woolgathering, Mama set in front of me a bowl of soup in a white Limoges bowl with tiny blue roses that spiral to a smudge in the bottom. She protested that she was sorry: The soup was not one of her best. A bird's portion of slaw was set to the right. I realized I could down what she had put in front of me before she even sat.

This time, I did call on what little discipline I had and waited for her to light. Mama sat across from me and bowed her head. We said a silent blessing, or at least she did, while I tried to feel thankful, my spoon poised above the bowl, ready for the flag to drop.

"Tell me about how you got your first book published," I blurted after the Amen, my head still lowered, focusing on the soup, and remembering I hadn't even had the wherewithal to eat a proper breakfast that morning. No wonder I was ravenous.

"Oh, I wrote the book in Manley Wade Wellman's class," she said matter-of-factly. "You know it got published by Grace publishing in town. But first I got a publisher from New York. What was her name? She was famous."

I waited for her to rifle through her memory. She shook her head, face in a ball.

"You know I went to the Three Arts Club yesterday," she said distractedly. "I've gotta get out of that club. I didn't know a soul there."

"Don't get out of it before you take me," I pleaded, remembering her earlier offer to take me to meet her successful artistic friends. What was that thing they said about it wasn't who you knew or what you knew but what you did with who you knew? Who knew? I might need an artistic friend one of these days, I told myself.

I shoveled the last of the okra and rice and turkey into my mouth and wondered what an acceptable interval was before I could get up and get another bowl. The slaw was long gone.

"Not one soul," she continued. "I got there late, and I was famished." Mama had yet to take one bite of her meal. "It was something about a documentary the lady made about the Farmville school closure . . . You must know about that, Marion, since you know everything about blacks." She snapped her eyes up at me.

I shook my head.

Mama was on a tear. I could get up and get another bowl of soup, and she wouldn't even notice.

"You know, I'm the oldest one there," she continued. "I don't know anyone from madame's off-ox."

"From who?"

"That's what Julia Royal always said. 'Madame's off-ox.'"

What kind or aristocracy had an off-ox? I wondered.

"But they do so many good things out there—documentary film." She paused, a look of wonder on her face as if she were discussing the human genome project.

"Hmmm. So how did you get your agent?" I asked again.

Mother furrowed her brow. She still couldn't remember the woman's name and it was bothering her. "I hate getting old," she sighed. "I can see her now. She was famous!"

I had trouble remembering people's names, too, all my life. Dysnomia, I always insisted. What does that mean? Just bothersome mental flubs, a little problem with word retrieval, nouns in particular. Who didn't have something like that? I'd been calling my husband every name but his own, including my first husband's, for ages. And I often called my children by their sibling's names first, eventually arriving at who they actually were.

Or maybe this was a more serious decline? Early onset?

My kids used to ask me when I said "thingamabob" and "doo-whackey," how I would ever be able to write a book without nouns when everyone knows verbs are much more important. Verbs and adjectives. I always drew a blank line so as not to slow down and looked up the nouns later. Thesaurus. Forgetting cleaned out space for other stuff to take residence, didn't it? Imagining a world without the ability to forget literally rattled my teeth.

I saw, however, that for Mama to forget, after a lifetime of easy remembering, an historian after all, must be tough.

"She came down here to look for new talent," Mama continued, still groping for the missing detail, "and Manley told us we should all go hear her talk, so we did. Afterwards she said any of us who wanted to could send her something from our work, so I sent her the first chapter of *The Curious Wine*, and she wrote me back in two weeks, and said if I would send her the rest of it, and if she liked it as much as she did the first chapter, she would send it around."

"Just like that? Wow!" I said, astonished. I was at the stove with my back to her as I fished out turkey chunks from the soup and I was a vegetarian that week.

Agents don't do that nowadays. Who goes on trips looking for new talent? How lucky can you get! Today it's all done anonymously through the Internet. You rarely get to meet an actual person, make a personal impression, be offered the world just for attending a talk. Especially when you rarely attend talks.

Then I remembered Mama'd had her book published by a local outfit, Grace Publishing. I asked, "So what happened?"

Mother looked puzzled. Then the sun came into her face, and she broke into a broad smile. I noticed her teeth were yellow, and resolved to buy whitening strips on my way home.

"Phyllis Jackson! That was her name. Phyllis Jackson. I can see her as plain as the nose on my face. She was famous. That year she had published more books than any other agent in New York City!"

She sighed and picked at her slaw, still smiling, as if remembering the name of Phyllis Jackson was all there was.

"So what happened, Mama?"

"Oh, Gene Grace . . . he was an ophthalmologist in our class who said he wanted to start a publishing company, but none of us really believed he would do it. He kept pestering me to let him publish my book. He had heard it in class, but I told him, 'No it was already out there with an agent,' and so that was that. He wanted mine to be his first, but then he went ahead and published another girl's book. Finally, after about a year, Phyllis wrote me back and said that a lot of folks liked the book, but that it didn't have enough sex in it. They wanted it to be more graphic."

She made a face.

I remembered quite clearly Mama telling us this when I was a freshman in college, going back into her bedroom night after night over spring break, Daddy laughing, Mama in there trying to spice up her book while we watched Ed Sullivan or Daddy's favorite, *Whose Line Is It Anyway?* Daddy was in love with Betsy Palmer that year, picked her out over that smooth, dark-haired Miss America, Bess Myerson, and I was secretly glad because I looked more like Betsy Palmer than Bess Myerson. At the end of that show, he would lean over and tell me, "You could be Miss America, baby," patting my knee and, for a minute, making me believe it. "If you'd just learn a few table manners," he would add with a snort.

"It was hard," Mama continued. "That was way before the day when everybody just laid it all out, practically filleted you, and I guess—I guess I just couldn't do it. So, I got it back and gave it to Gene. *The Curious Wine* was his second book."

"And *your* second book?" I asked to keep her going. "Tell me about that." Her successes seemed all too easy to me.

Mama's stories were spiking my envy. Still, I needed to know this.

"Oh, I was trying to write about my childhood. The first few chapters seemed to be filled up with General Carr. He lived a block away from us, downtown, next to the public library, and he was such a big personality. Founded Durham, you know. And when I showed what I had to Manley, he said, "Mena, there's no definitive biography on this man. You can sell this. The University Press will want it. Get busy!"

"I went to the head of Wilson Library, H. G. Jones, and he told me there were piles of stuff up in the historical collection on General Carr I could use for my research, so I spent lots of time up there. In the stacks. I loved research!"

I was like her in that way. I'd spent happy months-turning-into-years researching things about the North Carolina coast for the book I was then writing, *Serenity Point.* I'd interviewed the chief of police, a tight, dark-eyed man who had a ship in a bottle on the shelf behind his head, his fat fingers folded into a tent in front of him, big knuckles with smooth, dark hairs on each joint.

That police chief had liked being interviewed, I remembered. "A writer," he said with a Mona Lisa smile, giving me a special status I didn't feel I deserved. I was spending my time reading endless missives about coastal erosion and whether it would be the south end or the north end of the beach that would go first with global warming; about Blackbeard's adventures, myth and reality; mollusk shells, killdees, jellyfish, and the migratory patterns of pelicans over the Crystal Coast; about the slave trade since the early 1700s. Not a lot of writing going on.

I'd asked the chief about that year's police blotter. *Serenity Point* was a mystery, after all. He told me there'd never been a murder on Topsail Beach. There was one in my book. More than one.

Mama interrupted my ruminations.

"It was wonderful, up there all by myself reading those fascinating personal papers, umpteen diaries," she told me. "Your daddy and I would go there over Christmas vacation and stay in the Carolina Inn. He took his typewriter, and I would go to Wilson Library in the morning and do my research." She paused. I looked over, remembering a much younger woman.

"Then we'd get back together for lunch in the Inn. They had the best food . . ." Her face was losing liver spots before my eyes. I could see her short blond curls and lipsticked pout.

"And then we'd have a little drink, and Daddy would take a nap, and I would go back to the stacks. We'd go someplace different every night for dinner. There was never anything open on Christmas Day, you know, but Daddy and I would take a cooler and eat cold chicken legs in the room. Heaven."

It sounded wonderful. Mama's face looked like a faded corsage, full of meaning.

"How long did that book take?"

"Oh, ten years, and then Bill Whatshisname told me: 'Mena, you've just got to stop writing it. You've just got to end it; you could go on forever.'

"And that's true, Marion," she said, pointing a finger at me. "Sometimes you just have to lay a book down and quit. And that's what I did. I took it to the Press and they liked it; took it right away."

Blam! A second home run.

"And you got paid for doing the third one, right?" I prompted, already knowing.

"After Daddy died, I got this idea to write about Durham for the *Herald-Sun*. I pitched it and they told me to send them something, so I did and I ended up doing two columns a month for three years, $200 a month, which back then was good money, honey! What I wouldn't do with $200 more a month right now! That was the basis for the book, you know. The Durham Historical Society wanted me to put it together in a book. Paid me a little to do it. So, I did it."

She shook her head. "It was like sweating blood to pull that one together though."

"You've had such a wonderful career, Mama. How much money do you think you made writing?"

"Oh, I made good money. If I'd just started sooner, I could've really made some money. I don't know how much. Let's see . . ." She bit her lip, adding numbers silently in her head.

"And it's not over yet," I continued. "I really think that *Plan B* idea could make it big. You gotta keep at it. 'Get busy,' like Manley said."

What I was really thinking was that I needed my own Plan B. I also needed a mama. I believed if Mama focused on her writing, she would live a lot longer. Maybe she would damn well be one of those centenarians I'd been reading about all morning.

Mama giggled. "Oh, this is so much fun! Talking shop. I'm telling you, Marion. You can do it too. I tell the kids all the time: 'I may be dead, but your mama's sitting on a gold mine, and one of these days, she's going to publish and be really good too.' Because, Marion, you can write! And that's important. You've gotta give something else up and just do it."

"Like what?" I asked.

She ignored me.

"I don't know anything about that book you're writing now, Marion, because you won't let me read a word of it." She shot me a glare. "But I know what you ought to be writing about."

"What?"

"You always have to write about what you know, Marion, and all those years you and Chris lived out there in the woods, building that house, all those times in the sixties, which I never have been able to understand . . . that's what you need to be writing about."

I paused, then stood and took my dishes to the sink.

"I do have a lot of notes," I said, trailing off. I turned and faced her. "But, Mama, it's so hard to get published these days. It's not just as simple as 'you can write'!"

"What do you mean?" she asked, narrowing her eyes. "Of course, it's about whether or not you can write. If you can't write, the best query letter in the world ain't gonna do you a damn bit of good! You listen to me, Marion!"

I'd heard that tone all my life.

"Just do it. Get your seat on the chair. Pick something. Write an outline. You need an outline, Marion, and a prospectus, get to know every single character backwards and forwards. That's how you do it."

That's how you do it, I thought. That's not my process at all. I get to know my characters as I write about them. My way's as legitimate as yours, I could hear my rebellious self-equivocating.

Then again, Mama had published three books. Me, I hadn't finished one.

Maybe I should listen to her, I told myself. Take notes. That's what you came over here to do.

I picked up my ever-ready Bic and wrote the word "prospectus" on my pad; then I laid it down, feeling limp.

"Where do you want to go today, Mama?" I asked, desperately groping for a lifeline out of this subject.

She looked up, her face still illuminated.

"Do you want to go shopping?" I asked.

Chapter Fifteen

Our Writing Routines: Mama's Method

Easy reading is damned hard writing.
—Nathaniel Hawthorne

Continuing to clear up the paper maze after Mama died, I found pages and pages of handwritten notes she'd taken on how famous writers managed their craft, and how her way of doing things compared. Her main guides were Henry Miller, Ernest Hemingway, John Cheever, and Thomas Hardy. No women, I noted.

I was blurry-eyed from reading so many notes in her loopy hand, but again marveled at the discipline Mama had in recording what these authors said about writing, especially with the difficulty, that back then no one thought was a difficulty, of taking notes before the computer age. Jesus, how did we do it? And I, once a middle school teacher who'd taught a class on note taking. I spied her summary:

"I had not known that I could stand, to a small degree, in such exalted company, but some of my very own habits and beliefs about the craft of writing were discovered before I ever knew of theirs, and so many of them are similar. This heartens me.

Like Henry Miller, I prefer to write in the morning, and after a while, something takes over. Like Hemingway, I often re-write a paragraph twenty or thirty times to get the word right. Like Cheever, I brood, often for long periods. Like Hardy, I write sketches of characters, places, conversations, and often do not use them, but feel they help in the creative process of writing a book somehow. As all four attest, I know that writing is a lonesome road you travel all by yourself."

I paused and held my head in my hands, feeling the chill of a time long gone. Then I returned to my reading.

"When I had finished The Curious Wine, I had cut out two-thirds of it. When I finish this second book, only God, in His infinite wisdom, knows how much will be cut out. But some of what I am writing now is definitely already gone, thousands of words now, though I am only a third of the way through the first draft.

One of my cardinal beliefs as a writer is in the value of plot. You can have a book without plot. There are many of those on the market today, but I do not feel you can have a real story without it. ... Nobody can tell you how to plot your novel. You can be helped in planning it, as I was by the idea of a prospectus, a detailed outline that includes who, when, where, what, why and how. But the plot is yours entirely.

Equally important is character. Right now, I am very involved with two characters, and I have written at great length about them, not only how they look, when and where they were born, their family backgrounds, educations, marriages, children, but their idiosyncrasies. ... I have gone back into their childhoods, to their earliest roots.

Once the writing is begun, if these two people are full and whole, they will stop giving me trouble. They may change, and in all probability, they will change. But it will be for the purpose of getting themselves across to me, and then to whoever reads about them.

Think about it. Try telling a story to a child. If you do not have a plot: that is, some action, some surprise, a beginning, middle, and end, you will lose his attention. "And what happened then?" is a question he may ask you. If you cannot come up with something, he will either run away to greener pastures or he will block your words out of his mind and concentrate on some inferior aspect of your face, as my daughter Carol once did, interrupting a hastily contrived and rambling bed-time story with the remark, "Mama, you really do have a fat nose."

Meanwhile, Here's My Method

Writing is an exploration.
You start from nothing and learn as you go.
—E.L. Doctorow

When I am writing well, I wake up before the alarm, and catch the tail end of my dream. I lie in bed remembering, gently pulling the threads of my subconscious until I find one I can hold on to, one in which the sound of the phrase pleases me, and I can see it as a place to begin. I try to have an idea of what I will be working on before I get out of bed.

Then I go anyplace I can be quiet and by myself, and take to the computer. (It used to be a notebook. I swore writing longhand on lined paper was my vehicle. But now it's the keyboard.)

I either start with a blank page and grab the thread that's stuck in my mind and take off, or I go back to a line I left unfinished the day before, reread only it, and begin again. It's helpful to leave something dangling and unfinished the night before—even to stop in the middle of a paragraph.

Though I understand and respect my mother's emphasis on plot, plot is not foremost for me. Not initially. For me, it's the setting, and the characters that create the story.

Places have always held my attention, both in life and in literature. I am drawn to new places and sights and the feelings they inspire. Geography grabs me and doesn't easily let go. It's no wonder travel is my benefactress. The environment always wins. Demographics *are* destiny. People are formed by the landscape they grow up in.

I learn about my characters as I write about them, no long prospectus, no exhaustive character analyses. Often the minor characters become major and the major ones, minor. Some woman I think is sort of like me, feels bland and staged. Maybe I try to make her better than she really is—prettier, smarter, more sympathetic—while the minor characters can be the mixed-up ball of motivations and machinations that all of us truly are.

I am often as surprised as the reader by my characters and where they end up taking me, who they love and hate. What lies deep inside them reveals itself over time.

Like Mama, the best time for me to write is in the morning, next door to my dream state, "twilight time," I've heard it called. It's important that I not see or talk to anyone. Talking, even quick back-and-forths, unravels my intention. I forget what I am doing. I must keep to myself, stay in my pajamas, and write.

Before I get started, I am nervous, restless, unsure of myself. But once my fingers begin their rapid-fire hunt and peck across the keyboard, I am off. I can fly. I feel relaxed and happy. I let myself go, and see what comes out of me. Now it is effortless action, no self-consciousness. I am absorbed in something far bigger than me. If I am very lucky, I vanish, but the words keep coming.

Mine is very much a kinesthetic way of writing. On the Neurolinguistic Programming (NLP) scale I am a Kinesthetic, Kinesthetic, Auditory, which means that my easiest way of taking in *and* processing information is through my body, my muscle memory. I am a wiggler. Embodied cognition, muscle memory, and a deep letting-go move me along. And one big secret: Writing turns me on. Physically. I am often horny after writing.

But the way I best check for the accuracy of *my* truth is through how something sounds when I read it aloud. That seals the deal.

I approve of Annie Lamott's shitty first draft idea, and that this draft is not to be tinkered with while getting it down. Only afterwards do I go back and make minor changes. The major ones come later at a second, third, or fourth sitting.

Editing is a struggle for me. It is harder to sit still and analyze than it is to set forth and sail. I am the thinker never catalogued in the psychology books, the kind that puts out the talk bubble and then looks to see what I've got.

In this way, I am also more like my father than my mother. Daddy was a quiet man, but as a newspaperman, he had to write on a deadline. I never remember seeing him with an outline. He just put his fingers to the keys on his old stand-up Corona and let them roll, cranking out article after article for the *Herald Sun* or the *Reader's Digest* or *Woman's Wear Daily*, various magazines he contributed to for a few extra dollars each month. He had an idea and he came up with something, later going back with his fat black soft-lead pencil, marking through his excesses and redundancies.

I used to think that my way of writing was the wrong way, that I would never amount to anything as a writer unless I did things the way my mother did, slowly, neatly, methodically, according to plan, a well-reasoned outline, a prospectus.

It's a fine way to write, and Mama was a true talent. But it's not my way. Everyone has to find their own way.

Mama was highly visual. She saw it in her mind's eye. It was all laid out before she tackled it. She spent a lifetime not only trying to get me to write, but to write her way and to write what she thought I ought to be writing.

"Why in heaven's name are you writing about Ecuador?" she often asked me. "Write what you know. Write about the hippie days and building that house in the woods with Chris, which I have never understood!" She didn't care that I also built a house along the northern coast of Ecuador and that I knew a thing or two about that, as well. That was too far out, too foreign. It may as well have been the moon.

We shared the love of research, though. I often feel I could read about integral, even tangential subjects close to my characters' hearts forever, and that if I don't release the research-addiction and let my fingers do the talking, I will never write. It's a side road, and though fascinating, can become a hole.

Learning, after all, is my real love. I love to learn, not necessarily in school like Mama did, but by doing, by dabbling, by getting my feet wet in all kinds of situations and then looking back to see what came of it. I am what they call an experiential learner.

By midday I am usually ready for motion. So, I leave it where it lies, hopefully in the middle of a good sentence. I dress, grab a bite, and head for the bike or foot trail. Movement clears my head, helps me to rearrange my To-Do list. I'm a big one for what I call "creative cancellation."

In motion in the natural world, I am able to see things in a new way. Moving through space cleans my mental carburetor. I may do a few errands or give myself some small reward, a trip to a thrift shop, a nap. Or I might recall that I am a member of the human species and have other obligations and interests besides the story that is developing inside my head and engage with a family member.

If I am lucky, and have planned it right, I am away somewhere on a writing retreat, somewhere hidden, somewhere I don't have to engage with the "real world": other people, talk, expectations, shopping, bill paying, work, holidays.

Come nightfall, my second favorite time to write, I once again begin. Perhaps I edit what I wrote in the morning. Or maybe do more research, always looking for that thread and the intention I set for myself before I finally fall asleep, late, around midnight.

"Give me a dream," I tell my subconscious, "a dream that helps me know what Guillermo does next. Wake me with a feeling, a line, a lifeline."

Chapter Sixteen

Steppin'

Above all, do not lose your desire to walk.
I have walked myself into my best thoughts, and I know of no
thought so burdensome that one cannot walk away from it.
If one keeps on walking, everything will be all right.
—Kierkegaard

Mama was dressed in her seal coat, a brown leather and fleece hat, and gloves. She had on thick pants, support hose and black flats with clunky gold chains across the toes, completely inappropriate for a ninety-three-year-old woman. She got in my car, and we headed off in the cold sunshine to the nearby shopping center. All the way, she exclaimed "Woo!" if the sun hit her eyes or a car came up on us suddenly.

"Outta nowhere" she trumpeted. She was dodging bullets every minute.

I watched her getting in and out of the car. She insisted on doing it herself, but I noticed that it was getting harder for her to buckle the seat belt and pull the door closed.

"My fingers don't work anymore," she said exasperated. I, too, noticed it was different getting in and out of a car than it used to be. I remembered the days when I bolted out of the car almost at a sprint. Now, everything took thought: open the door, be careful not to hit the car beside you, swing your legs around, step out, turn back around, make sure you have everything you need, lock the door. This routine would only intensify if I lived to be her age.

The GNC was around the corner, so I suggested we walk there. It was a brilliant day. For the first time ever, she said, "Hold my hand, Marion," and slipped her gloved hand into mine.

It was hard to walk as slow as she did, but I tried, taking baby steps, breathing deeply. She walked past Sally's Hairstyling, a copy center, a Chinese take-out, and said "Whew" or "Woo, look at that!" as if she were sauntering in a foreign country, the Champs-Élysées, not this ratty little strip mall.

"You know I need some tennis shoes, Marion. The ones I have at home don't feel right anymore."

I thought of the ridiculous flats with slick leather bottoms she was wearing now, threatening her life.

Right at that moment we came upon a shoe store: Athlete's Foot. "Well, let's get some, Mama!" I said, excited. "We have the time."

"No, Marion!" she resisted immediately. "Not today."

We slowed down anyway and peered inside. A boom box blared. Three employees in their teens or twenties were standing around rapping, waiting for a customer.

"Well, we're here, Mama," I encouraged, "and you said you need some shoes. We may as well go in."

Mama put her face smack up to the glass and shaded her eyes with her hand.

"Come on, Mother," I said, wanting to help her in some tangible way on this visit. God knew, she needed all the stability she could get. She needed to keep on walking. She needed tennis shoes.

Finally, she said, "Oh, all right."

I could tell Mama couldn't see a thing through the window, because if she saw the age of the salespeople jiving over in the corner, she would become indignant and refuse to enter. She would write the whole venture off in a flash. Nonetheless, we walked in. I steered her to the women's side of the store, a step or two ahead, looking for a shoe she might want. Most of them had red, black, and blue lightning bolts on the sides or built-up jelly soles, but I did see some plain black and white ones—and a few pairs on sale.

Two hard benches lined up in front of the walls. So far, no one had come to help us.

"Look, Mama, look at these over here."

I held up one pair, then another. She squinted.

"I don't know," she trailed off.

A twenty-something guy with thick arms and a crew cut, wearing a see-through blue mesh shirt and khaki pants, came over.

"Hello, ladies. Can I help you with something?"

Beyoncé crooned in the background, and the other two guys were grinning conspiratorially in our direction. I felt like they were saying, "Look at those two little ole ladies over there."

"Well," Mama smiled sweetly up at our salesman, "I'm Mrs. Webb." She shook his hand. "And I'm looking for a tennis shoe, something I can walk in."

"Yes, ma'am. Did you have anything particular in mind?"

"Yes, something I can walk in," she repeated.

"Look, Mama," I pointed. "These here are for stability. It says so right up there."

Mesh-shirt agreed. "Yes, ma'am, we have shoes built especially for stability, and that's what I would recommend for you."

Mama sat down and stuck out her feet. She took off her right shoe, and he measured her foot, which I noticed was turned slightly inwards with a huge knotty bunion.

"See my feet," Mama said, almost embarrassed. "They don't work like they used to."

"Yes, ma'am. That happens as we get older." Mesh-shirt was careful with her, gallant. He squatted at her feet and smiled up at her. Even with her shoes off, she was warming to him.

"Size eight," he said.

"Eight! Why I never wore more than a seven-and-a-half in my whole life! Narrow, too. Do you have a narrow?"

"Well, Mrs. Webb," he remembered her name. Points. "It measures an eight today. And a B. Not a narrow. Let's look at those first."

"Hmmph," she grumbled as he disappeared into the back room.

"Me and Arthur went shopping for shoes recently, Mama, and he wore a size bigger than usual this time, too," I said to reassure her that maybe this guy knew what he was talking about.

"Now that's another thing I'd like not to hear you say, Marion." She bent over to look at her toes. "'Me and Arthur.' That's wrong, Marion. Not good English. Burns me up."

Mesh-shirt returned and pulled out a black leather pair. He removed the tissue and plastic shoehorn, then sat cross-legged on the floor to help Mama try them on.

"Sometimes, Mrs. Webb, our arches sag as we get older."

"You got that right. Everything sags!" Mama corrected. He showed not the slightest smile, but held her foot as if she were Cinderella and he the prince.

"Plus, our feet swell significantly during the day," he added. "Now this Reebok," he was trying the sale pair first as she was clearly eyeing that shelf when he'd first walked over, "is good for stability." He laced her up.

She grabbed her cane and we helped her to her feet. "It's too big," she pronounced. "Do you have some Dr. Scholl's?"

"Well, we have these Arch Cushions," he said and turned to retrieve some insoles from the wall. "We prefer these, Arch Plus, over Dr. Scholl's, Mrs. Webb. They're softer and not quite as invasive. Support your foot better, take up a little less space."

"Hmmph," she sniffed again, and he took the shoe off, inserted the insole, and put it back on.

"Nice little batch of arthritis you've got in that ankle," he said, briefly stroking her foot. "This will be less work for you, Mrs. Webb. Keep your foot from pronating in."

This salesman was twenty-five years old, and he knew feet. He knew old people, too.

"What's your name?" I asked, trying to connect.

He reached for his card. "Mark." Under his name, it also said exercise physiologist. An exercise physiologist selling shoes. I guess that made sense in this economy. Hell, at least the guy had a job.

Mama stood. She walked slowly around the entire store. Another customer who came in after us stopped to watch her, as did the other salesmen. One of them, a cute guy with a pencil mustache and an S-design carved in the back of his hair, smiled at me and winked.

"I saw you two ladies walking by here just the other day," he said pleasantly. Beyoncé was still crooning. Mama didn't hear him. Or her. And we hadn't been anywhere near this mall in years. But the guy was being friendly, so I smiled and nodded.

"Lemme try on that gray one," Mama pointed with her cane to a jazzier model higher up on the wall underneath *Stability*. Mark bounded up to get it.

"How's that shoe different from this one?" she asked.

"It provides even more stability."

"Well, for God's sakes, put it on, Mark," Mama instructed. "I need all the stability I can get!"

As Mark laced her up, she looked at me as if she'd just noticed I was there and said unexpectedly, "Marion, don't let me hold you up, now."

"What do you mean 'hold me up'?" I asked. "I came over to take you wherever you wanted to go, remember?"

"Oh." She remembered. She was comfortable in Mark's hands.

A second guy, who looked like a salesman in training, sat down on the adjoining bench to watch us. Whenever Mama said anything to Mark, and Mark answered back, the other man marveled. I couldn't tell who he was marveling at, Mama or Mark. They were both quite marvelous.

Mark talked to Mama about diabetic socks and neuropathy. He was kneeling down—still the prince.

Again, Mama got up and walked around the store in the new gray pair.

"You steppin' now," called the black guy with the S in his hair from across the store. "Go right on."

Mama raised her eyebrows.

"Those look nice, Mama. They'll go with any color pants."

Mama told Mark she'd "take 'em" and he began to clear up the boxes and tissue paper.

Mama put on her perky Jackie-O persona. "You know, Mack never exercised," she told me. I gathered up her cane and pocketbook. "Said it made him tired." She smiled at the memory.

She paid and I hung her heavy box of New Balance shoes on my arm, hoping they would, indeed, give her new balance. I imagined her tippy-toeing around Dunbarton in her sporty new "tennies."

"You should wear your leather coat with these," I suggested, taking her arm to walk her to the door.

Before we got there, S-curve called out, "You're a mighty special person, Mrs. Webb."

Mama turned. "And just why is that?" she challenged, bold-faced.

"Because your name is Webb." He was pure eye-candy.

"What?" she asked the obvious.

"My name is Webb, too." He flashed a gleaming alabaster smile out of his perfectly beautiful ebony face.

"Well, lawsy mercy," Mama said. She smiled back at him, seventy years and many different cultures between them.

"Bye," she said sweetly to the assemblage and twiddled her fingers as I held open the door.

"Bye, Ms. Webb," they chorused, standing in a semi-circle behind us as we left. Mama, it seems, had made their day.

As we tottered towards the GNC for the two-for-one supplements, Mama whispered, "He might just be our cousin."

"Maybe so," I said. I felt happier than I'd felt in ages to have this crazy little woman hanging on my arm.

"And I'm gonna tell you something else, Marion, that I know you'll just love."

"What?" I asked brightly.

"Because you like anything black, you know."

I chose not to take the bait.

"I didn't know anything about the Webbs and black people, but most of the Fullers in Durham are black." She announced this as if she were telling me a state secret. "Blind Boy Fuller was one of the first jazz musicians around, you know. Famous! And if you look in the phone book for Fuller," she referred again to her own maiden name, "practically every Fuller you see is probably black if you check their addresses."

"That's great!" I said, and meant it.

"I knew that would please you," she says as we pushed through the glass doors to GNC.

"Why, good afternoon to you, Mrs. Webb!" I heard her man, Kevin's, greeting. He sounded truly delighted to see her, rushing over to help with her pills as she winked at me, and patted my hand.

"They know me in here," she confided. "We're all connected, Marion. Every single one of us."

Chapter Seventeen

Returning the Fucking Lamp

When people don't express themselves, they die one piece at a time. —
Laurie Halse Anderson

"How was today with Mena?" my husband asked, microwaving the leftover pesto and frying the fish. My mother's mission that day had been to return a lamp to Home Depot.

"Pitiful." Sitting at the dining room table, I hung my head and began my story with its ending.

"Just before I left, Mother stormed into her house, and even rebuked my offer to help her go get her MRI next week, 'or any help whatsoever in the future!' she said. She said she was going straight in the house to cancel the damn MRI *right then*."

The picture of her stomping in, a rickety little ole ninety-three-year-old lady with a cane, a big pocketbook, and a yellow plastic bag from Best Buy, flashed in my mind.

"Fine!" I hollered after her, exasperated and got back into my car. I'd had an inkling this kind of thing might happen today.

"Remember, Art, this morning, when I asked you to please cook dinner tonight and you asked, 'Any particular reason?' You know, I *knew* I was going to be *tired* tonight after visiting Mama." I tossed back a slug of beer.

"Even after meditating and purposefully saying to myself I wanted to be there for Mama today no matter how irritating she is, I allowed myself to get caught in her bad mood. Hell, all I was trying to do was help her out with something she wanted to get done: return a lamp to Home Depot and get a new Oscar Peterson CD at Best Buy. But then she pulled her old bait and switch two-step—where she acts so pitiful and asks for my help, and then when I help her, she finds a way to put me down or criticize me, or suddenly gets all paranoid and acts like I'm messing in her stuff and says she never asked for my help in the first place. It pisses me off so bad!"

By now, I was almost crying.

"Kirsten calls it 'the dependent/independent two-step,'" I went on, "the 'Why haven't I heard from you, now (swat) go away!' rag."

"Back up. What happened?" Art asked.

"By the time we'd finally gotten on the road to Home Depot, I innocently asked her where the contract for her book with the Historical Society was."

My husband put a plate of food in front of me.

"'I don't know, Marion,'" she said sharply to me, "'but when I find it, I'm not going to let *you* see it.'"

"Huh?" Now, even my husband was confused.

"As if I give a damn," I muttered to him, stirring my fork around in my noodles.

"But damn if it didn't bite. I let myself feel hurt. Unappreciated. I told myself I wanted to get the hell out of there. Every one of my childhood wounds lifted up their ugly heads and screeched in my ear."

He laughed.

"So much for my resolve," I told him. "So much for being centered. Ha!"

By this point, Art was almost tearing up. He said he'd give anything if he could have a straight conversation (i.e., argument) like that with *his* mother, sweet Lillian, who was slipping away from him slowly with Alzheimer's.

Truth be told, my husband's family had *never* had a disturbingly honest talk like that with each other. They avoided assertion like the plague. Art once told me if you asked any of them how they were really feeling, they would jump up and set the table or go outside and cut the grass or something; anything but talk about feelings.

As he began to miss his mother out loud, wrapping himself around the reality that he will lose her even before she dies, I realized he was right.

But I sat, still angry that my mother rebuffed me; that here she was in her nineties and I in my sixties, and I couldn't ask her to please let up and quit criticizing me when I tried to help her. And even if I did, she couldn't manage it.

I ran our conversation over and over again through my head.

"Before all that," I told Art, "were the two hours of faithful listening to her talk about my sister, with all the right head nods and sympathy I could muster. Mama thinks Carol is mad at her, and she even once stooped to saying—grandiosely, I might add—that everything would be all right with Carol when Mama died. I queried this, but basically let it slide, stayed out of it."

I thought back on the scene.

"Then, abruptly, she asked if I could take her to her MRI next week. I gladly agreed and gave her my available dates. Just trying to help. She stood up, grabbed the wall phone, and began a series of calls to her doctors, so I went into her bedroom, flopped down on the bed, and turned on CNN. I was *tired*.

"Every now and then, I would holler out, 'Mama, do you really want to exchange that lamp today?' That was the original purpose of the visit. She would holler back in a pointedly flat voice, 'Yes, Marion.'

"But I didn't see hide nor hair of her except for the one time I snuck into the kitchen and stole a brownie out of the fridge. An hour later, she was still on the phone trying to arrange the MRI.

"Finally, with just ninety minutes left before I had to come home, I fell asleep. I took a catnap in front of the TV. That was all. At some point, Mother came in, fully dressed, and tapped the bed with her cane. 'I'm ready,' she said, raising her eyebrows and looking at me like I was the one holding things up.

"I struggled up and carried her bags and the lamp we were returning to the car.

"Mama was driving. 'Practice,' she says to me. Terrifying. On the way, she began to talk about her book on Durham and how the Historical Society was not doing enough to publicize it."

This was a familiar refrain.

"She tells me that some woman at Barnes & Noble, who got a copy of the book because you took it around, Art, completely unsolicited by me or her for that matter, called her and asked her to set up a time to do a reading.

"That was so nice of you, Art," I added. He nodded, accepting the compliment.

"I was happy for her. Mama's been pleading poor for so many moons. This was good news. Every penny counts when you're living on a fixed income. That's what she's always saying."

Art, who loved to save pennies any way he could, nodded more strongly, with an I-tell-you-this-all-the-time look on his face.

"I suggested that you'd be willing to do that with other bookstores in the area too, and asked if she had any more copies you could take around.

"'He'll have to call the Historical Society,' Mama snapped at me. Just this morning on the phone, she told me she had two more copies in the dining room she could give to you, and that the less she said to the Historical Society the better."

I saw my husband had finished eating, while I had not taken a bite. Or a breath.

"In fact, she'd been hoping that the Historical Society would forget they're supposed to pay her royalties by the end of the month, because if they forget, she gets a greater percentage of the sales, and she needed it. Hell, she's been soliciting my help with her money situation for months. I try to remind her of all this.

"'Marion, I'm going to do the right thing!' she countered. I repeated her earlier comment about laying low with the Historical Society.

'I have to take another look at my contract. I'm not sure what it says exactly.'

"This is the fateful moment I asked the question that made it all go to seed: 'Do you know where the contract is?'

"'No, Marion,' she was practically snarling, and then she said, 'but when I find it, I'm not going to let *you* look at it!'

"'I don't want to look at it,' I told her. 'I just wondered if you knew where it was. Look, Ma, I don't need to have my hand slapped all the time. I'm just trying to help you out, and I don't want to look at your damn contract at all.'

"'Well, you're so nosy,' she said.

"'I'm so what?' I cried. I could literally feel myself slipping off a cliff. I didn't even want to be there. I'd given up half my day to come help her out, and, once again, I was being insulted.'

"'Marion, don't yell!' she commanded. 'You always yell.'

"'I'm not yelling,' I said to her. 'There's just emotion in my voice.' But I realized that I'd stepped into the trap, and that now I was caught in it. I was swirling down the drain.

"'Yes, you are yelling!' she yelled at me. 'And that's what you always do.'

"You should have heard her," I said to Art, and as an aside. "I was not yelling, Art. I swear I was not. By that time, I was not saying anything. But if anyone looked in the window, they could've seen smoke coming out of my head."

He laughed.

"Mother's driving so slowly, trying to remember how to get to Home Depot, and I was staring straight ahead, trying to calm myself and resolving not to say one more unnecessary word to her on this trip."

"Want another beer?" Art asked.

I nodded. "It was a stalemate."

"So, what finally happened?" He got up to grab another Corona. I love it when he listens to my tales of woe.

"Oh, we managed to make it to Best Buy, and I guided her, silently, to the CDs, and she got one.

"But we never did return the fucking lamp. I left it in the car and she didn't mention it. Instead we got back in, and she turned the car around, and we crept back to her house. Five miles an hour. That's when she got out of the car in a fury and canceled all future visits."

My husband set the beer down on the table and motioned for me to stand up.

"Come on, baby. You need a hug!"

I stood and fell into his arms.

§

The next morning before I woke up, Mama called and left a message on my phone:

"Maa-ri-on," she said in her Scarlett O'Hara accent, "I want to apologize to you for the way I behaved yesterday."

Fine. She could apologize, I thought. I let her trip me into balling my heart up into a fist, and I was still feeling the effects. "Go on and apologize again, Mama." I said silently.

"Honey," she said.

Was I her honey?

"Can you call me before you get all caught up in your life today?"

She sounded plaintive.

"We forgot to return the fucking lamp!"

Chapter Eighteen

The Fall

Maybe it is not about the happy ending. Maybe it's about the story.
—Athena Orchard

I'd just finished making potato salad for my younger son's twenty-fifth birthday party when my older son, Tom, called.

"Ma, did you hear about Mimi?" he asked, his tone flat.

"No. What?"

"She fell again. The EMS people are here, and Kirsten and I are here too. Eno Bradsher called me on my cell." He said all this in one breathless run-on sentence.

"Oh my god! Is she all right? Did she break anything?" I dropped the spoon on the floor, seeing the events of the evening rapidly rearranging.

"We don't know yet. They have her strapped to a board. And she's bitching. That's a good sign."

I could hear Mother's voice in the background. "Get my white blouse, could you? And that green pocketbook." She sounded strong.

"We're going to the emergency room with her. Durham County General," Tom told me.

"I'm coming," I said. "I'll meet you there in half an hour."

This was Mama's third fall requiring the ER in the last three years.

I hollered to Arthur to go to the party without me, got into my Beetle and wound the back way through Durham County, practicing open-heart breathing and trying to be as "here now" as I could before the fireworks started at the hospital.

The ER waiting room was full of petitioners hanging off crutches and clutching their sides. I was ushered into a small green room where Mama lay on her back. Tom and Kirsten paced back and forth on either side of her.

"Is that Marion?" Mama whimpered. When she saw my face above theirs, she broke into sobbing.

"Hi, Mama. It's me," I said gently. She looked tiny and vulnerable, her eyes full of questions.

"They haven't X-rayed her yet," my daughter reported.

"Coming in any minute though," chimed in Tom, his tone brighter than the facts, trying to allay his grandmother's concerns.

"Oh, Marion, I hope I haven't broken anything," Mama whispered, grasping for my hand. "I fell! It was horrible. I was just going to answer the door. I'd woken up from a nap in the chair, and I fell in the hall, on my butt, right off my feet, backwards, and I just lay there saying, 'Oh God, oh God.' I don't know how long I was there, but it was a long time. I cried and yelled, but nobody could hear me."

"Even the person at the door?"

"No, the walls are too damned thick! And then I inched somehow, inch by inch, back on my back into the bedroom and finally got to the phone and speed-dialed Eno." Eno was one of her oldest friends who lived in another state.

She burst into tears again, remembering. Tom and Kirsten crowded in. We made a cocoon around her.

Just then a small, cute man in a white coat came in with a gurney. Somehow, I always notice cute, no matter what the situation.

"Are you here for the x-ray?" I asked.

"I am," he smiled, his eyes on Mama.

He unleashed the gurney and rolled her out, Mama praying out loud, "Oh Lord, oh Lord, please don't let me have a break."

§

Tommy and Kirsten caught me up: what they found when they got to her house, how the EMS had ruined her white rugs with black grease from the wheels of the gurney ("Looked like they came straight out of the La Brea tar pits," Tom allowed, using Mama's phrase), and whether or not we could recoup the damages.

We sighed, seething with nervous energy. Kirsten walked around looking into drawers full of syringes and gauze and cleaning solutions. We looked at our faces in the wavy mirror on the back of the medicine cabinet, and finally at each other.

Then my darlings began a descent into gallows humor. Kirsten walked like a duck around the examining room, contorting her face into a multitude of funny positions, pulling down her eyes, making rear-end noises under her arm just like she's done for laughs since she was five years old. Tom cackled at her every move like he, too, has always done. I sat in a chair and smiled.

Fifteen minutes later, Mama was rolled back into the room, the same orderly with her, telling us all with a broad smile, "There's no break."

The "Thank the Lords" began. We clutched each other in a jubilant hug-fest. The orderly said he'd be back to help Mama sit up in just a little bit.

"Oh, no! I couldn't possibly do that!" Mama shrieked.

He smiled just as if he'd heard her, backing out the door, but I could tell by his face that that was mere tactic, that he was coming back to get her up, period, and was trying to ready her for the inevitable.

"You can do it, Mama," I said, stroking her hair. She just as resolutely assured me she could do no such thing.

After a quick confab, Tom and Kirsten left to go get burritos. When the orderly returned, he listened to her protestations even as he was cranking up the bed.

"Stop it. Stop it," Mama screamed as she realized what was happening. I put my hands behind her back and helped her lean on me. "Just pretend we're dancing," he said. His eyes twinkled, ever the professional.

Several start-stops later, Mama was sitting. Her legs dangled down like a rag doll's. Her face contorted in pain. She looked up into his face with pleading eyes.

"What's your name?" she asked him.

"Darren. We're just going to dance over to that chair," Darren said soothingly. It did look like a dance as he sidled her around him, Mama swooning in his arms. Darren lowered her to the raised seat.

"There," he said. "I'll be back in a few minutes."

"Thank you so much, Darren. I could never have done it without you. Such a nice name, Darren. How did you get that name?" Mama still stared down into her lap, regaining her breath.

"I was born before they were expecting me," Darren told Mama.

"Huh?"

"My mother didn't know what to name me. Then *Bewitched* came on the TV. So, she named me Darren."

"It's such a nice name," Mama repeated, glancing up. "But please. Don't leave me, Darren. I have to go to the bathroom. Where are you going?"

"Oh, I'll go get Rachel to come back in and help you with that," he said, as the door sucked shut.

Mama and I waited in a moment of silence. Then she tuned up with "If I could just get to the bathroom!"

I reminded her how fortunate she was that she hadn't broken anything. But she was having none of it and continued to agonize.

"Go get somebody, Marion!" she ordered.

"I have a deteriorating hip myself, Mama," I reminded her. "I'll look out into the hall and go to the corners, but I can't go running around all over the hospital now. Besides, somebody needs to stay with you."

As usual, I was reacting more to her tone of voice than to her actual plea. But I went.

In the hall, unshaven men hung off stretchers and slumped over wheelchairs, unattended—dumped—one of them moaning out loud, all either knocked out on some drug or visibly in pain. I limped to both corners of the hall and peered around. There was no one in sight. It was Saturday night and the staff was doing triage. Obviously, there were far worse situations than Mama's stacking up. I returned and told her so.

"They don't give a damn about a ninety-five-year-old lady," she muttered, snapping her lips shut like a purse, closing her eyes.

"If I could just go to the bathroom," she said for what felt like the 400th time. "I promise, Lord, I wouldn't ask for one other thing."

"For how long?" I heard the cruelty of my remark even as I tried to make my voice sound light.

Mama opened her eyes and looked at me. "Until the next time I have to go," she said evenly, word by word, refusing my point.

My compassion was sagging. I tried to slap myself back into shape.

Soon Rachel came, and together we walked Mama into a bathroom, slowly, painfully inching her over to the johnny, then down onto it.

"What's next, warden?" Mama muttered.

"When you finish, Darren will be back and we're gonna get you home," Rachel chirped a little too lyrically.

"Home!?" Mama wailed. "I can't possibly go home! I need care. I need to stay in the hospital."

"Well, we can't keep you with no break," Rachel said. "If you want to stay in the hospital, we'll have to get an order from your doctor, and it might not be till morning before we could get you a bed."

"Hospitals never used to be this way." Mama's head flopped forward again. She didn't sound like herself.

§

A half hour later, we were still stranded in the examining room. This time I was willing to walk however far and found a wheelchair half a mile from us.

Kirsten and Tom dressed Mama. Then we rolled her out, passing Darren as we left.

"Bye-bye." He nodded, saluting.

We got Mama into my green bug because it had the biggest front seat, and I drove slowly—oh so slowly—over the potholes and railroad tracks that constituted downtown Durham. Mama closed her eyes and winced in advance of every bump.

"You're a good girl, Marion. A really good girl," she told me in a stage whisper as we rolled in the dark down Mangum Street.

Once again, she began recounting the days of her youth along this old, stately thoroughfare—how regal and beautiful the homes were then, everything now a part of urban development; who lived in the biggest homes; the parties they had on each and every block; the fun she'd had as a girl.

The drugs had hit.

Back at her condo, in her white eyelet nightie, I tucked Mama into bed. It was decided Tom would be the one to stay the night.

Kirsten and I stumbled out into the cold and hugged each other. We hobbled home at 3:00 a.m. Mama was going to make it. She was going to live another day.

Chapter Nineteen

Nurse Jane Fuzzy Wuzzy

Anybody who has survived his childhood has enough information about life to last him the rest of his days.
—Flannery O'Connor

When I was sick as a child, Mama was at her best.

That was when she became "Nurse Jane Fuzzy Wuzzy." (Nurse Jane Fuzzy Wuzzy was Uncle Wiggly's loyal muskrat housekeeper, a caretaker and nurse to all of Uncle Wiggly's characters in the old children's book series.) She gave me toast and ginger ale and Triscuits, and if I was on the mend, lime sherbet. I remember her cool, smooth fingers on my forehead as if it were yesterday: entering my room when my fever broke and washing my neck with a "rashwog"— my childhood word for washrag. She would plump my pillows, and if I was ready to eat something solid, bring me a baked potato without butter on a small pewter tray and yet another glass of ginger ale. For Mama, ginger ale was the cure for whatever ailed. As I got better, I could prop up and read or draw, and later write on a lap table she would bring me. I enjoyed her ministrations. I don't remember her giving them to me this attentiveness at any other time.

If I was seriously sick, I would lie in my single bed with the counterpane tight around my body, arms out, fingering the little tufts that rose up like dandelion heads, staring at the ceiling, my head filling with fevered dreams and visions. I never doubted that Mama would make me better. Not the doctors who came on house calls then, but Mama.

If I came home from elementary school with a sore throat, she would give me a teaspoon of whiskey and sugar. My friends were shocked when I told them. But it helped, or at least helped me forget my sore throat. I never thought it strange at all, just the right thing to do. Cool, too, for my mom to be so different from the other kids' mamas.

When I was eight and broke my arm, she let friends come into my bedroom one by one and write messages on the cast. And the time I had mononucleosis, which ironically saved me from a terrible car accident I surely would have been in—one that busted up a lot of my friends when they careened over the side of a cliff onto the Hope Valley golf course—Mama conscientiously nursed me for six weeks.

Of course, that's what mothers did and what mothers still do. But for my mother, this was her time to shine, to give me the unparalleled, tender loving care and focus that I didn't receive at any other time in my life, certainly not when I was well and healthy.

Mama made great chicken soup, great soup, period. She readily turned to *Heloise's Hints* for what she should put on our poison ivy bites (calamine) and wasp stings (tobacco) and what we should or should not be fed as we battled our various maladies.

At other times, though, Mama was busy. Mrs. Hunt/Pick just like her own mother, her attention elsewhere.

After my father finished work at 3:00 p.m. and walked home the back way along the railroad tracks, he was the one to have time for us, at least when he wasn't mowing the yard or raking up leaves, his two manly chores.

Of course, Mama would have said that was because he wasn't in the kitchen, and she would be right. But still, both my sister and I grew up feeling closer to our father because of the attention he regularly lavished on us—even when we weren't sick.

When we were sick, Daddy didn't have the slightest idea what to do. He would come into our room once or twice a day and perhaps read us a story, but I don't remember him holding me or giving me medicine. He probably scratched my back, his tour de force, but I don't recall.

Or Daddy's first-time babysitting job when Carol was an infant. Not knowing what to do or how to do it when she inevitably pooped in her diaper, he tied her onto her bassinet with his bathrobe sash, leaving her to squirm around in her shit until Mama came home. "She was perfectly happy," Mama told the story, incredulous. From the very first telling, we both knew that was because she had the eye and smile of her daddy.

When we were sick, it was Mama.

On some level she must have realized this, because later when I was grown and doing just fine, thank you, or so I thought, and Mama wanted some attention for herself, her habit was to probe underneath my gaiety for the "fly in the ointment." So, she could "fix it." There seemed never to be any pure pleasure in my triumphs. She always cautioned me not to be too proud of any honor I'd earned, not to let anything "go to my head."

Couldn't it go to my head for just a minute, I remember wondering? Couldn't we just revel together in the happiness I was feeling without qualification, without warning of impending doom?

"What is really going on?" was her perennial question, looking intently at me like a lie detector. What should we be looking out for? What was likely to come tearing down the happy path we had chosen and gobble us up? What could she help us with, if we would only listen to her superior wisdom (which we seldom did and sometimes rued the fact later after the gobbler had gobbled)?

A lot of Mother's warnings did come true. She was, after all, older and wiser.

On the other hand, I missed seeing and feeling her unadulterated joy at my joy; her bursting pride when I had achieved something important; her delight, just as she'd described her own mother's happiness for her, when I was involved in some delicious romantic escapade. Instead, Mama was busy finding out which side of the tracks the boy was from, urging sexual caution, and doubting that he, whoever he was, would in any way be suitable material for her daughter.

"What about Gilly White?" she would ask over and over again, "or Neil McBride?" a boy down the hill from us whose father was a doctor, but who prompted not the slightest palpitation in my heart.

There are two times, in particular, I remember:

One, a book I read when I was sick in bed, maybe that mononucleosis episode, from Kahlil Gibran—a verse that's served me my whole life:

> When sorrow is at your bed, happiness is at
> your board.
> When happiness is at your bed, sorrow is at
> your board.

Maybe that was what Mama was trying to tell me. It changes. Don't get too excited.

§

The other memory was an Encounter Group I participated in during college. We had to walk around the large circle of people gathered in the gym as they shouted out compliments to us. Each time we would shout back to them the things our parents said to us: "Oh, sit down. Don't stand out. Who do you think you are? Don't get a big head. Oh, no you're not!" This was in order to exorcise what the leaders called our "Pig Parent."

Yes! That was it. Even if she was trying to be my Protector Parent, it felt like she was robbing me of my moments of happiness, making me feel like I was less than I was, reminding me it wouldn't last.

But then, what did I expect? That Mama should be some kind of Earth Mother? That she should hang on my every word, say what I wanted to hear?

Surely, she was never that. She was always a woman who wanted to do things besides be my mother or Henry's wife. She was also, eternally, a woman skillfully warding off impending doom

Still, when I was sick and it counted, Mama was Nurse Jane Fuzzy Wuzzy. And, if not my fairy godmother, then surely my faithful custodian, my minder and tender, a guardian for sure.

Maybe even a guardian angel.

Chapter Twenty

Aftermath

If you cannot get rid of the family skeleton, you may as well make it dance. —-
George Bernard Shaw

Ten days after Mama's fall, I returned from a business trip to find my cousin Liza had prevailed upon Mama to get another x-ray and that she had been moved to my sister's house to continue her recuperation.

Mama was still in terrible pain, far longer than she expected to be, and had to have round-the-clock care, and Carol always wanted Mama to come live with her. She frequently voiced frustration that Mama didn't want to leave her condo and come to Raleigh.

Now Carol's getting her chance, I thought.

Over the phone, Mama's voice sounded smaller and smaller, as she told me in minutest detail the pills she was taking, the pain that didn't go away, the x-rays that had been scheduled but would have to wait 'til Thursday. "Please come when you can, Marion," she whispered.

Immediately after touchdown at the airport, Arthur and I drove to Carol's house.

Mama was on a chaise lounge in the sunroom facing the window. She turned, but didn't see me until I was close.

"Oh, Marion," she said as if I were an acquaintance, she hadn't laid eyes on for years. Her hair, normally coifed and curly, was flat against her scalp. I noticed her legs were covered with dark bruises. Mama was usually so fixed up, even in her bathrobe, her legs always covered in support hose. I lowered my head and peered at what looked like shale. Her toenails were long and thick, petrified rocks.

My toes will look that way someday, I thought to myself.

Mama kept her eyes closed and began to talk. She flailed her right hand for her pill bottles. "I've been holding off," she whispered. "But now I need a Propox. I'll be more coherent if I take the damned pain medicine."

I helped her find what she needed. Every move was jerky and slow. Even with my help, it took her five minutes to swallow a pill.

John, Carol's husband, invited us to dinner, so my husband dropped back into the kitchen where the three of them busied themselves whipping up a meal. After three days with Mama there, they were relieved to have someone else in the house. I heard them talking in the background. Mama required someone to help her up two to three times a night.

"Home Instead has been coming some," Mama told me, "so that Carol and John can go to Prayer Meeting and to church." She went on about some lady I didn't know who had a horrible time with her hip replacement—a story I didn't particularly want to hear with my own operation still coming up. But I listened anyway. She'd told me this story ten times already.

Her voice was bite-sized and husky all at once, with lots of long pauses. She swiveled from side to side trying to locate where things were, asking me to rearrange her cascade of pillows. I rubbed her legs gently.

"Liza doubts I'll ever stay alone again," she whispered and grabbed my hand, her eyes still closed tight, her face contorted in terror.

I tightened, resenting, at this point in time, that my cousin had flat-out imparted *her* vision of Mother's diminished future directly to her.

"What?"

"She said that. You can ask her. She said that."

Even if she was right, I knew full well the enormity of the psychological aspect of healing, and I saw my little mama growing smaller and more afraid and dependent before my eyes.

"I know I ain't going to live for a long time," she said, echoing my thoughts. "I have to have around-the-clock-care now. Home Instead, well, they're very good babysitters. That's all they are—babysitters—but I want to use them as much as I can to spell people so they can live their own lives. Carol and John have been so good. I want to pay for the care while I have a penny in the bank."

Her face was drawn into a ball. I tried to adjust to this new Mama, to hold on to her hand, to be there and listen, to grow comfortable not having the answers anymore, lifelong problem-solver that I was, shorer-up of broken dreams.

"I'll go by your house and get you whatever you need, Mama," I said, as much to remind her of her house and her former life as to be helpful. "What can I get for you?"

"If you could bring my picker-upper," she said quickly, "and that tray with the pockets—it's back in the pantry. And maybe the light thing," she continued. "Though I cannot read. I can hardly even see."

"You have your eyes closed, Mama."

"I know," she said and fluttered them open for a second, then clamped them shut again. "I don't know why I'm doing that. I think I just don't want to see how bad it is. I don't want to look at it."

"You were doing that some before your fall too. Maybe you oughta look," I reminded her. "I'll bring you books on tape."

"That'd be good," she said without enthusiasm.

The doorbell rang.

"Oh, law," Mama squealed. "Who's that? I don't want anybody to see me yet. Nobody 'cept ya'll."

Before I could turn around, my cousin Liza strode into the room in a dark pantsuit and sat down on a straight chair at the end of Mama's chaise.

"Hi, baby," she said to Mama. Mama's eyes homed in on hers and locked. Liza worked in an orthopedist's office; to Mama she was The Expert. She'd arranged Mama's second x-ray in which they did find a small fissure—a compression fracture they called it—one they hadn't found in the hospital, but one we were assured would heal.

Mama immediately told Liza about everything wrong:

"Did you get a little of that stool softener going?" Liza asked.

"Yeah, but it's not doing any good."

Liza took charge, asking more questions. I leaned back in my chair and observed not only what was going on in front of me, but with my insides as well. This was *my* mother, and I didn't like the way the questioning was going.

"This is a struggle for you because it's changed your whole life," Liza continued. Mama looked plowed under.

This was about Mama, not me, I reminded myself. Still, Mama had asked me earlier to ask Liza about this, so I chimed in.

"Liza, Mama said you said she will never live alone again. What about that?" I asked in as light a tone as I could muster.

"Well, that's what I think," she said and hiked her eyebrows, her dark, spiked hair doing a little dance. "I don't see it happening. And you know, Marion, I am going to say what I think."

"But, Liza," I protested. Both of us were now talking in front of Mama, who had retreated behind her eyelids. "It's just ten days since she fell, and she has in fact broken something. Her bones will heal, but her spirit is a part of her healing, too. I think it's just too soon to be telling Mama that she will never go back to her own home."

Liza ignored me and looked back at Mama. She patted Mama's foot. "Well, I'm just as sure as gun is iron that your mama's going to need help for a long time to come. Who has power of attorney, baby?" she asked Mama, abruptly changing the subject to something even more macabre.

"John has general power of attorney," Mama whispered.

"Well, you need someone to have health care power of attorney too," Liza went on. "Someone to say what is going to happen if you suddenly aren't doing too good."

Like you start to die is what Liza meant. Everybody understood this.

Idiot, I thought. You are talking about this much too soon.

I tried to take back the reins. "I have a copy of Mama's living will at home," I said in monotone.

"Well, it's probably out of date, and we'll need to redo it. Now, Mena, you do whatever you want, but I'd be happy to be your health care power of attorney if you want me to." Liza ignored me, as if I didn't exist.

Like hell you will, I thought, still angry that Liza was taking this tack. May as well just go ahead and die now, Mama

"That'd be fine," Mama said. Her eyes looked truly terrified now. "I just don't want to be any trouble."

"Liza," I said, "I'll get a copy of her living will and bring it over here, but I don't think we need to be talking about that right now. We're talking about Mama getting well. We were talking about whether or not you want to go home, Mama, whether or not you *could* go home."

"What would happen if your mama started to fail next week?" Liza asked me loudly, not bothering to hide her rolling eyes, like I was an imbecile. "I'm going to push on this."

My body was almost yelling, "This is *my mother*!"

Instead I said quietly, "If that's the case, I'm going to have to push back. Mother's going to last more than a week. She's very likely going to get well. There's time to make the necessary changes. We don't have to scare her to death."

Mama's eyes were still shut. She opened them briefly, looking completely dispirited, her pupils miniscule.

Liza leaned back. She didn't like my argument, or me. She was used to taking charge with no impediments. But she saw she'd met her match, and she shut her mouth.

I imagined getting a call in the future and hearing that Liza had pulled the plug on my mama, and that Mama was dead and that they're so-o-o-o sorry they couldn't reach me in time.

I was burning up inside.

My sister, Carol, came into the room, oblivious. She asked Mama if she wanted to watch the 700 Club. Mama looked terrified and took longer to respond than she would have earlier, but then she timidly declined.

I thought, Yeah, Carol. I'm visiting my mama. We can leave the TV off. I saw more clearly what it meant when you are old and failing, lose your independence and have to depend on other people.

Carol shrugged and left with a head shake. Mama had been a bad girl, and as if on cue she returned to whimpering and complaining.

"I'm depressed. I haven't gone to the bathroom. I don't want to be any trouble. I shat all over myself one night and John had to help clean me up and change my clothes. It was humiliating. But I said to him—he was so good—I said, 'John, we're finally getting our shit together.'" Ever the storyteller, even then. We all laughed.

"Well, Mena," Liza leaned forward again, "I've got to go, but I want to tell you one thing."

Mama blinked. "I just want us all to be on the same page," she whispered.

"Oh, we'll be on the same page, Mama," I assured her. "We just need to talk a bit all together."

Liza looked skeptical. I knew Mama couldn't see her face because she was in her own tight cocoon.

"We'll all be holding hands and singing "Kumbaya" at the end of the day. Don't you worry, Mama," I continued. I doubted what I was saying, but I had to keep this woman—my 'cuddlin'—no longer kissin', from sealing my mama's fate before Mama could find out what it actually was.

"I just don't want to make any trouble," Mama said and began to cry.

"Now listen," Liza went on, her voice on speakerphone, but her eyes again tender. "We can do a lot of things. We can get you the help you need, and we can take care of all the papers, and we can make sure you're not dehydrated, and that you go to the bathroom. But you've got to bring something to the table, too." Liza leaned back.

I did too.

"I don't want to see you crying anymore," Liza said firmly. "You can get mad at me if you want, but stop this crying. That's not going to help you. You can hit me if you want to." She stuck her arm out. Mama recoiled. She didn't look like she could swat a fly. "But you gotta stop this pity party. I don't want to hear any more of it."

Mama's eyes opened. She cocked her head to hear Liza's voice. She looked about three years old.

"I know it. I know it." Tears rolled down her cheeks. "I think of your father, Uncle Bacon, all he went through at the end with that cancer, and I think of Mack, and Mama." She went on to list all of our dead relatives. "It just makes me so sad."

"I know that, but you've got to quit your crying. You've got to be good."

"I'm trying to behave." Mama's drying tears lay like paste on her face "I'm being busy every minute over here. Behaving."

"You have to decide what you want, if you want to get well or not."

I nodded vigorously. "That's right, Mama. A lot of this is up to you!"

Liza leaned over Mama for a good-bye kiss. Then she left without a glance at me. My sister talked outside with her for a good while.

When Carol came back in, our husbands took over with Mama, while we went off to her bedroom to talk. I wanted to tell her everything Liza had said and how I felt about it. I wanted to find out what had gone on in my absence to diminish Mama so drastically.

Carol was chuckling. "You know what Liza said?" she asked.

God only knows, I thought, but shook my head.

"That Mama looks like Uncle Bacon in drag."

"Yeah?"

"She says her father did the same thing at the end, closed his eyes all the time, whimpered and whined." I could not imagine my Uncle Bacon, gruff ex-POW-turned-tobacco-magnate, whimpering. Even once. Pain and death deteriorated their victims and then transformed them. I saw that now.

I told Carol what Liza had said in front of our mother and made my complaints. Carol shrugged.

"You can't change Liza, Marion," she said. "Besides, Mama trusts Liza a lot more than she does you or me. Uncle Bacon in drag. Ha!" Carol laughed again. She wiped her hands on her apron. "I've got to go finish dinner." She left, undisturbed.

This was too strange for me: Carol, the born-again Christian, who thought gays were damned—though half our cousins, living and dead, were gay—getting true pleasure out of Liza calling Mama "Uncle Bacon in drag"; Mama shrinking before my very eyes, all sense of control vanishing. Hers. Mine.

"Please. Let me be of help?" I made a silent prayer to God, not for the last time.

Then, I rose again to go sit at my mama's feet.

Chapter Twenty-One

Home Again

"I am not going to die. I am going home like a shooting star."
—Sojourner Truth

"How do you kick the coffee habit," my son asked. "Joy needs to know."

Joy was now carrying my grand baby—Blessed Be!—so I dutifully launched into Mama's method. Just a week before her fall, she'd become a real green tea girl.

"How do you like that stuff?" I asked her.

"Here's how," she instructed. "First switch to Lipton's regular tea. It's a black tea, which is more palatable. When you get to green tea, fill it up with boiling water and flavor it up anyway you like it just to disguise the hay taste. Keep on. After a while you won't notice it. You may even like it."

"Okay, I'll tell Joy. Did you hear? I'm getting Grandma a new chair. For when she comes home." Tom said. He sounded excited.

"Praise the Lord. You just never know when you have it good, Tommy," I told him.

§

I'd been watching Mama's decline and talking on the phone to my kids about it three times a week ever since the fall. But now it was decided: Mama was coming home from Carol's. We were getting her some outside help.

When I went over to see her at Carol's a few days earlier, she was sitting up on the same chaise lounge, her hands flailing in the same patterns in the air around her.

"Just don't put your stuff down, Marion," Mama exhorted. "I have to create a little island around me. Gotta know where everything is."

I could tell she was better by the strength in her voice.

"How are you doing, Marion?" she asked when she was sure what she wants would be within arm's reach.

"Good, Mama." I smiled at her brightly, glad to be seen at all.

"I'm a little bit better," she pivoted quickly back, "but be careful around here."

"Why,"

"No reason. I'm just behaving," she confided, "I've been busy behaving."

"The lady doth protest too much," I said.

"Now listen, you can get the chair out of my room so Tom can bring in the new one before I get home. And then call Bobby Van Arsdale, would you, to see how Van's widow did in Gulfport?"

She started her list as I picked up my pad.

"Could you try to find the Bible in the little chest beneath yours and Kirsty's picture? There's a prayer in the front of it I saved, I'd like to get."

"What is it?"

"It's for old people to let young people know what they wish would happen. Like be patient when we tell stories over and over. And that time has come, I guess."

Her eyes drifted away toward the window.

"Whatever way the wind bloweth, that's the ways it blows," she said softly.

We both turned to the beauty of the day.

"This morning. I was watching the men cut down that tree," she pointed in a feathery gesture. I saw a pile of logs neatly stacked beside a truck in Carol's back yard. "They're doing it in stages. It was a welcome change just to watch it."

She turned back, her face excited. "And did you see the chair Tom's bringing me?"

I acknowledged that I did.

She moved on to how she is desperately trying to get through that large print PD James book I got for her; is excited by the mystery, but then added, "I'm worn out after half hour of reading," she shook her head, "both because of my cataract surgery and the Fuch's Dystrophy, but now my wrists poop out too when I have to hold that book up."

"But the day wasn't a complete loss," she ended. This is one of Mama's belittling phrases that actually means 'it was a good day.'

"My neighbor, Joan McCuskins came over to visit me, Marion. I love Joan."

§

Mama ricocheted between complaints: no reading possible, brand new eye floaters confounding her already bad eyesight, her pain level high, end-of-life worries flooding her consciousness, and excitement about seeing a tree surgery, the details of her old friend's visit, and the anticipation of a brand, new chair. I rearranged myself and focused; breathed with her to get into the river of her words.

"Her precious little Charles: he was her eyeballs!" I heard her say about a son of a friend of hers, as I emerged from wherever I've been woolgathering, and realized I hadn't heard a word for the last ten minutes.

She talked, and I applied myself to listening until the sky turned a dark bottle green. Outside lights in neighboring houses began to twinkle.

Soon, another half hour passed. Mama held the clicker to the TV up in the air, not punching anything. It was her command stick, the tube silently dishing up more pictures of drowning people in New Orleans, and those still standing on rooftops trying not to drown. For a moment, it seemed a fully appropriate backdrop to our conversation in the darkened sunroom. Wherever I looked, I could see the evidence of things falling apart.

"Maybe we should eat," Mama offered, so I went to the refrigerator to dish her up a small plate of fresh tomatoes, scalloped potatoes and okra.

"Not too much, not too much," she warned from her chaise, now glued to Larry King Live, where two former presidents are trying to raise flood relief, the sound up high.

For better or worse, Mama was going home. Everyone's torn up. Nothing's certain. Nothing. Ever. But Mama's going home.

Top left - Baby Mena and Mother, Caro
Middle right - 313 Main St., Durham, NC
Bottom right - Rose

*Top two photos - Married to
Henry Bond Webb aka Mack*

Top left - Easter
Top right - Newspaperman
Middle left - Confidantes
Bottom left - Popsicles at Nags Head
Bottom right - Mack: Pre-picnic

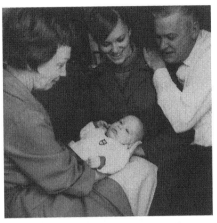

Top left - In the country
Top right - Tom Krueger
*   arrives*
Middle left - A couple of
*   lovebirds on the porch*
Middle right - Mama and
*   Kirsten*
Bottom right - Older
*   Together*

Top left - Mena and Bev Webb
Top right - Halloween
Middle right - Ma, Carol and me
Bottom - The Beach

Top - Her Favorite Hat
Middle - Last Party
Bottom - Namesake

Writer

The Way We Were:
Remembering Durham
by MENA WEBB

April 2003 Publication Date!
ORDER YOUR COPY NOW!
(See Reverse Side for Details)

Top right - "The Curious Wine"
Middle left - Good Luck Club
Middle right - Fayetteville reading
with Hap and Margaret
Bottom right - Durham's Mayor

Inner Circle

Top left - Mack
Top right - Kirsten
Middle left - Tom
Middle center - Carol
Middle right - Corey
Bottom right - The Scallfolding:
  Kirsten, Mena, Carol, Marion

Marion

Top left - Nags Head and Topsy, 1952
Top right - Brownies
Middle left - High School Photo Day
Bottom left - Costume party
Bottom right - University of Vienna

Top left - The Sixties
Top middle - Citizen's Peacemaking Award
Middle left - Corey, Marion, Kirsten, Tom
Middle right - Art
Bottom left - Art, Corey and Marion
Bottom right - the house

Chapter Twenty-Two

Mediating Mama

Family quarrels are bitter things. They don't go according to any rules. They're not like aches or wounds, they're more like splits in the skin that won't heal because there's not enough material.
—F. Scott Fitzgerald

Tom called me at nine o'clock on Sunday night.

"'I can't stand it one more minute. You've got to come and get me,' was what she said. Ma, can you please call them?" Tom asked, bone-tiredness in his voice.

"Sure, baby. I'll do it. Sit tight."

I dialed Carol and John's number and heard a hullabaloo in the background even as John picked up in his cheery telephone voice. "Hello! Sure, you can speak to her. It may take a minute."

I heard Mama's muffled voice and my sister screaming. Then Carol grabbed the receiver and broke down in sobs. "She doesn't love me, Marion. She has never loved me."

This particular brouhaha had begun a few days earlier, but we all thought it was over, tucked away, better because Mama was going back home to Dunbarton.

Now it was obvious. She needed to get out of there fast!

The next day, Tom picked her up and brought her home. All of us were called into service to spend more time with her, including overnights to supplement her paid help from Home Instead.

My night detail came the following Friday. I quietly let myself into her condo.

Mama had said earlier over the phone, "I'm exhausted, Marion. Just go on upstairs when you come in. We'll talk in the morning."

But when I opened the front door, I heard the TV playing softly in her bedroom and saw the lights on, so I went back.

Mama shrieked.

Not only could she not see my face in the flickering light from the tube, but I realized I still had on the orange glow-stick necklace someone had given me at dinner. I must have looked like the Specter of Death.

I ripped it off. "It's just me, Ma."

"Oh God, Marion, you scared me to death."

I sat down beside her. "How're you doing, Ma?"

"Not good," she responded, clutching the remote, the flickering images of the Golden Girls flashing across her face, her eyes watery, her mouth downturned.

"But I don't want to go into it tonight. I already told Tom all about it, and I swore him to secrecy. I know if I tell you, everybody in the family will know." She was baiting the hook. Instead of taking the bait, however, I took her hand and began to pat it.

"Okay, Mama. No need."

"But I'm not doin' good. Not one bit!"

"Is there anything I can do for you?"

Then she spilled. It had all come to a head the night before.

"We had a perfectly good dinner," she began, "and had washed up and gone to have our tea and coffee in front of the television. That O'Reilly show that Carol and John like to watch was on. Somebody named Ann Coulter on it. Have you ever heard of Ann Coulter?"

I nodded and kept the phrase: "that bee-atch" to myself.

"Well, O'Reilly was going on and on about how NBC wasn't going to let Ann Coulter come on their network anymore—"

One for NBC, I thought.

"—and she didn't care because she said it would just help her sell more books. And then they started talking about how you couldn't even say Jesus's name at Christmastime because of all the liberals, and how the blacks have gone and invented this holiday called Kwanzaa, and about how the country is going to pot and the support for the war is declining. . . the show is very conservative, Marion."

No shit, Sherlock. I continued to pat her hand.

She launched into a tirade: "And then all of a sudden John said, 'You know who they're talking about, don't you, Mena? They're talking about your children and your grandchildren. They're the liberals.' And

I said, 'John, don't you dare speak to me about my children like that!'
And he said, 'Like what? They *are* liberals.'"

I thought to myself, No, John, wrong again. I'm a radical.

"'And they're what's wrong with this country. And if I were
you, I would do something about it.' And I said, 'Like what, John?' And
he said, 'Talk to them about it; change their minds, you're their
mother!'

"And I said, 'Listen, John, my children have the right to think
anything they think. This is a free country. And if you want to talk to
them, why don't you stop being a pansy-assed hypocrite and talk to
them yourself?'"

Why had this gotten so out of hand, since Carol and John had
long proclaimed the rest of us as being "lost" with a capital L?

"Why didn't you just get up and go to your room, Mama?" I
asked and eased the remote out of her hand, turning off the television.

"I tried, but John blocked my way. He was loud, and he got
down in my face, and he was waving his arms. He got really angry,
Marion. It scared me. And when I finally got in my bedroom, they both
followed me in and told me it was my duty as a mother to keep you all
from going to hell. What does John know about being a mother?"

"Obviously nothing," I said. "I'm so sorry you had to go through
this, Mama. This is not a nice way to spend your golden years, as they
say."

"Golden, my ass!" she spat. "Baby-shit yellow years." She began
to cry. "I can't believe I've gotten myself into this situation."

"Me either." I was not surprised though.

Mama, Carol, and John had had a tempestuous relationship for
decades. Lots of love and lots of anger. Plus, Mama was a handful. I
couldn't see her living at their house really working well for anybody.
But I remained silent and let her talk.

"Then John started lording it over me—about all he and Carol
have done for me over these last years."

True, paying most of the mortgage on her condo for twenty
years, essentially giving her their car, offering her their home.

"And to you all, too!" she said.

Yep, giving my children $5000 each one year for Christmas,
contributing to their college funds, lending them money here and
there.

"It was infuriating. I could hardly get to sleep. I lay there all night trembling and thinking, Oh Lord, what have I done? Oh Lord, what can I do now? They don't want me here. I'm so glad to be home, Marion!"

Two hours later, I climbed the stairs, promising her we'd figure it all out in the morning.

§

Over toast and tea, I listened to Mama for another spell, occasionally making suggestions, recommending negotiation, telling her I would again look into more respite care, trying to buck her up before I left for the day.

When my husband and I returned later that evening for our joint overnight stint, Mama was a changed person. Kirsten had been with her in the afternoon: a good-bye visit before she and her boyfriend, Rob, flew off to Nicaragua for Christmas. Kirsten had sprinkled her fairy dust.

"That Kirsten is a lifesaver," Mother exclaimed. "I swear I think I can do it."

"Do what?" I asked, carefully lifting from the paper bag the dripping pot of mushroom soup I'd brought for dinner, while Art rooted around in Mother's liquor cabinet for a bottle of Bushmill.

He poured two shots in two highball glasses, one for him and one for Mama.

"Go back over there and be good,'" she said. "I think I can do it now."

"What? You're going back?"

"Not now. But I can if I want to."

"What did Kirsten say?"

"She said it was true that Carol and John *had* done a lot for this family, and that they were interesting people, and that they probably needed a lot more appreciation from all of us."

Nothing I hadn't said, but then Kirsten was the granddaughter, and everyone knows granddaughters hold far more sway than daughters do.

While I heated up the soup and thought that wonders would never cease, Mother and Arthur sat around telling stale jokes and laughing like they were on Comedy Central. We spent most of the meal reciting maxims. Mama said she had grown up with maxims all her life, "A stitch in time saves nine," "A penny saved is a penny earned," "Give me liberty or give me death." By bedtime, all was well again.

§

The next morning Carol called me at Mama's house, sobbing.

"Mama has never loved me," she said over and over again on the phone, along with a lot of other things I couldn't understand, because she was choking on tears while I was trying to breathe and listen and get her to slow down all at the same time.

My family has a penchant for two-hour rants. It was exactly two hours later before I put down the phone. John had gotten on once or twice to ask me if I was a liberal or not, and once Mother picked up and said she didn't like her daughters talking behind her back, but it was Carol's turn, and I told Mother to get off the phone and let Carol finish.

Carol's story included all the things Mother had said over the weeks that had cut to the quick, some real doozies like, "I'd rather die than live here," and "Marion and Tom are my allies. You two aren't."

That last one even hurt me. I knew our mother was decidedly not Aunt Bea. She was seriously hard to deal with. But that was horrible. And untrue.

John kept inserting himself and saying things like "Your mother living here is untenable,' and then Carol would snatch the phone back and say "That's not how I feel. I just wish she could be nice."

John denied the "you'd rot in hell line," and I got them to see that his talking about Mama's children and grandchildren was just stupid.

"John's got an anger problem," Carol sobbed. "He's just angry."

"Join the club," I said.

"But I've never been angry in my life," Carol insisted. "Not until Mama came over here. Now, we've lost it three times. She's so mean. They should've named her Mean, not Mena. You just wouldn't believe it, Marion."

"Yes, I would," I said when I could get a word in. "I can believe it. Why did you want her to come live there in the first place?"

She took a deep breath. "Oh, I don't know. I guess I thought we could learn to love each other better. I had this fantasy that—"

"Note the word 'fantasy,' Carol," I interrupted. "People don't just change toward the end of life. They get more like themselves. I've now read three books on this. It's a fantasy, plain and simple, this everybody coming together and being sweet to each other."

"I just wish she could be nice . . ." Carol's voice trailed off.

I told her that Kirsten came with her magic, and that Mama did think she could go back over there, and that she did appreciate them. We all did.

Carol listened, asked a few questions, then sighed. "Okay, Marion. Not sure she can come back any time soon, though."

"John'll settle down. It's hard having Mama full time, Carol. Don't blame yourself. She does love you."

"And Marion," she added as a finale, "I did not say you and Tom and everybody else were going to hell!"

Maybe not this time, I thought to myself, because you've said it right to my face before. If I didn't take Jesus Christ as my Lord and Savior, no matter what other good I did in this world, I was going to hell, and she and John would miss me up in heaven.

Not sure why, either, I remembered thinking at the time. They don't miss me right here on earth. We didn't really see each other that much.

"Good," I said. "That's good. Bye, Carol. Do something good for yourself. Take John out on a date." Art and I had just written our book: *Two Dates a Week: Rekindling the Spark*.

She harrumphed. "What?"

"Do it. You all need to do something fun. Go out to your favorite restaurant. Take him to eat at Pyewacket. He'll love it. Buy him a bottle of that salad dressing he loves. You don't have Mama to worry about all the time anymore. Put her out of your mind."

"Easy for you to say, Marion," she dwindled off. "Easy for you to say."

And then she hung up.

Chapter Twenty-Three

Black People I

If you expect to succeed as a writer, rudeness should be the second-to-least of your concerns. The least of all should be polite society and what it expects. If you intend to write as truthfully as you can, your days as a member of polite society are numbered anyway.
—Stephen King

On Tuesday after noon, I rang Mama up.

"Hi, Mama, whatcha doing?" I asked.

"Sittin' here with my teacup," she answered, sounding glum. "Thinking about getting my ears blown out so I can hear on this phone."

"Are you just eating breakfast?" I imagined her with her characteristic half a Foster's biscuit and green tea.

"Yep. I'm feeling a little whickery though, 'cause I waited so long."

"Why did you?"

"I don't know. These days I just seem to lie in the bed for hours and hours thinking about the past, which you know I love to do."

"Nothing wrong with that."

"Nope. And when I get up, I just don't know what to do anymore. I'm more and more screwed up in my head, Marion, but I refuse to say it's Alzheimer's."

"It's not Alzheimer's. But you do need to eat. And before one o'clock in the afternoon."

She agreed. "Yep. If I don't get something in me in the morning, it's 'Katy Bar The Door.' My body won't take it! But yesterday Hazeline came and we made the best soup ever! Garlic gumbo we called it. I may even have some of it left when you come over on Thursday."

"That'd be great."

"If you're lucky." I heard her rattling her cup in the plate. She continued to talk about soup-making with Hazeline, one of Mama's caretakers.

"We decided we would call it 'Hazeline and Mena Webb's Famous Soup Kitchen' when we take it public," she announced. "You should hear the way Hazeline talks, Marion."

I didn't reply. What about Hazeline's last name? was what I was thinking.

"She's always saying, 'If you say so,' and 'You right about 'dat, Ms. Webb.'"

This should please her, I thought. These are the only two things Mama ever really wants to hear. Hazeline would be good in the diplomatic corps.

"And then she said, 'If I say so myself' and tells me some story of her own. She's got a husband named Big Daddy. It's Big Daddy 'dis and Big Daddy 'dat."

"Mama, that's just her vernacular," I said.

Mama smacked her lips.

"Oh, I know it, Marion," she said. "It's just stock phrases—kinda comforting to me. If you get what you expect, you're not so shaky."

"Do you like Hazeline?" I asked. Mama liked only some of her caretakers.

"I *love* Hazeline. Hazeline and Gloria and Suzanne. They're my favorites. Though sometimes Gloria can be a know-it-all."

Takes one to know one, I thought, seeing Gloria as the best friend Mama had, and 100 percent her match. Gloria was diplomatic, but she didn't take Mama's guff either. She stood up to her, which Mama needed.

Mama went on talking about black people. I thought back on all the stories she'd told me about black people, and how they'd framed and propped up her life ever since she was a baby—now too, an old lady on the way out.

To begin with, there was Rose Bumpass, her wonderful cook and confidante, whose picture I now had looking down on me so kindly over the piano. Mama told me so many stories about Rose: how she used to bury her head in Rose's big bosom for comfort; her own mother escaping into perennial doing, not really being there for her in that way. History did repeat itself.

I thought about the cook we had early on in my childhood before my parents realized they couldn't afford one: Australia, a warm, hefty woman like Rose, who offered me comfort in the same way. I remembered Australia's daughter, Olivia, just my age. She played with me down on the banks of the railroad tracks until we both hit puberty and Mama and Daddy discouraged our getting together anymore. I'd been so confused and angry about that.

We'd grown up right across the railroad tracks from Hayti, Durham's bastardization of the word Haiti, what everyone in town called the black section then and now.

One night our doorbell rang, and there stood a woman screaming because some man had thrown lye in her eyes. Daddy took her straight to the hospital. She had come from The Cabbage Patch, a shack directly across the tracks, that I later found out was a whorehouse. Daddy had been so kind that night.

Then there was Fannie Mae, our childhood babysitter, just a few years older than Carol, who came on Friday and Saturday nights when Mama and Daddy went to the club. Even though they instructed Fannie May to spank us if we were bad, she would always tell us to put a comic book in our underpants first before she made a half-hearted show of swinging the switch. We would all laugh and giggle and go on playing together because that's what we did. All three of us were "bad." Fannie Mae was hardly a babysitter anyway. She was a fun-loving baby herself.

I thought back to when we took Fannie Mae to the beach with us, standing up to her ankles in the yellow sand, a tight black one-piece over her chocolate skin, squinting in the sun. Fannie Mae was freaked out by sand fleas. Every year she refused to traverse their space and go into the water.

I recalled, too, the time Mama got a bee in her bonnet when I was a teenager and wanted to have a maid in our house to serve us dinner (aping some of her richer friends), though the kitchen was so close to the dining room, you could almost put your hand through the swinging door and reach the pots on the stove. I was embarrassed that Mama put this poor teenaged girl, just my age, in a black-and-white maid's outfit, complete with a stupid frilly hat, and made her come out and serve us lamb stew, ringing a little bell. The girl was smart enough to quit after two times, seeing we were far too plebeian to have a maid, and definitely eschewing the outfit.

Then there was Willie at the country club, the bartender who was one of Mother's favorite people in the world. She'd talked to Willie on the phone up until about a year ago when he died. And Lonnie, who came and tended her yard 'til he crossed over, too.

I remembered the anonymous black woman who came to one of Mama's book readings after Daddy died at a time when Mama was deeply depressed. When she stepped out from the line waiting for Mama's signature on her book, the woman took Mama into her arms for an embrace, and said, "You just look like you need a hug." Mama told me that woman saved her life that day.

All the black people in Mama's life, from birth to death, had been there for her, had held her up and comforted her. Now Mama was telling stories in black-talk.

My blood was boiling, and I wished she would just shut up.

Two of my best friends in this world were Black. They were initially professional colleagues, all of us trying to teach the world a little something about diversity and multicultural education, and then we became fast friends. I preferred hanging out with them more than with most of my white friends, a "wannabe" to the bone. I love their intelligence and how courageous, fierce and forgiving they were. I thought about how much fun I had with them.

Mama continued to rattle on about Hazeline. In black-talk.

"I wish you'd just stop, Mama. Stop right there," I finally managed.

"Why, Marion?" She was on a roll and sounded confused.

"All this talk about 'those people.' Don't you know saying 'those people' is racist, Mama, and so is talking like they do, mocking them? We're all the same to God. Just us chickens here, whatever the color. No one higher than another."

There was silence on the other end of the line.

Finally, Mama responded. "Oh, Marion, I know you're right, but Marion, what can I do? I was suckled on racism right with my mother's milk. We are born in a certain time and place and that informs our story from the get-go. I don't mean anything by it." She paused and I could hear her taking a sip of what I imagine now to be very cold Lipton tea.

"I love black people. I do. I love Gloria, for example, even though she bosses me around."

Individual black people. Hers was the standard anthem of defensive, racist, white people, I thought, grumpily.

"Gloria's great," I trailed off, now feeling ambivalent about taking her on.

But the black-talk returned. "Every Wednesday, she says, 'Get yo' clothes off, Ms. Webb. We gotta' bathe.' She likes to boss me around. I'm glad I'm so interested in people. Me and Gloria, for instance. You can learn so much from watching, listening."

Before I signed off, I said, "You sound better than you did when I first called, Mama."

"Well, it just depends on how vulnerable I am in the moment, you know. Mercury comes in waves; some days are better than others. And I like talking."

"Maybe I could get over there for a minute tomorrow. Can I come tomorrow, Mama?" I really did want to see her.

"Oh no, Marion," she says gravely. "Don't show your face over here tomorrow. Wednesday's bathing day. Gloria's coming. She go'n take my clothes off and stick me in that shower. Nobody better be here when Gloria comes."

§

Two days later, I showed up for our regular Thursday date expecting a shopping trip. Mama was using a walker now, and as far as I knew there were no doctor's appointments on the docket.

"How are you, Mama?" I asked as I entered her bedroom, thrusting my phone and keys into my bag.

"Trying to rise above my present circumstances." Her favorite line.

She was sitting in her chair, all coifed up, smelling like a rose, still in her pink bathrobe.

I went into the bathroom and sat on her throne. I liked how old people got thrones, at least in this room. I looked at her silk granny pants drying on the silent butler across from me, and the Edwardian picture of the bather, delicately dipping her toe into the creek and raising her skirts just above her knees on the opposite wall, a picture I intended to have on my bathroom wall someday.

Mother's bathroom had a golden glow, her jars of lotion and tins of loose powder in pink plastic containers from the fifties were laid out in a line on the countertop underneath a wall-to-wall mirror, ringed by movie-star lights.

It was like the Taj Mahal in there: rich, safe, happy. Made me ready to grease up my dry old self and have some corporeal pleasures and pleasantries. I got up and peered at my face, which, under these lights, looked a lot better than it really did. Lighting. That was the trick.

"Are we going anywhere today, Mama?" I hollered out.

"No, I don't think so today. I got the rhuematiz sumpin' bad today."

Was that her vernacular? Or Gloria's?

"I'm sorry, Mama." I emerged from the bathroom, went over to her, and sat in front of the chair. "Your hair looks nice," I said, taking up her stockinged feet in my hands and beginning to rub. She allowed this for a while.

"I got something else I want you to do today, Marion. If you will."

"What?"

"I need you to go upstairs and he'p me clean out that file cabinet up there. There's a lot of good stuff up there, some of my old writing, and I want you to have it, whatever's up there. And get rid of the other junk, the old bills and stuff."

I brightened. "Sure, Mama. That'll be fun!"

"Have you eaten?" she asked.

"Yeah, I got something on the way. I thought we were going out. Have you?"

"Naw." She looked like a kewpie doll. "But I'm not hungry. There's some of that garlic gumbo left in the refrigerator if you do get hungry. I'm just gonna sit here and watch this horrible news."

I looked up. People were still standing on their rooftops waiting for rescue in New Orleans. Black people. The sound was off.

"Pitiful," Mama said, shaking her head. "So pitiful."

We both watched the silent movie for a few minutes. I'd seen so much of the Hurricane Katrina aftermath in New Orleans over the last few days, I was happy to have something else to do.

Before going upstairs, I made my obligatory stop to look inside her refrigerator and saw the tiniest amount of garlic gumbo stuck in a little glass bowl covered with foil. Not much left. Musta been good, I thought, climbing the stairs to my task.

When I pulled open the heavy top drawer of her file cabinet in the storage room behind her closet, I reached haphazardly inside for a folder. This paper was the first thing I pulled out.

"In these days of rootlessness, with people forever on the move, searching for better jobs with more fringe benefits, better houses to live in, bigger cars to ride in, longer hours for play and less for work, the sense of any identity with a place seems to be disappearing. I don't see many people who've lived in Durham all their lives and who remember how it was when they were children. There are some, I know, and occasionally I meet one of them on the street, and we stop and talk. We speak of the old days, which seem good to us no matter what they really were. Time dulls the pain of some memories and sharpens the sweetness of others, and it's the sweet ones we remember, happy days that were long and golden, and all we had to worry about was homework. All we had to do after school was play.

Standing on a corner while people mill around us, we stare at an empty lot full of rubble and commiserate with each other over the razing of another landmark; and then we groan and roll our eyes and shake our heads because they are narrowing Main Street instead of widening it. In some of the empty lots that urban renewal has left in its wake, the city fathers have planted grass and seedling trees and evergreens in an attempt at beautification, we suppose. But look: they are littered with paper cups and sandwich wrappers and cigarette butts.

Black people come to sit in the sun and eat their lunches there, and when they are finished and it is time to go back to work, they simply walk away from the trash. Again, we shake our heads, not only at the offenders, but at the policemen who will not enforce the law against littering.

The blacks are a colorful lot, like bright jungle birds in their brilliant shirts and tight, flared jeans. Gold hoops swing from their ears, and sometimes even from one wide, dark nostril. Both men and women wear high-heeled shoes that thump and clatter as they walk, and beneath the jet explosions of their hair, their eyes are either wary or insolent.

Remembering when Negroes rarely came to town except on Saturday, I am made uneasy by their presence, and I can sense that my friend is too. But to speak of it would be in bad taste. We shrug, and look away, or up at the sky, which seems to be the only thing that is constant in our town. It's still the same bright September blue it was when we were young and untroubled by change.

§

It felt like providence that I picked up this writing then. Not a lot of sociological understanding, certainly, full of racial privilege and prejudice, not politically correct. The 'jungle birds' phrase offended me. The whole piece offended me. But it was honest, from Mama's time, I remind myself, from her post-colonial viewpoint. I am bowled over by innate prejudices, sewn in childhood, and how they shape us to view things. But I must be careful, I remind myself, not to limit anyone to a single term of 'racist.'

And boy, could that woman write: "jet explosions of their hair"! She looks at the tree, but she sees the twig.

"Please, God," I offered up, as I headed down the stairs with that essay and a garbage bag full of trash, "just let me have some of Mama's writing genes!"

Chapter Twenty-Four

The Funnies

I love people who make me laugh. I honestly think it's the thing I like most, to laugh. It cures a multitude of ills.
It's probably the most important thing in a person.
—Audrey Hepburn

Mama's sense of humor was her saving grace.
"Man plans and God laughs" was written on a scrap of paper she had magneted to her refrigerator for as long as I could remember.

That one and a *New Yorker* cartoon with a man at a desk saying into a phone, "How about never? Would never be all right with you?" This one especially appealed to me, a working introvert with far too many commitments.

If finding life funny was among God's true gifts, Mama had that one in spades. She loved to laugh at the foibles and eccentricities of human nature, the ironies, the jokes on us all.

§

For Mama, the dirtier the better. She asked me repeatedly where that friend of mine was (his name shall remain a secret) who knew so many dirty ones. "Can you please bring over that joke-teller guy?" she would plead, particularly when she was in a slump.

Even my childhood shower curtain was risqué. It featured black and white drawings of half-naked Parisian women pulling up their stockings and striking a pose, their high-heeled feet hiked up on wrought iron chairs. I conjured up some fine story lines looking at that shower curtain when I was banished to do my requisite "business" every day after lunch. That may have been where my imagination truly took off!

Once when I was five years old, the punch line of a joke she told me, but I can't remember now, was "shit, shower, and shave," so you know she didn't hold her tongue around children.

We grew up laughing. Crying, too. In short, we grew up emotional.

Daddy, whose sensibilities ran as deep as a boy's were allowed to be, appeared restrained and managed to evoke a certain unflappability in our midst. He boasted he could turn his mind on and off at will with a switch inside his brain, often encouraging us to try it when we were overwrought.

But when the three of us "girls" were up late hashing out some problem of human existence he thought we should well enough leave alone, Daddy would dance through the living room with his underpants on his head to distract us (an extra pair—he kept another on).

Mama's number one path to "enlightenment" was in laughing her head off, even if she had to alter her consciousness to do it. Can we say "highballs"? Not to mention pot.

§

The first time Mama and I smoked pot together was on a trip to Topsail Beach, specifically arranged so that she could get away and have this experience where none of her friends or disapproving family members would know. (Sorry, Mom.)

Lest you think I was the pusher, this was entirely her idea. She even requested I get her some "kind bud," a term she had learned from my youngest, lifting up her nose and saying no matter what it was, she was only going to partake of the finer things in life.

Later, at an oceanfront cottage called The Waves, Mama laughed so hard over the "50 Most Handsome Men" issue of *People* magazine we'd found on the coffee table, that wiping her eyes she said, "If I knew pot would do this, I would have been smoking it a long time ago." We evaluated each one of the men in the magazine, most of whom Mama thought looked ridiculous, unworthy of the honor. "Look at him, look at him," she laughed outrageously. "Look at *that* guy," she exclaimed, nearly falling off the bed, at a muscle-bound guy in a hardhat with his jeans unbuttoned.

I wrote an anonymous piece about this "trip" in the "Reader's Write" column of *The Sun* magazine (published in Chapel Hill, NC), which you can check out at the end of this chapter.

Mama smoked pot a few more times with me and my daughter at our Good Luck Club, when the girls in the family had a sleepover and drank and ate and told stories from our lives. "Well, good luck!" we would all say to each other at the end of everyone's recitation. Thus, the name.

Mama even asked for her own glass pipe. She hid it in a sunglass case far back in a bottom drawer of a dresser, afraid someone who wouldn't understand would find it while cleaning, or after she died. (Kirsten and I made sure to confiscate it when that happened.)

She never smoked alone, afraid she would go crazy. One time she did have a "bad trip" at the beach when the weed was a little too kind. Kirsten sat at her feet and talked her through the paranoia. Still, she imbibed several times after that, always a sucker for some laughs.

Underneath, Mama was just a girl who wanted to have fun.

I thought Mama's pot-smoking thing was a deep, dark secret, but I can't tell you how many folks told me after she died that she'd spilled the beans.

"Kell—eh . . .," Mama confided after one of those "good luck" afternoons to her friend and the publisher of her two last books. "Kelly, I'm high as a kite." Kelly told me this right after Mama's funeral, and laughed. Mama knew whom to confide in.

Regularly, Mama surprised me by thinking some singularly unattractive man who had "tickled her to death" was "cute."

"Funny goes a long way, Marion. Funny'll just save your life!"

The Sun
May 2003

My eighty-seven-year-old mother was, and is, an all-time classic party girl. She comes from the "time to take your medicine" school of highball drinking: always at 5 p.m., not a minute before.

When my son went to college, my mother would kid him about his pot habit. (She guessed what was going on.) The next Christmas, he presented her with a tiny blue-and-white Chinese urn containing two tightly saran-wrapped joints. "You said if you ever smoke this stuff, Grandma, it has to be the very best," he told her. "Well, here it is."

My mother beamed, thanked him, and said she'd save it for her deathbed.

She didn't, though. The following October, she and I arranged a beach trip to get away from it all, and to smoke one of those joints.

Sitting on the motel bed with her legs out, favoring her arthritic fingers, my mother kept saying, "I don't know what the fuss is all about. I don't feel a thing."

Then my aching, forever put-out, prone to depression and endless bouts of romanticism, not to mention jealousy and anger that life didn't turn out the-way-she-thought-it-would-mother, got up and danced around her cane. Why in the world, she asked, had she never heard of Ramsey Lewis before whose music billowed out of the boom box? "True genius!"

That night Mama laughed until the tears ran. "If I'd known pot could make you laugh this hard," she said, falling back on the bed, almost limber, "I would've started smoking it a lot sooner. Lord, if my friends could see me now!"

Just before I pan-fried some scallops, Mother said, "We need a little more of that stuff."

I told her I didn't have a roach clip. Mama stood up and walked steadily into the bathroom, sans cane, healed as surely as if she'd been dunked into the Euphrates. She came back with a triumphant smile and a hair clip, ready for another round.

"You know," she said, never one to be outdone, "I think your father tried some of this reefer back when he was a young man in New York." She smacked her lips and lit up. The smoke curled up over her horn-rimmed glasses.

My mother is saving the other joint for her deathbed. But I've told a few family members about our beach trip, and now every one of them is dying to smoke with Grandma.

Chapter Twenty-Five

Pre–Hip Surgery

A person who publishes a book willfully appears
before the populace with his pants down.
—Edna St. Vincent Millay

The time for my hip replacement was fast approaching. With the long recuperation period the physical therapists were promising, my to-do list was king-sized.

On the week before my hip surgery, I'd marked down: "Visit Mama."

Right beside it, I had written "One half to six hours, depending on how it turns out."

I wondered: Will it be an actual visit face-to-face or a good long chat on the phone? My free time was especially precious. There was a lot to do this "last week," as I found myself calling it.

On the Sunday before when I'd telephoned, Mama was scheduled to make a return visit to my sister's house, first time since the brouhaha. But now on the phone she said, "'Law, Marion. I may not be leaving 'til Tuesday or Wednesday." She sounded chipper.

"Well, good, Ma. Maybe I can see you for a little bit then before you go."

"No. I don't see how you can do that!" It was a bark. I heard chastisement, maybe even rejection in her voice.

"Marion, you've got to take care of yourself!"

Okay. Maybe it was caring I heard. I was hungry for her concern.

"I know, Ma, but part of what I want to do this week is see you."

"Well, I don't know," she backed off. "I won't know exactly when Carol is coming for me until she calls me later today."

"Okay, Mama. Let me know after she calls."

"I will," she sang, and rang off.

When she hadn't called by eleven the next morning, that afternoon being the disputed territory, I wondered if it might be better to just have the damn visit on the phone. She sure didn't seem to need to see me. So maybe I didn't need to see her either, I thought petulantly.

Butt-headed, I called anyway, lamenting: *I won't be able to go anywhere for weeks, maybe months after this hip thing, and I might die on the operating table.* It's always a possibility. Heck, if "I could die tonight" was a regular Buddhist mantra, then surely "I could die on the operating table" was just plain fact.

After a tedious morning of grant writing, I was ready to bolt out of the house—drive somewhere, anywhere, gas prices and global warming be damned. I had to check something off my list for my own well-being. I needed to get out.

"You forgot to call me back," I heard myself stating first thing when she answered the phone, reflecting the true state of my mind. Laid flat.

"What?"

"You forgot to call me back. Remember? When is Carol coming?"

"Oh, not until Wednesday. I'm going to play bridge tomorrow. Did I tell you? Isn't that great?"

"Great. Yeah. Would you like me to come see you this afternoon?" I asked her in that totally unsatisfactory "Do you love me?" tone of voice.

"Sure. Maybe you could take me to the grocery store."

We arranged a three o'clock meeting.

I had things to do, I told her importantly, and only a short time for our visit.

"Fine," she said, as if she didn't really care.

My early afternoon was filled with nightgown shopping. I couldn't very well be expected to get into my sordid old pajamas after the operation.

I ducked into a gourmet shop near Mama's to grab a bite before arriving. It wouldn't do to get there hungry when we were going to the grocery store. I paid an arm and a leg for an expensive mushroom soup, just broth with a few spinach leaves floating on top, no actual mushrooms. But I spent most of the time in the shop ducking behind a rack of circulars to avoid catching the eye of a loquacious friend who stood blabbing at the cash register. No time to talk with him today, I said to myself, pretending to read intently about amazing vitamin supplements as if it were pornography. I was late for Mama's, and tired.

When I pulled up to her condo, I struggled to clean out the front seat, transferring everything from the backseat to the trunk in order to make room for her walker. Then I limped, sans crutch, to her front door, rang the bell and waited, trying to peek through the blinds to see if she was coming. They were closed so tight, I could only see little circles of indiscriminate light here and there. I heard no sounds. I rang again, then slumped against the doorjamb.

After ringing three more times, I finally heard the walker stumping forward from the bedroom, Mama saying, "I'm coming. I'm coming." She opened the door and I fell inside.

"Come in," she said affixing a bright smile on her face and backing out of my way. I saw her affix it.

We went to the kitchen where I dropped into a chair. "Are you ready to go?" I asked, breathing heavily.

"I was thinking I wouldn't go after all," she said. "I can make it with the food in the fridge, I think, though there's nothing in there."

She opened the refrigerator and peered in. I felt like putting my head down on the table for a cry. Maybe Mama was right. I didn't really have time for this visit. Maybe this was too much for me. I propped up and tried to look attentive. Grown up.

"I haven't gotten a thing done today!" she launched in, as if this was the most important thing in the world. "I try to do one thing and then the phone rings. I answer it, and after that I don't remember what I was doing before, so I go off and do another thing. And then the phone rings again. Hmmph!" She sighed. "I need to drink water. I don't drink enough water. I haven't drunk enough water today. I haven't taken my eye drops once today either."

"What are you looking forward to about being back over at Carol and John's?" I asked to change the direction of the conversation.

Mama blinked. She thought. "Well . . . I won't have to grocery shop," she said finally.

"Is that all?"

She blinked and thought some more. "It's all I can think of."

"What about John's good cooking?"

She shook her head vigorously. "No, I have to have a salt-free diet now, and John and Carol pour salt on everything. Did you hear that man on NPR today talking about Jesus?" she asked abruptly.

I had, in fact. On the way over. A man named Ehrman was discussing his book *Misquoting Jesus*, which unraveled the idea that the Bible was inherently perfect. He talked about who changed the original words and meanings in the Bible and why they did it.

"Well, that made me feel a whole lot better," Mama said. "A lot of Christians don't really even know the meaning of what Jesus said to begin with."

"Yep," I acknowledged.

Mama shrugged. "Sometimes I feel bad about it. I don't believe the way Carol and John do."

"You sure don't have to. Freedom of religion, you know, Mama. That man on the radio who studied Christianity all his life now describes himself as a 'happy agnostic.'"

"What's an agnostic?"

"Someone who doesn't take a position one way or another about God."

"That's me," she said and settled down into the chair opposite me. "Even though I *do* pray to him."

We struggled to place the third chair exactly between us so we could both put up our aching legs.

"Carol still talks about God a lot," she says.

"How much?"

"Just all the time."

"What do you say?"

"I don't say anything anymore. I just nod and smile and I go off someplace else in my mind."

"That sounds like a good idea."

"It's the only thing I can do. Every now and then, she has some kind of a breakthrough, and she'll see she's preaching to me, or has said something judgmental, and she apologizes; says it was her sin-nature talking. She has this sin-nature. I guess we all do."

"Well, that's good," I said.

"Very convenient is what I say. Do anything you want and then later say it wasn't you, it was your sin-nature."

"Well, everybody's got a sin-nature, Mama. And forgiveness is good. But then everybody's got a Buddha nature, too."

She ignored me.

"I've just got to get my head straight, Marion," she went on. "Get centered, you know." She said this drolly and cocked an eye in my direction.

"What for?" I asked.

"I need a mission, a purpose. I need a reason to get up in the morning."

I waited.

"Did you know I am playing bridge tomorrow, Marion?" Mama brightened.

"Yeah, I knew."

"First time in over a year. If I could just play bridge once a week, I could make it." Her voice trailed off and she stared into the distance. "In Raw-leigh. But I don't know anybody over in Raw-leigh."

"Why don't you stay home here? Where your friends are?" I had asked her this hundreds of times. "You're doing so much better over here."

She was, too. Her pelvis had healed. Her depression had lifted. She had gotten a cute new haircut and was no longer in her housecoat at noon every day. She was fielding hordes of friends, unwrapping new offerings of food, talking on the phone, watching Comedy Central and old *Golden Girl* reruns late at night. She had great helpers.

She was still talking primarily about herself, but that was nothing new.

"I know," she said quietly. "But I can't."

"Why not? So, you won't have to grocery shop?"

"No, Marion. I don't know."

"You know you can order groceries and have them delivered."

"Really?"

"Yeah, Sarah's parents do it."

"I wonder how much that costs," she scoffed.

I decided not to talk to her about staying at Dunbarton anymore. People do what they're gonna do on their own time. No point in fighting it, even though what she was doing made no sense at all, not even to her. Mama wanted to stay at home.

"Let's talk about you," she said suddenly.

"What about me?"

"Your operation."

"Yeah. What about it?"

"You're gonna be all right, baby."

"Thanks, Ma. I know I will."

"When is it?"

I'd told her this a thousand times. "Next Monday."

"I'll be in Raw-leigh."

"Yeah, I know."

"But you get Arthur to call me the minute you get out, you hear?"

"I will, Mama."

"I'll be praying for you."

I nodded.

"Everybody over there will be prayin'."

"That's good."

She reached across the table and squeezed my hand.

Chapter Twenty-Six

Mama and Eudora Welty

Beware of a man with manners. —Eudora Welty

Mama hated Eudora Welty. Not because she didn't like the woman's work. She did. She'd had her *Collected Short Stories* in the bookcase beside the fireplace, as well as a book on the coffee table about writers and how they wrote, which I loved, called *Parting the Curtains* with a chapter by Eudora. I remember poring over that book trying to find someone who wrote like me, a writer who made a quilt out of pieces of patchwork. Mama even mentioned Eudora in conversations about the virtues of Southern writers with her friends. Female writers.

But she hated her. The reason: Eudora didn't recognize her the second time they met at some function or another. She often described the author as a self-centered, pompous ass because in some receiving line, Eudora Welty didn't remember Mama.

All of my life, I thought of Ms. Welty, with her long, horse-like face, as stuck up, rude. It never occurred to me to think of my mother that way. After all, who *wouldn't* remember my pretty mama, who was so cordial and mannered and bright all at the same time? If they were paying attention, that is.

Only later did my friend Ellen talk to me about Eudora.

Ellen had grown up down the street from her in Jackson, Mississippi. She was often in her house, and had many enlightening stories to tell about this famous writer, a charming, elderly Southern lady who invited you in for iced tea and egg salad sandwiches, and just happened to be a genius. Being charming herself, Ellen couldn't be wrong, could she? She had *known* the woman.

Much later I read a tribute to Eudora by one of my all-time favorite writers, Ann Patchett. In fact, it was Eudora's story, "A Visit of Charity," that set off Ann's course in writing at the age of thirteen, and she described Eudora's face as "long and gentle."

When Eudora came to Nashville, Ann's hometown, Ann was there with her mother in the audience to get her copy of the book signed. She approached the famous author for her signature, but she had the book opened to the wrong page, and Eudora admonished her, saying, "No, no, dear, you always want to sign the book on the title page." Maybe it was because she was in seventh grade and hadn't ever met Eudora before, and Eudora was already her hero, that Ann didn't carry a sting from Eudora's public admonition. She was so impressed, she put this heart-stopping experience "up against anyone who ever saw the Beatles."

When Eudora died in 2001, Ann, an accomplished author herself by then, flew down to the funeral of her idol. She proclaimed later at a talk in the bookstore, "If my house were burning down, the one thing I'd rush in to save would be my copy of *The Collected Stories of Eudora Welty*, which I had signed at the first author reading I ever attended, the year that I was thirteen and the author was seventy. I could discourse endlessly on why my books are in no way improved by my signature, and my words are just the same on the page whether or not I've read them aloud. And while I know better than anyone that I am no Eudora Welty, I know how profoundly I was shaken to see her, how I felt that my book had been transformed by the touch of her hands."

Eudora was so cool, Ann and her friends in Jackson gathered for the annual one-night stand of the night-blooming cereus flower every year in her honor, and called themselves "The Night-Blooming Cereus Club."

My mother made instant judgments. She held grudges. She could be petty. She felt she was the center of the universe, and a lot of the time, she arranged it so she was. She made pronouncements about people. Though many times, she was right, a lot of the time she was wrong, too. She was Judgy-McJudger personified, sometimes based on the most surface of qualities: someone with a beard or long hair; someone being a Democrat; someone being boring according to her; someone not remembering her name in a receiving line.

I remember her judgments to this day. Many have become part of me. I hear my own Judgy-McJudger in my head, too.

But it's complicated.

Mama's "often right" part of it stays with me also.

§

Mama was psychic. Maybe it was little things, like always knowing who was on the other end of the phone when it rang, or having déjà vu experiences in which she described, in the minutest detail, what we would see around a particular turn in the road, one neither she nor we had ever traveled.

Once she was studied at the Rhine Research Center at Duke under Dr. J.B. Rhine, who provided the first professional study of parapsychology in a university environment. Mama tested as mildly psychic, maybe more than mildly; I'm not sure. I only know she was pronounced psychic.

I had to admit that a great many of her own pronouncements, especially about people, had borne up over time. She saw things, secret things, things folks were trying to hide or maybe didn't know they had themselves: flaws and foibles, motivations, leanings, weak spots. Not just surface things. Deep things.

But I never remembered hearing Mama point out someone's unconscious strengths. It was always their deficiencies, their failings. And it galled me. She never gave anyone the benefit of the doubt.

Even when I knew she was right, I balked. She was only partly right, I would tell myself and her. When she spoke about someone's shortcomings, especially people I knew better than she did, I would remind her that there was always another side to the story.

Mama would just say, "You wait."

§

Years later, I realized that even if she did only see the fly in the ointment, was on guard for it all of her life, the fly was usually there. Maybe not the whole fly, but an essential morsel.

Eudora Welty was a master of short stories, notable for their sense of place, sharp dialogue, and fierce wit. She sounds like Mama: particularly in the dialogue and wit department. I admit I haven't read nearly as much of this revered figure in contemporary American letters as I should have. Now I will.

Maybe Eudora was one of the few people Mama was wrong about. Certainly, she had little to go on in her opprobrium: simply not being remembered in a receiving line. But then, maybe it was something else, something no one else saw, that Mama picked out about this eminent Southern tale-teller. Who knew? I committed to reading Eudora's complete works. And while doing so, I would at least give Mama the benefit of the doubt.

Maybe somewhere down deep, I would see that Eudora Welty *was* a pompous ass.

Chapter Twenty-Seven

The Good Luck Club

Female friendships that work are relationships in which
women help each other belong to themselves.
—Louise Bernikow

Once or twice a year, Mama; my sister, Carol; my daughter, Kirsten; and I would have a sleepover, climb into our pajamas and talk. Each woman got her chance to spill the beans—if there were beans to spill—or just laugh, drink, eat and commiserate. We were girls telling jokes, acting crazy, depressed, happy, cynical, silly, or *whatever we really were* in the company of our peers. Afterwards we found we could deal better with the pile on our plates, and sometimes gather the courage to smash the plate altogether.

My grandmother's generation had called this conclave The Little Helper's Club: their tribe of womenfolk who helped each other with whatever life threw their way—some predicament, their husbands, or children. They may not have had much power in the outside world, but they had one hell of a responsibility inside the family frame. They got things done, moved themselves and their families forward. The name morphed into the Good Luck Club for Mama, Carol, Kirsten, and me.

True, we had a few fiascos when one of us got too honest or pushy. There were meltdowns, or one would leave with her feelings hurt. The group was for support, for God's sakes! So, we would self-correct and behave.

But as everybody knows: Girls rule! Certain things seem to transpire only when women are alone together. Here are a few snippets.

In Mama's living room: "It's fascinating to me to watch the dynamic, the various things that go on between husband and wife," Mama said, settling back into her club chair and putting her feet up on the needlepoint footstool. "All for different reasons, of course. It's like a dance to me.

"A dance implies something a little more beautiful," I said.

"Yeah, some of it isn't so beautiful, just a jumpin' and a jivin'," Kirsten added, pushing back a long strand of her russet hair. This time she'd brought her new baby daughter, Mena Claire, to our gathering—her gift to her grandmother, a baby, a namesake.

"Mena Claire throws me into a total trance. Look at me: I've got the smile of a complete simpleton on my face."

Mena Claire gooed at her. She looked like a Scandinavian baby with her red cheeks and ribbed t-shirt.

Mama changed tack. "I need your help, girls. I don't know if I'm going through retribution, hell on earth, or revelation, but I'm beginning to realize what a plain ole stinking person I can be! There's a little blue car over at the McCuskers', and I don't know whose it is. My first inclination was to call Mary Jo and say, 'Come on, Mary Jo, since you never come by and see me anymore, I would certainly like for you to just tell me who is living at the McCuskers' now.' I feel like someone should tell me that."

"Mama," I chastised. "Mary Jo's not leaving you out. She's busy. She works. She does so much for you." I identified with Mary Jo.

"No. Nothing is the same any more, Marion. It's not right for Mary Jo to all of a sudden ignore me, not after all these years together. It's not right. I helped her get that house, introduced her to people around here. Now, I may as well not exist. And then I think: Let it go, Mena. Don't get your knickers in a knot. But can I really change at this stage of my life and be a nice person instead of a mean old bitch?"

"Well, how do you think you're going to handle it, Grandma?" Kirsten, the expert questioner, proffered.

"I just made the first move," Mama said. "I aired my beef to my two kinsmen. Tell me the truth, not something just to spare my feelings. Here I am. I have lived this long and I'm not any better than I ever was. In fact, I'm worse."

"Hmmmm. I can see how that would be troubling," Kirsten mused out loud.

"I do not want that sweet little namesake of mine to ever know what a real bitch I can be," Mama warned.

"But that's her birthright, Granny. It's important for her to know the foibles of even the greatest. Maybe it doesn't sound good, but it's human. Everyone harbors grudges and complaints. We all have our low and small-minded moments. That's okay. It's human. I don't like being around saints."

"Do you know any saints?"

Kirsten thought. "Yeah, one. Joan."

"They're flat as batter cakes," Mama said.

"Poke Salad."

"If I were sober, I would know what that is. What do I do with it?" Mama asked.

"Put it in your nose," Kirsten said.

"Nose?"

We descend into silliness.

§

Kirsten reminded me of one of the bad Good Luck Clubs.

"When Granny brought the idea up, I was in adulthood, and the idea sounded very appealing. It was a bit hard to schedule with our lives going in such different directions, but worth it. I looked forward to it: The Little Webb Women.

"But for me it was better to call it the Good Luck Club. We needed luck outside of it, yes, but also *in* it, too. We were all on such different pages philosophically."

"I remember one particular fiasco," she went on, "but I think it served to bond you and me more, Ma, because we could have a whole mother-daughter conversation on the side when Meemz was just rambling or processing, and she couldn't see us or hear us anymore. ('Meemz' was one of a million names Kirsten had for Mama.) Or when it was irritating to deal with her, how slow she was. I was grateful you were there; otherwise, I probably wouldn't have done it at all. Ever.

"There were some really sad moments: that big meltdown, seeing Meemz crying on the toilet. She had pissed herself and couldn't get up and had to let her granddaughter help her, because you and she had gotten into a big fight."

"What was it about?" I asked. "Memory's foggy."

"I think it was the first time you told her how painful it was for you that she was always harping and talking about Carol, and you never got your turn. You both yelled at each other sumpin' fierce, Ma, and Meemz was heartbroken— thought she'd been such a bad mother to both of you. It was devastating. You can have a really fuckin' bad night at the Good Luck Club too. There are certain levels of craziness and honesty that are fun, but then there's also the black hole."

"Yep."

"But I definitely remember fine ones too. Remember that time at Christmas, when we were all decked out in red. We looked so good, we took twenty pictures of our reflections in the mirror. And we gave Meemz her own special pot pipe, and took pictures of our feet."

I sighed. Good times we would never have again together.

"And that weekend trip to the Blockade Runner at Wrightsville Beach!"

That trip was the last Good Luck Club with all four of us together. I recorded it, and then later took it down verbatim in my journal:

At the Blockade Runner, Wrightsville Beach:

Kirsten and I had settled into a gorgeous beachfront room the color of the sea, and Mama and Carol were on the way. We'd immediately drawn the blackout drapes, gotten between the sheets with our eye masks and earplugs for a nap. But when I woke up abruptly wondering where Carol and Ma were, I tried to get online in the dark. Stumped, I called the desk for the password and woke Kirsten up.

Now I hear Kirsten murmuring, "Rude!" as she gets up, grabs her stuff, and heads out.

"Kirsten, are you mad?" I jumped up and hung my head out the door.

"Yep. A little. But I'm going downstairs to get over it." She disappeared with her towel and hat.

She was deservedly pissed.

Oh well, I said to myself: the oh-well-path-to-enlightenment.

I finally got out to the pool where Kirsten sat with a Bloody Mary and a much-improved mood.

"Have one. I've got an open tab."

I ordered a $12 piña colada.

"Ridiculous, but at least it's big. I love coconut," I sighed.

"Already," Kirsten said, "I've learned four things I didn't know about you before, Ma."

"What?"

"That you'd like to play the squeeze box; your favorite state is to be moving somehow over the planet—car, bike, boat, whatever; and you like a breeze blowing over your body at night. And now the coconut."

I was feeling the liquor.

We finally got Carol on the phone. They were just over the bridge in Wrightsville. But within minutes, they arrived and came out to join us, Carol holding Mama's elbow as she toddled forward with her walker.

Mama made her first toast. "Here's to crime!" She turned up her hearing aid. We were sitting under a white latticework roof facing the ocean.

We talked about good anti-depressants: Lorazepam, Doxepin, Selectra.

"You can have anything you want out of my drug bag, Kirsten," Mama offered.

Carol said something about God.

"I have a totally new vision of God," Mama interjected. "I've decided I think he's a neat guy. This morning I said to him, 'I'm going to the beach with my womenfolk. See to it I have a good time.' And He said, 'Okay. Keep your mouth shut.' And I said, 'You know I can't do that.' And He said, 'Yeah, I know. But try.'"

We all laughed.

"Do you remember the Arlington Hotel at Nags Head?" Mama asked, taking me back to the good ole days. "Do you remember Mrs. LaPier's Boarding House?"

I nodded, dreamy.

"What a good idea liquor and fries together are," she added.

We all stared at the sea, the alcohol seeping deliciously into our veins.

"Do you remember Nutt Parsley, Carol, the preacher who christened you?" Mama went on, ensnared by memory.

Carol shook her head. "No. But I am fascinated with his name."

"Oh yes, Nutt Parsley. He came from a prominent family in Wilmington," Mama smiled, satisfied.

Kirsten was looking up. "I really love hawks."

"That's profound," Carol interjected.

"Why?" I asked.

"Compared to doves," Carol said. "They get all the press, but hawks are the ones who get the job done!"

Somehow before we knew it, someone was telling us that Clark Gable shaved his nipples.

"Wasn't he gay?" Kirsten asked.

"Hmmph. Whatever." Mama shook her head. "All I know is that I would have loved to have known Clark Gable. And I mean in the Biblical sense."

Carol agreed.

"I like men," Mama stated, "for what they're good for. I especially like to look at their hands and their butts. Always remember, you can't drive a ten-penny nail with a tack hammer," she added, taking a sip of her drink.

"You can have a big penis, and still not know what the hell you are doing," Carol suddenly added. We looked over, surprised. Carol usually eschewed conversations about sex.

Then together, we listed every euphemism for "penis" we could think of.

Mama talked about when she first realized boys had a "monkey wrench," a new moniker to us.

"Do you still notice their packages, Mama?" I asked her.

"All the time," she said and raised her eyebrows. She haltingly lifted her feet up to the railing.

"You know," she added, shading her eyes with her hand and sighing, "Right now, I am as happy as I can be."

Chapter Twenty-Eight

Executor

Experience is the hardest kind of teacher.
It gives you the test first, and the lesson afterward.
—Oscar Wilde

"Hey, Mama. How're you doin'?" I asked over my cell.

I was up early and on a tear, now parked in the lot in front of TJ Maxx. It was the last day before our family beach trip, and I was in a hurry to return things: a battery-operated bocce ball set I'd bought on a whim for my grandson who's only six months old. A book on "intuitive eating" that I intuited on my second glance I already knew, but nonetheless had not been doing for the last thirty years.

I needed as much money as possible to satisfy any extra little longings that might crop up when I sat staring at the never-ending ocean waves breaking at Topsail. Nature and commerce.

"Oh, I am so glad you called!" Mama said on the other end, but in a low, muffled voice. I could tell I'd awakened her.

"How *are* you, Ma?" I repeated, swinging my car keys from the end of my fingers, waiting for her report.

Women in groups of two and three were already schooling up near the store's entrance waiting for it to open. At ten I would join them, and plow through the herd to exchange my earlier purchases for a few tall vases my garden's purple bee balms and yellow canna lilies cried out for this morning.

"Not worth a whit," Mama plunked down. "Listen, I need you to come over here and help me with all this funeral shit. When can you come?"

"How about next Thursday afternoon?"

"It's going to take longer than that."

"What is?"

As far as I knew Mama just wanted to change the executorship of her estate over to my sister and me, rather than have her son-in-law do it. That was a quick drive to the notary at Pip Instant Printing, a half mile from her house, a form to fill out, a signature. Even with Mama taking thirty minutes to get in and out of the car, the entire junket ought not take more than an afternoon.

"I want Carol to be involved. You know, I told you I wanted both of you, if you think you could work together . . ." She'd said this so many times over the last few months, it was a chorus line.

"We can work together, Ma."

"And I don't know if she can come on Thursday."

"Call her and find out. That's my only day next week," I tell her, "except maybe Friday." I hated to give up my Fridays.

"Well." She paused. "I just don't think Thursday would work."

"Why not?" I persisted. "Have you asked her about it already?"

"No, but, Marion," she raised her voice in exasperation, "she'll have to drive home in all that traffic if she comes on Thursday."

"Get her to come at noon." When had my sister ever made it anywhere before noon? "We can be finished by four and she'll miss rush hour."

"We won't be able to finish at four, Marion." She sounded downright dejected. "There's so much to do!"

"What?"

"There're the funeral arrangements. There're all these forms."

"Can we prioritize?" I went on. "What's first for you? Second? Third?"

"I know what prioritize means, Marion." She sighed over the phone.

"Mama?"

"Huh?"

"Tell me what's first on your list." I was determined to wring this out of her.

"Oh, the executorship, I suppose. And I gotta be quick about it too. I couldn't stand it if, if . . ."

"Well, let's get 'er done!"

TJ Maxx opened, and the sidewalk of waiting women with big pocketbooks emptied. I checked my watch and opened the car door, gathering my purse and returns while juggling the phone.

"But that won't take any time," Mama continued. "I could just drive up there myself. Be done in ten minutes flat."

I remained quiet. My point exactly, Ma. *If* you could drive. Which you can't.

"How about next Friday?" I offered again, stifling my sigh.

"Oh, look, if you don't want to come, Marion," she said, desultorily, "We'll just have to wait 'til week after next. Do it on your schedule."

"We might," I answered, locking the car. "Except then, I'll have even less time."

"You will?" She suddenly sounded frightened.

"Yeah, I have to go to Nashville next week."

"Oh."

To her, this was insoluble. "Well, if you don't want to come . . ." She picked that thread up again, then trailed off completely.

"Who said I didn't want to come? I've given you two options. What's wrong with them?"

"We'll just have to do it on your schedule . . ." she repeated limply.

Mama was obviously disgusted with me and my—what? Perversity? Job? Schedule? The fact that I had a schedule? The uncertainty of it all?

No, she was disgusted with the business of dying. Who wouldn't be?

I pushed back. "Who else's schedule? You and Carol don't work, Ma. I do." This was something I felt she could truly not understand.

"Now, Marion, don't you yell at me!"

"I'm not yelling." I checked. I wasn't. "I'm saying I called you just to check in, to see how you were, give you a few times to get together next week. Nothing seems to satisfy."

"If you can't, I understand how it is—"

"How what is?"

"Just go on to the beach," she said. "I can't talk about this anymore right now."

"Okay," I answered. "Good-bye."

"Good-bye." She clicked off.

I stood in the parking lot letting my anger simmer for a full minute before heading into the store, wanting nothing more than to "return" that entire conversation.

(Note to Self: Have you ever noticed how "executor" and "execute" have the very same letters?)

§

Later that afternoon, I picked up Kirsten at Jiffy Lube.

Even before the air conditioner cranked on, Kirsten told me she was seeing "Mimi"—another of her names for Mama—that very night, and I launched into an annoyed rendition of our phone encounter.

Kirsten chuckled sympathetically in all the right spots.

"I don't know what she wants me to do," I said and shrugged.

"I think she wants you to go through the whole death and funeral and the aftermath twice, Ma."

We changed the subject.

§

When I got home, my husband hugged me and poured us a drink.

"You've got to listen to your mother's voice mail." He clinked my glass.

"She apologized, eh?" I clinked back.

"Yeah. A real *mea culpa.*" Art turned back to the counter and cut a thin slice of lime. "What did she do?"

I shrugged. I couldn't relive it.

Still, when Art went to bed, I went downstairs and listened to Mama's message.

"Ma-a-arion," she began in that Anglican bleat of hers. "I just called to say I don't know what came over me this mawnin'. I hadn't had anything to eat. I think that was it. My blood sugar was low. I was wrong, and I don't want you and Arthur going off to the beach mad at me or me be mad at you. I'm NOT mad at you, baby. That's what I meant to say. I'm sorry, dawlin'. Mea culpa." Click.

§

The beach trip was a blast. When we returned four days later, I called Mama again. To check in. (Danger, danger.) And also, of course, because I'd missed her. I sat dialing the number from our window seat.

"Hey, Mama."

"Well, hey!" Her voice lifted.

"Whatcha been doin'?"

"Oh, I've been busy!" she crowed. I envisioned trips to the grocery store, drinks with neighbors in her kitchen, little chunks of leftover cheese cut into micro-size servings with water crackers for hors d'oeuvres; or maybe being squired somewhere to lunch by her new best friend, the gay undertaker, or getting a lift with Creel's Wheels to the library for some large-print books. Outings. Rendezvous.

She regaled me with the details. To top it off, Mary Jo had regained her good neighbor status by planting impatiens in Mama's tiny front yard, red and pink, emerging from a half-buried terra-cotta pot she'd cleverly buried in the ground.

"I've never seen such a thing!" Mama exclaimed. "I wake up every morning just so happy to be living in this beautiful, well-cared-for place," she sighed.

I understood already that at age ninety-five, maintenance of your home and body and mind, your material and spiritual existence, took on heroic proportions.

"And lately, John Satterfield keeps callin' me, wanting to come over here," which she pronounced 'ch'eah'. John Satterfield was one of Mama's courtiers.

I laughed. "Good for you, Mama."

"Hmmph," she snorted. "He keeps saying he's got to get over here to talk about old times. And I say 'No, John. We've done that. We've talked that dead horse to death.' 'No, we haven't,' he says. 'Besides, nobody else remembers it but us.' And of course, I do like him bringing me all that wine and candy. I want it. But not at the price I have to pay."

Her throaty voice indicated Mama was barely out of bed—at noon. She probably hadn't had a thing to eat, and her blood sugar was surely low again. But she was practically giddy, sounded like she was 'in her cups.'

We talked about a book we'd both been reading called *Round Heeled Woman*, and our opinions about Jane Juska, the lusty sixty-seven-year-old protagonist and her adventurous want ads for sex.

"She doesn't even bother to disguise who she is," Mama said incredulously. "A week of great conversation and 'Maude and Haroldesque sex' is how she describes the affair with the thirty-seven-year-old. I wonder what's wrong with him."

"Nothing. I bet she's cute." Mama was ninety-five, and she was cute, batting off her suitors.

"I think good talk is sexy myself," I continued. "How many times do you get to talk about all kinds of things, intelligent things, controversial things, and then get to screw on top of it? That's the best sex to me. Usually it's one or the other, but not both. Have you ever had both together?"

"Just once," she answered quickly.

"Was it before or after Daddy? Or during?" I asked just as quickly. I knew it wasn't with Daddy. Daddy was a man of few words who saved his for stories for the newspaper, Clark Kent personified. He obviously had a lot of them swirling around in his head, but he wasn't prone to sharing.

Neither was Mama. "I'll never tell."

We laughed.

Today Mama was alive and well. And maybe she'd slept with at least one other guy besides my father.

We talked about books and libraries and famous men and the old South and the state of the world; about relationships between men and women (our favorite topic), between men and their fathers, and once again I tried to weasel out of her the recipe for her incomparable Black Forest brownies. (She was still not telling, leaving the sacred recipe to "The Prince.") She told me the man she most wanted to talk with in heaven was John Updike.

It was a grand visit over the phone.

"Oh, before you go," she signed off without a hitch, "Carol's coming Thursday afternoon when you do. We can all three go do the executor stuff then. Won't take long. See you then, baby. Love you."

Chapter Twenty-Nine

The Tipping Point

Not everything that is faced can be changed;
but nothing can be changed until it is faced.
—James Baldwin

Mama took a second fall—the bad one—in December of 2011. She was ninety-six. It landed her in Durham Regional Hospital. This was followed by a stint at Hillcrest Assisted Living, ostensibly to recuperate from the new crack in her pelvis. But it was evident Mama might not get home this time.

Over the years, she'd had a number of falls, illnesses, drug reactions, bad biopsy results, increasing deafness, psychological traumas of numerous kinds, a screw loose here or there, and the eventual loss of her eyesight.

On Hillcrest's intensive care unit, we watched her slow progress and received bad reports from her helpers. Mama floated in and out of consciousness, lost in the low-gravity waterbed.

"She isn't trying," they said, while Mama gave us impassioned reports of just how hard she *was* trying, and how mean and inept all of the people around her were. Her worst nightmare had come to pass. She was at the nursing home.

The visitors, the cards, the meetings with the staff to strategize ways to get her to increase her effort and stop her limitless bellyaching before they kicked her off the Medicare Hall and we had to find some way to start paying them the full $10,000 a month this place required, initially helped. Exhortations. So did regular visits from her favorite staff person: Ira Christmas, a young African-American physician's assistant who went to Duke. Ira liked Mama. She loved to argue with him about Duke and Carolina. Arguing gave her life.

Still, even when she'd been moved to a pale yellow room at the end of a hall on the Longview ward, too far away from the nurse's station, and we brought in a little of her art and a few things from home, I had trouble imagining Mama ever living on her own again, or us being able to afford the round-the-clock care she would surely require if she were to return home.

She occasionally dressed herself with help and had a glass of wine and a Triscuit, trying to talk about something besides the predicament she was in. We brought in one of her favorite Home Instead helpers, Gloria Wardrick, for continuity and plain ole friendship, thanks to the largess of her sweet godson, Tom Kenan. She liked having somebody familiar to fuss at.

Six weeks later, she fell again trying to get to the door of her room. She wanted to stick her head out in the hall and holler for somebody to get in there, she said. She wasn't supposed to get up by herself, and she knew it, but she insisted everyone was ignoring her buzzer.

It may have been true. Equally true, there were only three caregivers on a ward for twenty-five old people, some in much worse shape than Mama. As they kept reminding her, this was assisted living, not the high-touch Medicare Hall. They were essentially telling her they couldn't be expected to be at her beck and call all day long.

One of the nurses found her fully dressed, crumpled on the floor in front of her closet that day.

"I was just looking for my brown sweater," she told them meekly, lying. I imagine she was feeling guilty. And dumb. Just as she had begun getting a bit of her oomph back, now the other side of her pelvis was fractured. Mama's goose was cooked.

After a trip to the hospital, she got a different room at Hillcrest, also yellow, but closer to the nurse's station. Someone in the family visited every day; me four or five times a week, Carol when she could. Mama's niece, Alice Raney, came frequently after her shift at Duke Hospital. She tended Mama with patient, loving care.

The grandchildren and great-grandchildren came, sitting on the bed and dangling their legs, Mama feeding them candies some friend had brought but she couldn't eat. She asked them a lot of great-grandmother questions, which they gamely tried to answer.

As she became more mobile in her wheelchair, we took her out to eat as much as she would go: to Southern Seasons or Watts Street Bakery; and many parties were held in her room with wine and various other delicacies brought in just to please her. Cards decked her walls. There was gaiety and laughter.

But most of the time, Mama was pissed.

Each visit was met with voluminous tales about her caretakers, both those she loved and those she hated, recited with her eyes closed and a twirling finger that jabbed the air to make a point. She also told us about her visitors, how she was connected to them, what they had done together in past chapters of their lives, as well as pronouncements about who she wished would come, and the things she wished she could do just one more time.

When the weather was warm and she was willing, we rolled Mama out on the second-floor terrace, where she was struck by the silky air on her skin and the beauty of the sky. Even the rush hour taillights on I-40 delighted her. Her old eyes saw only a ribbon of red trailing off into the sunset, a pseudo LSD trip, phantasmagoric and fantastic.

Out there on the roof, Mama was at her best. Whoever designed that little escape hatch was a visionary and has our eternal gratitude. Mama was on the edge of the cliff, but there she was happy.

At the end, being outdoors made a vast difference, even to Mama, the consummate indoor girl.

Chapter Thirty

Hillcrest

Most things will be okay eventually, but not everything will be.
Sometimes you'll put up a good fight and lose. Sometimes you'll hold
on really hard but realize there is no choice but to let go.
Acceptance is a small, quiet room.
—Cheryl Strayed

Mama'd been at Hillcrest now for four months.

"Hillcrest should be called Hell-Hole Nursing Home," she mumbled when I walked into her room. She lay despondent, staring out the lone window that faced a tall brick wall and one pink japonica bush. I tried to see what she was seeing. It looked like a cross between a picture in *Southern Living* magazine and a prison view.

"Why do you say that, Mama? What's happened?"

"These people are *mean.*" She strung out the word.

"How so?" I had interacted with many lovely caretakers. There were a few dolts, yes, and one who's condescension earned her the title of "whale turd" from Mama, which the attendant decried to us in the hall, truly stung. Of course, she was overweight, Mama's second favorite prejudice. But I could only shrug, and half admire Mama's nasty way with words. I'd heard that nurse, and she was a whale turd.

But most weren't like her. As the brochure said, Hillcrest offered "Elegant Retirement," whatever that meant.

Mama's lip protruded. "Most of the people who work at Hell-Hole are kinda sadistic or they wouldn't be here."

"Now Mama, you know that's not true. What about Ira? Or Ella? (That wasn't her name, but Mama insisted on calling her that because she looked like Ella Fitzgerald.) Or Sheila? You know you love Sheila."

She nodded, barely. "They try to be nice. They come in and say 'How's it going?' But then they bring me things I can't eat. I say take them back. These Triscuits are too salty. They take them away, but then they bring them again. They don't listen. They don't care."

She'd turned to me. Her eyes were bleary. She was sad and dwindling.

I need to get her out of this room, I told myself, but Mama was largely past outings, certainly this late in the day, especially since the fiasco of the last one to Pop's restaurant downtown where her foot got caught, in those stupid flats of hers, in the tiny 1950s wheelchair elevator, practically taking her toes off.

She continued on. "The people here don't really have much to do. Most of them just wander around yelling."

"You mean the patients or the workers?"

"All of them. I know I'm a spoiled old lady and I'm sorry; not sorry for the actual spoiling, but what it's made me into." She shook her head. "I'm not a nice person."

"Let's go up to the balcony, Mama, get you out of this room. It's pretty outside, almost sunset."

She protested, but I grabbed some pony beers out of her midget fridge, and she allowed me to lift her out of the bed, grumbling, and into her wheelchair. I covered her with blankets and shawls, then stuffed her sunglasses, hat, the beers and some snacks into a bag, which I hung on the handles.

Mama sit-walked the wheelchair with tiny steps, making our progress glacial, but giving her the needed control.

In the elevator, she turned and looked up at me, "The world's gonna be just fine after I'm gone, Marion."

Maybe. But would I be? I felt tight in the chest.

We approached the glass doors that led to the roof. She added, "And I'm gonna quit trying to jerk it into shape while I'm here, take it as it is."

Already her spirit was lifting.

Outside, we spread our little cocktail party on a bench. I arranged her chair so she could see I-40 and all the cars zipping below us on their way home. The sky was striated with pinks and blues, wispy white clouds laid on top like Mechlin lace. Mother put on her sunglasses and ball cap and covered it with the multicolored shawl I'd brought her back from Ecuador. She'd made it one of her favored possessions and took it everywhere, which pleased me no end. As she reached up to adjust her glasses, she looked like an old Middle

Eastern woman with her ancient hands and too-long fingernails with chipped rose polish.

I remembered the last time I brought little Mena here to see her, her beloved three-year-old namesake. Mama kept trying to get her to hold her hand. Little Mena kept looking at that hand and trying hard not to recoil, which to her inestimable credit she managed to do, taking it into her small, smooth one. Mama's hand looked like a scary drawing in a picture book of a witchy woman's.

Still, little Mena obliged her, kissing her cheek and sitting up on her bed while Mama gave her compliments and M&M's. "Just like Granny snuck me some pep'mints every time I visited with her," Mama mimicked. "Sweets: every old woman's special sauce."

Now Mama crooned with pleasure at the sunset, "So wonderful. Look at that beautiful red thing shining up there."

I turned. It was the exit sign.

She finished her beer and set down the bottle. "Wish I had my Dynamite," she says.

"Your what?"

"Dynamite Chardonnay. That's my favorite. One of them. I got a lot of favorites."

"Well, I've got us two more Coronas. Want one?"

"Sure."

I twisted off the cap and handed her the bottle along with a cracker dipped in hummus.

Mama sipped and nibbled. "If it wasn't so chilly, I could sit out here and ruminate all day long."

"Want my jacket?"

"Naw, I'm okay. My thought process is pretty damned slow these days. But you know what?"

"What?"

"I don't have to do one thing if I don't want to."

"That sounds nice."

She winced. "But the pain. Jesus, Mary, and Joseph, the pain."

"Where does it hurt, Mama?"

"All over."

She drifted into talking about her parents: Granny and Skipper, and then about her maid, Rose, who she called Big Chief. "You know she was a genuine Cherokee, Marion. Not just black."

"No, I didn't know that."

"She was the best damn cook in all of Dixie, and she tol' it like it was, too. I've still got a chapter in me about Rose, one that's just paused like a Victrola. Just need to set the needle back on it. About Mack too. That's what I wish I could do: write about Mack before I die."

She broke into song:

"Am I blue? Yes
You'd be too,
If these tears from this man
Done come true."

"Are you singing about Daddy, Mama?"

"Mack, yes. And every other man on earth." She nursed her beer, holding it carefully in the folds of her shawl. The sun graced her face.

"My life was all about 'man and woman.'" She stirred her finger around in the air. She seemed happy now. Or drunk.

"It's shocked me, all the wrong ideas I've had about people."

She launched into a story about some male employee at Hillcrest I didn't know.

"He's like a little ape. Bow-legged. He walks like this." She showed me with her fingers. "He says, 'Hello, Ms. Webb' when we pass in the hall, and I smile at him, because even though he's polite, he's ridiculous."

I winced.

"Like most men," she went on, "they're happy as long as they've got the remote, their penis, and their jobs." Mama sighed. "Gimme another cracker, Marion."

As I handed it to her, she added, "And some place to put their penis, too. But," she said brightening up, "I wish him well. He's got so much to learn, but he's got the opportunity to learn it."

We were silent.

Again, she began to sing.

"Remember you vowed
By all the stars above you,

Remember?
Remember we found a lonely spot
And after I learned to care a lot
You promised that you'd forget me not
But you forgot
To remember..."

Her voice was tinny, but as usual she knew all the words.

"I was so young and malleable, Marion, always laughing and happy-go-lucky; bouncy, just like a teenager."

My head was tight and full of tears. I wished I had more beer. I didn't want to lose my mama.

She peered over her glasses at me as if she could sense what I was feeling.

Instead she said, "You wonder what happened. Don't you?"

"Uh-huh." I had a tight leash on my words so as not to start blubbering.

Mama took a swig. "I grew up, that's what happened. So much of life is ugly, Marion. But it's necessary. Let's go back in. It's getting cold out here. And I think I got some Dynamite in the refrigerator."

§

Propped up in bed, we ate a dinner of Marcona almonds somebody brought and cold chicken from her dinner plate, the only thing she said she could touch. Her new Paul McCartney CD, *Kisses on the Bottom*, tinkled in the background.

"You know what I want for my birthday, Marion?"

"No, what? We were thinking about getting you a massage."

Mama smiled. "Yeah, I could be rubbed into insensibility, take a little nap, revive, eat..." She smacked her lips. "Man, that was good!"

"What?"

"That little piece of chicken."

She reached for her wine glass. "Promise when I'm about to go, you'll sponge some of this Dynamite into my mouth."

"I promise, Mama."

"No, what I want for my birthday, Marion, is simply peace: P-E-A-C-E."

"Okay . . . "

"If we did more about getting it, we'd be happier, I reckon."

"Hmmm hmmm."

"I'll tell you what I've learned."

"What?"

"I have discovered that cold chicken can be pretty darn good, even when it's been inoculated, like you know this chicken has been," she seesawed back. "And I want to go home for my birthday, Marion." She'd told me this often. "Do you think you can arrange it? Just one last time?"

"Yep."

"If anyone could, it'd be you."

"Yeah, we're already talking about it."

"Carol's gonna be out of town." She rolled up her eyes. "Florida."

"Oh."

"Did you ever manage to get the stone lions back in place?"

"Huh?"

"The ones that lay on the hearth."

I had no idea what she was talking about.

"The two lions. The dog and the deer," she insisted.

She must be talking about the sitting room at Hillcrest, I thought, which she swore she hated to go into because there were too many old people in there. There was a stuffed deer and a dog statue on the hearth, though no stone lions.

Her eyes closed. She kept them that way most of the time these days. Fox News silently flashed cold colors on her skin.

"Go on home, baby, and get some sleep. I gotta get me some, too."

I pulled back the tray over her bed. "Do you want anything else to eat, Mama?"

She opened her eyes. "Maybe I'll just eat one more Triscuit."

"Is that all?" I rose to get her one.

"Maybe a little something smeared on it too. I'm still hungry. And just a little sip of that CoCola. Sure can't live on Marcona almonds and cold chicken."

I smiled and went to get her what she wanted.

"Le's go home, baby," she slurred, "And le's eat some *good* food. Nothin' slapdash."

"Okay."

Mama sighed. "It's a deep subject," she said.

Chapter Thirty-One

The Last Lectures

Some writers take to drink, others take to audiences.
—Gore Vidal

The talks had been advertised in the Hillcrest bulletin for a month, an article with a darling picture of Mama peeking out from her black seal coat. I poked my head in the Activity Room on my way to get her and saw the chairs set up in a circle, snacks and drinks arranged on a table near the door. The activity director was bustling around. It was ten minutes 'til tee time: 6:00 p.m.

When I got to her room, Mama was dressed to the nines in her best rainbow shirt, black pants, and jacket, plus the ruffly poodle scarf she liked so much—her "beads and feathers," as she called her accessories. She sat in her wheelchair, holding onto her purse for dear life, royally pissed.

"I'm not going!" she announced in a stentorian voice.

"Yes, you are, Mama." I tried to sound matter-of-fact, reassuring. "There are people in there already. Waiting for you."

"I don't care who's in there. I'm not going anywhere!"

My cousin Alice Raney and I fussed over her. We offered her a glass of wine. Alice fluffed her hair.

My husband, Art, had single-handedly arranged this four-part lecture series based on Mama's book about the history of Durham, *The Way We Were: Remembering Durham*, and he was late, nowhere to be found. I was seething.

"Hi, Mena. Ready to go?" Art careened around the doorjamb, still in his dirty work shirt. Before Mama saw him, he ducked into the bathroom and put on a black button-down and tie. Coming out and combing his gray hair back into a ponytail, he leaned down to kiss Mama's cheek. She recoiled.

"You promised!" she said, eyes squinched.

"Promised what, Mena?

"That you'd cut off that hair before we did this!"

"No, I didn't, Mena," Art said gently.

He was good at not letting Mama get his goat. She had been trying to get him to cut his hair and shave his beard since we got together thirty years ago. Their relationship had been tense in the beginning, this long-haired Midwesterner who replaced her first and still cherished son-in-law, the one I should still be married to. But in these last years, they'd had fun together and grown to like and appreciate each other.

"Let's go, Mena." Art stepped around behind her chair. She shrieked "No!"

Alice and I looked at each other, then cocked our eyes out the door where several residents, behind their walkers, were heading steadily toward the Activity Room.

"What d'ya mean 'no'?" Art asked, still cheery. "We've got this, Mena. We've practiced."

They had, many times over the last month when Art visited: making the selections from her book, who would say what, planning out the agenda for each part in the series.

Art had ordered copies of the books, both *The Way We Were* and *Jule Carr: General Without an Army* from Preservation Durham in case she made a sale. Mama was particularly happy about that: the possibility of a little extra money.

In fact, all along she'd seemed excited and only occasionally intimidated, once when she thought about Pelham Wilder, another Hillcrest resident and former Duke Chemistry Professor Emeritus, being in attendance.

"He's also written something about Durham," she'd confided, shrugging.

But now, she sat frozen in fear.

Art rolled her toward the door.

"Stop! You'll regret this, A-ar-tha'," she bleated. "You'll regret this 'til the end of your days. Mark my words!"

"It's okay, Mena," Art soothed, and marched her onward. Alice and I followed timidly, carrying her books, praying.

"I will not say *one* word!" Mama issued her final decree.

Art pushed Mama inside the brightly lit Activity Room. I headed to a table behind the microphones, the spot where she was to sit, and spread out her books, steadfastly trying to ignore her like a recalcitrant child. I wondered what in hell Art was going to do.

Mama faced forward, her face balled up, her arms crossed tightly over her chest in her cute little black jacket. She looked like she could kill somebody.

We chitchatted with the few folks already there. More drifted in with their aides and orderlies, the staff issuing welcomes and offering everyone drinks.

To my left was an entourage, the mother obviously the Hillcrest resident in her motorized wheelchair with breathing-tube, and also a Fine Feathers chartreuse suit. The father, also nattily dressed in brown linen, introduced himself as Mr. Lucas, the erstwhile principal of Hillside High School. I remembered him from when I worked in the school system. His daughter was there too. We all small talked until Art realized that her brother was a famous pro linebacker, and then a highly animated sports conversation ensued.

All the while, Mama didn't move an inch, except to shrink in on herself and intensify her scowl. I operated on the ostrich principle. If I didn't notice Mama, maybe nobody else would. But of course, she was the star attraction and could not be missed.

Finally, the room was full, including the esteemed Pelham Wilder, who rolled in late. I noticed that Mama nodded her head at him, almost imperceptibly, but not quite. She looked like the original Steel Magnolia, minus the magnolia part.

Art brought the room to order and started with a lovely introduction to Mama's work and her book, catching the assemblage up on the fact that in those days, Chapel Hill was the gleaming city on the hill, the intellectual, cultural place to be, while Durham was a mere backwater: mud, whores, drinking, and debauchery.

Mama didn't budge. Art began to read the first chapter: "Peeler's Place, Best Known Shady House," about Pinhook, a tract of land today known as Erwin Square. The writing was wonderful and we all visibly relaxed and began to enjoy ourselves.

Every now and then, Art paused and said, "Would you like to say more about that, Mena?"

He stuck the microphone in front of her face, but she either acted like she was deaf and dumb, or declined sharply.

"No," she said, more than once.

Though I was embarrassed by her performance, I was equally impressed by Art's ability to carry on and engage everyone in the room. With her amazing words in print, Mama was almost superfluous.

Now Art was telling folks a story he and Mother shared prior to the talks about Bull Durham Tobacco. His smile and genuine friendliness, plus his obvious admiration of Mama's work, only made his black shirt and silver ponytail look debonair.

Suddenly, without warning, Mama reached over and grabbed the microphone from his hand, saying, "That's wrong. Let me tell it."

He handed her the mouthpiece.

Mama tuned up and started to play.

We were off.

Mama's last lectures were on.

Chapter Thirty-Two

Up on the Roof

Every man's memory is his private literature.
—Aldous Huxley

Mama and I are on the roof again at sunset. Today she's in good spirits. Both of her blue eyes are open. Her face is turned up sweetly. She is talking about Mack again: about his trips on the surveillance plane to the Far East, "the Orient," Mama calls it.

"Mack always wanted to go to places with foreign-sounding names like you." She peers over her glasses. "He didn't get to go except with the army for all that secret stuff, and then with Carol and John to England, Scotland, and Wales. We went to Blenheim Castle where Churchill lived, and your daddy had a little smile on his face like he was just bustin' over with happiness. Of course, he never said anything like that, not Mack. He just kind of glowed. He loved planes. Liked to fly."

After the first moon landing, Daddy'd always told me he wished he could go to the moon, however improbable it sounded.

"Our happiest times were right after he retired. Damn newspaper didn't pay him enough; never did! But by and large, he was a happy man most of the time if he could be left alone to do what he wanted to do. You know, Mack was always into a lot of cloak-and-dagger stuff. He'd be gone for ten days at a time."

"Maybe I'll use the Freedom of Information Act to find out more about my father," I say.

She rolls her eyes.

"What did you do then, Mama?" I ask, turning to her. "When he was gone sleuthing?"

"Oh my. Little stuff. Making curtains. But I wasn't really domestic, Marion. I was always looking for a time or a way to write."

"Yeah, I know." I think of my own lifelong search for similar puddles of time.

She takes a sip of beer. With her other hand, she holds up her head and tenderly strokes the skin around her eyes and hairline.

Cars rush by under us on Broad Street.

"Work has always been my salvation. Now I can't read or write." She says it simply. "You need to get writing, baby. Quit running around and write! I know you're gonna do it someday. Just wish you would while I'm alive."

A majority of my running around has to do with caring for you, I think, wishing I could slow down, too.

"I wish you could bring me a really good cup of coffee next time you come," she adds.

"I can get you one now, Mama." Hillcrest is catty-cornered from Whole Foods.

"Coffee. My last joy," Mama intones. She had dumped her green tea experiment.

Thank God she has a few joys left, I think.

"But no need, baby, next time." She closes her eyes. The beer bottle glints gold in her hand. She is ruminating.

She talks about my children, her grands. "Tom was the perfect first grandchild," she announces. "Filled the bill. I worry about him now," she says. "He's a fool for those children. He's such a good man, Tom . . ."

She worries, too, about Kirsten's predisposition to worry—this from the *star* fretter in our family. "It's some kind of lack of faith," she says.

"She's a six on the Enneagram. The questioner," I offer. "She's good at research."

She looks doubtful. "Gimme that hat, will you? Can't see a thing."

I hand her her Yellow Cab cap. She puts it on, lowering the brim to a jaunty angle.

"I'm so afraid I hurt her the other day with something I said. She's so tender."

"Yeah."

"Rob has a perfect head," she announces. "It's a perfect oval."

What is a perfect head? I wonder. I'll have to take another look.

"And that Corey." Mama shakes her head. "I just hope I live long enough to go to that wedding, but I don't think I will."

"Yes, you will," I encourage.

She lapses into one of her favorite topics: the sixties and why I became a hippie; what that whole time was all about. "Never did understand it!" she says for the thousandth time.

I think about all the keg parties we had to get those logs up in the cabin we built.

"Do you still worry?" she reverts back to our earlier topic.

"Not nearly as much as I used to. But I would say I'm still periodically a reluctant member of the worrying clan."

Mama lays her head back against the seat. She fingers the brim of her cap. "Why do you think that is?" she asks, priming me so I will take the conversational ball and keep it in the air for a while.

"Well, you know, Mama, you always said, 'Demographics are destiny.'"

"But we worried. And now you say you don't." She sounds annoyed.

"I worry some," I concede. "But coming from all that, I had to get out!" I hear myself. I sound panicked. "And the 'Don't worry, be happy' movement came along just at the right time."

"Yeah, the sixties philosophy." She opens her eyes and takes a look at me. "'Practice enjoyment.'"

We watch the sky turning darker.

"It's always been a struggle between enjoyment and duty," Mama says.

"Since when?"

"Since way back. Ella's always sayin', 'All the way back to when God's dog was a puppy, Mrs. Webb.' Like she knows sumpin' about way back. Which she doesn't. She's only about forty-five."

"A baby," I confirm.

"My great grandmother was always saying to me, 'The devil's standing right behind you, Mena, waiting to tempt you.'" She takes another sip of beer. "And he was, too. Eternal vigilance is the price of freedom, you know, Marion."

"Yeah . . ." I say, but I'm uncertain about this. Keeping your eyes open, yes, but eternal vigilance against evil? Not so sure that makes sense. What you focus on materializes. Might just bring evil down.

"Everything you hate, just sweep it under the rug and close the closet door. But it creeps out, you know. What you do in your youth creeps out in middle age."

"When is that?" I ask, wishing I were still in it.

"Nowadays, youth's 'til about forty-two," she says with finality. "Middle age 'til sixty-six, then old age up until decrepitude at around ninety-five."

Ma is ninety-seven.

"You made it work with Arthur, baby." She suddenly turns to my marriage. "I congratulate you on that."

I nod.

"It hasn't always been so, and you made it that way. Lots of people split up for less. I am grateful to Arthur for giving me a reason for being. The talks."

She adds: "Arthur's tired. He's a good man. You're becoming very dependent on Arthur." She points her finger.

I think about that.

"And Carol." Mama sighs. My sister was diagnosed with bipolar disorder just last year. "I don't know why there is no answer for my daughter, no path for her. I see it as never changing, and her husband sounds agitated, angry, almost at the breaking point of self-control."

"Well, he's probably worried about what's gonna happen next," I say, remembering some of the recent manic episodes, the scenes.

"I think she will someday know more than she does now, Marion. And I hate for your children to think of her as the Crazy Aunt. She has such horrible suffering and pain. In her heart she just wants to help. She tried to with money."

"Carol's so generous," I agree.

"I want you and Kirsten to be a team for Carol. Promise me you will."

"We will, Mama. I promise."

"I just say to myself, 'Hang in there and be calm, Mena.'"

I stay silent.

"Way back in my day, we always relied on religion, but nowadays, I don't know about all that. The Scotch Presbyterians always believed in religion. Your people. And we accepted the crazy people."

"How?"

"How they were treated in our town was 'Don't pay attention to them, but watch out for them.' It's inherited, all that wild swinging back and forth. All of us loved each other, but we were bad for each other, so many crazy people on both sides. We were all crazy. We just reiterated that terrible malady for each other." She outlines for me all the probable bipolar and depressed people in both families as far back as she can go.

We are silent for a long while.

"You know, Marion, your father is always with me. He is more with me now than he was when he was on this earth. I'm not kiddin'. He called me Ms. Peevy. And Knottyhead, you know." She downs the last of her beer. It's dark now, but she shows no signs of wanting to go in. "But it wasn't all beer and skittles with Mack."

I say nothing, hoping for more.

"Your daddy was shy. He had an inferiority complex with his brother, James. James was always praised. Mack just never figured he was as good as James. And isn't that too bad, because he was head and shoulders above James?"

"Why was he jealous?"

"The older brother thing. He didn't talk about Jim in any good way. 'Jim and his little blue drawers,' he would say. What he meant by that, I don't know. Daddy got the blues too. But he loved children. He knew children would accept whatever he had to give. They wouldn't judge him or reject him."

"Was Daddy competitive?

"Fiercely."

"Did he ever apologize?"

"Not directly. The one thing he maybe wanted more of was sex. Maybe I was low sex. Who knows? But he was never demanding. I was *very* romantic."

A soft rain starts to fall.

"We better go in, baby."

"Okay."

"Can you get me a few things before you come back?" she asks, fishing for her list in her pocketbook, which is never far away.

"Sure."

I read it by flashlight.

Boost—plain chocolate
Seedless grapes
Hearing aid batteries
Meridian wine
Low-sodium Triscuits
Resolve Spot Magic
Klondike bars

"They don't have the good chocolate Boost here," she informs. "And they dump salt on everything."

I push Mama's wheelchair inside. All the way to her room, she sings softly: "Glow Little Glow Worm" until we meet Ella at her door.

"You go on home, honey." Mama waves me away. "Ella will take it from here."

I watch her smile up at Ella who pushes her around the doorjamb, out of sight.

Chapter Thirty-Three

Black People II

The single story creates stereotypes, and the problem with stereotypes is not that they are untrue, but that they are incomplete. They make one story become the only story.
—Chimamanda Ngozi Adichie

I was riding with Mama and my sister through Duke Forest on an earlier Easter morning, Mama groaning in the backseat about trying to write something about Merritt, Moore and Spaulding and the other blacks who were prominent in Durham's history.

"I haven't any business writing about those people," she'd wailed, shaking her head. "It was like sweating blood to pull that one together."

I looked back and saw real tears falling down her cheeks—my mama, who had always excused any racism she might have inherited with the "but I was raised on racism with my mother's milk" line.

"I didn't know anything about them," she was saying, as my sister gave me a look in the rearview mirror, silently mouthing, "Praise the Lord."

"Those people lived two blocks away from my house all my life, and I never even knew they were there!"

That day I admired Mama's honesty about what she was learning about Durham's black families: the Black Wall Street, and Durham's African-American forebears; and also, about herself. So, I cooled it on telling her what was wrong with the phrase "those people."

After she died, I found the following draft crumpled up behind a file drawer recounting those times:

> *"I knew Elna Spaulding and Howard Clement. I'd met both of them years ago at a Junior League meeting. Spaulding was the speaker and Clement was the heckler*

*sitting on the back row in Durham's YWCA building, long
since demolished, one more victim of urban renewal. But
at that time, it was a popular meeting place for civic
organizations.*

*It took like what seemed forever to get a date that
worked for them to talk to me for the book, but both were
worth the effort. Going inside the North Carolina Mutual
building is, indeed, a real trip, and Howard Clement, one
of its retired executives, is yet another. Oh, how he
pontificates! But he does it well, with a great deal of flair,
a handsome man, and very attractive now that he's
changed from a bombastic activist into a somewhat
avuncular executive.*

*As for Elna Spaulding, she's the same beautiful
woman with the same lovely voice who spoke to that
eager group of Junior Leaguers so many years ago about
violence prevention, before I retired from civic
responsibility and good works so I could try to become a
writer.*

*They answered all of my questions graciously.
They enabled me to write that damned chapter for the
book. I wish I could tell them in person how I will forever
be deeply in their debt."*

§

Tonight, however, was Mama's final lecture at Hillcrest. She
and Art were presenting Chapter Seven of her book—the chapter
about Merritt, Moore, and Spaulding in *The Way We Were:
Remembering Durham,* to an ever-growing crowd, a mix of residents
and folks from the outside. My friends Phil and Ellen, and their
friends, one of whom had worked for Daddy at the newspaper, Bill
Kirkland, came, and my cousin, Randy, and a reporter from the
newspaper, plus a goodly number of other folks I'd never seen before.

To accommodate the extra people, Hillcrest moved the talks
from the Activity Room to the large parlor, where we were now
gathered along with the iron dog and the stuffed deer.

I had seen a great deal of change in Mama in the last month since the lectures began, a diminishment, and though she was on again, off again in her enthusiasm about the talks, she had received great feedback as well as a mushrooming audience. We'd adopted the habit of bringing chocolates and champagne back to her room for an after-party each week. But just like the first night, tonight she was balking.

We had come early to ply her with chitchat and liquor and make it seem natural and fun. But Mama was nobody's fool. She knew what was coming, and she didn't like it. Just as she felt like a fraud for writing the chapter on Merrick, Moore, and Spaulding at the last minute under duress from her publisher, I thought she now must feel equally inadequate to the task of participating in a live program on her research, although I knew she was in good hands with Art as facilitator.

Before the panic set in, Mama had been entertaining us in her room with memories. One remark, in particular, however, that 'it was no wonder Merrick was so intelligent because he was half-white,' had my sister and me white-knuckling each other on the sofa in the parlor, afraid of what might come out of her mouth in public.

The crowd was large, but not one black person at Hillcrest had shown up. There were always a few at earlier presentations. What was up? I wondered.

As usual, Art began to read from Mama's book, this time about the three most compelling characters in the history of Durham who were not WASPS, and about 'Hayti,' the black section of Durham across the tracks from where I played as a girl.

Mama fiddled with her fingers and stared into her lap as Art read. Carol and I held hands, trying to breathe.

Fifteen minutes in, six or seven latecomers wheeled into the parlor, every one of them black. They settled in at the back of the room.

I wondered if that had been their strategy all along, safety in numbers. After all, this was some white woman telling them about their own history, though some of them were not even from Durham, had simply ended up there from somewhere else and were interested in the town they were going to die in.

I scanned their faces trying to gage their reactions as Art read and Mama fidgeted. Those I'd assessed as being *compos mentis*, able to hear and understand what Art was reading, appeared inscrutable. There were also some, both black and white, who had "fallen off the cliff," as Art put it. Gone. They weren't getting much out of anything these days. But they liked to come to the activity room anyway, and more power to them.

After Art got rolling, Mama began to look up shyly and smile. She took the microphone away from him to tell the people about a little black-owned business where her Mama got groceries on Roxboro Street, and began to rattle off every single item on the shelves, her attention to detail in high gear.

I looked at the audience, all of them intent on her and smiling, and wondered if she would ever stop. She kept saying "and on the shelf above that . . .." Art deftly took back the mic in a way that didn't disturb her or anyone else, and returned to the story of Merrick, Moore, and Spaulding.

At the end of the talk, the applause was enthusiastic. Mama's final lecture was a roaring success, everyone coming up to shake her hand and introduce themselves. One woman from Duke bought Mama's book on the spot. Mother held onto her hand and looked up as delighted as if the Prince had just brought her the glass slipper.

Carol and I were regaled with stories about our father and mother from folks who had known them in the "olden days," and about Durham, until we all finally escaped and retreated to Mother's room for the celebratory champagne.

The night was a victory for Mama in every way. She had endured. She had not only survived, she'd been heroic. We stayed late, laughing and talking, realizing what an accomplishment this was and how much we loved her, and appreciated Art, and also realizing: Mama was not going to be around much longer.

Chapter Thirty-Four

The Mother-Daughter Wars

Most of us have been hurt into memoir. —Mary Karr

For over six decades Mama had been trying to fix me, so I would look "presentable."

"Ma, how long have you spent trying to get me to fix my hair?"

"Forever!"

"And have I done it?"

"No!"

She could stand then without help. Her hands were on her hips, her lips pursed, her brow a corrugated pigskin. Her eyes pierced me like a butcher knife.

"Well, here's how I see it, Mama," I'd started as gently as I could to avoid getting stabbed.

"You're what now? Ninety-two? You can either continue trying to get me to fix my hair for the rest of your days—"

She nodded, following along.

"—or you can let it go and we can talk about other things in the time you've got left."

Mama stopped for a minute, and I watched her thinking. Finally, and uncharacteristically, she said, "You're right, Marion," and we moved on to another topic.

I don't remember Mama ever talking about my hair again in such a focused and critical way, hair that was never cut right for my face or wouldn't stay in place, hair that had certainly never, ever been the way Mama wanted it.

But today she had lost her resolve and was fussing about it again.

She had been moved to her recliner, and her legs were up. A cola, a can of Boost, chicken broth, and a Corona pony sat on her tray. All liquid. I wondered about this.

She said my hair looked bad, that I need a haircut. What's the matter with me that I didn't get it? I was definitely not presentable. I was an embarrassment to her.

"I tell people, 'That Marion: She jumps high, wide, and fine.' You know, you've been hell-bent for leather all your life, Marion. I don't know how you got that. Wait for no man."

"You always wanted me to be just like you, Mama. You wanted me to be your clone. And I wasn't."

"That must have really hurt you."

"It depended on my vulnerability in the moment." I repeated her line.

"It was the best I could do. That's all any of us can do," she said and shrugged. "I had a bum lunch and I have some scathing reviews of last night's dinner, too."

I saw her right foot was swollen. She noticed my glance. "Dr. Manning thinks I should have an x-ray."

Someone had painted her toenails a bright coral, her big toe angling in to push the others out of line. Each had become a fat "little piggy."

Everywhere else, she was growing extremely thin, all flesh-colored bones and canyons, mottled with veins and bruises.

"What was the matter with last night's dinner?" I asked, not sure I should pursue it.

Mama shrugged. "I am now traveling with something that is a total anathema to me. Everything in my life is so fragile now, not rooted and grounded anymore in what I like and what I believe. I have no control over some of the things that go on around me."

I waited for more.

"And I can't find anything," she continued.

She hardly gets out of bed anymore, I think, never by herself after the last fall.

"They never put anything back where I tell them to."

"Don't they listen?"

"They give me lip service, but they don't really listen. It's frightening. Yeah, yeah, yeah—it's all a bunch of crap. They put things where they want to put them, and never where I can find them. And they're poisoning me, too. But what are you going to do?"

She sighed. I remembered reading that sighing is good for your brain.

Then she answered her own question. "You just arm yourself with good vibrations."

"Are you armed?" I asked, knowing the answer.

"No, not really. May as well be a horse's ass while I am!" she announced.

I said nothing.

"I just burped up a chicken tender," she added, brighter now.

I was glad to hear she was eating solid food.

She laid her head back and began to recite:

> The quality of mercy is not strained.
> It droppeth as a gentle rain
> on the place beneath
> It is not strained.

There was a silence, and she began again.

> The fear of the Lord is the beginning of
> wisdom.

"Pow, pow, pow," she added, mimicking Daddy, who always said that.

Suddenly, her favorite song came on the radio: "Mac the Knife," by Bobby Darin. We both stopped to listen to the words. "When the shark bites . . ."

Her niece, Alice, entered. After pleasantries, she began to lightly massage Mama's neck. Alice's hair was perfectly coifed. She was wearing a turquoise checked suit coat with matching skirt and scarf, stockings, and pumps. I looked down at my baggy outfit. Alice was dressed like the daughter Mama wished she had.

The day was sunny. In spite of the difficulty, we planned an outing. On the way out of Hillcrest, as Mother inched herself forward in her wheelchair, she saw me waiting ahead for her.

"What do *you* want?" she asked bitingly, forgetting I was even there.

She told Alice and me right there that she didn't trust me.

I said, "That's okay, Ma." (Though it wasn't.) "But I *am* trustworthy."

She sneered, eyes closed, the last word on the subject. Then she added, "I just know what I know what I know. And one good thing about all this is that I won't have to do a thing, and you will have to do everything!"

I'd listened to these barbs all my life.

I knew my mother loved me, but she also disliked me.

At this point, I didn't really blame her, because for every relationship that is teetering on the brink, there are two parties who have worked to bring it to that point. I had my hand in it, too.

I'd certainly shouted, "I hate you!" enough times, slamming the door so the whole house rattled when she restricted me or banished me to my room.

I openly chastised her choices, particularly in the sixties. I fought back with open acts of rebellion, though I wasn't really aware of it at the time.

Nonetheless, we buy our definitions from others, especially our parents, and if a parent ignores, neglects—even while "doing for" a child, or belittles them or their accomplishments, it leaves a mark well into old age. I knew that firsthand.

I googled it, and was surprised to find loads of literature on the fact: a high percentage of mothers dislike their daughters.

Often, it's because the mother herself is suffering from issues that have been left unattended. She develops a very controlling nature, and as the daughter grows and the mother feels her tight reign loosening and her daughter slipping away, she'll seek to regain complete control.

It's more accepted that sons go off to their own lives. There is not the same societal uplift when daughters chart their own divergent course. Seeing their daughters enjoy a world of freedom and adventure can bring up a lot of negative feelings for women who did not have as many opportunities.

When I talked with my own daughter, Kirsten, about Mama disliking me, she said, "Truthfully, Ma, many parents are guilty of disliking their children at one point or another. Raising children is extremely difficult work, and children have a way of pushing our buttons. We may love our children a lot, but the fact remains that we may find some aspects of their personality bothersome or downright unlikable."

Of course, she was right. We are certainly not always cut off the same bolt of cloth, most especially Mama and me. I wondered about Mama's relationship with her own mother, Granny, who always seemed so sweet. But then, she did try to abort Mama by bumping down the stairs.

I knew mothers who disliked their daughters were not evil shrews. They were victims, too. I reminded myself that her constant criticisms of me helped in some ways. I didn't physically flee, but I learned about emotional flight, detachment, not to be confused with denial. I learned that boundaries were wonderful things. I made a conscious decision to no longer allow Mama to pull my emotional strings and bring me down. And most of the time, it worked.

I didn't deny it, though. Denial didn't face the reality of what is taking place. Rather, it lived in a fantasy world and made excuses such as, "Oh, it's not that bad."

It was bad.

Sometimes, all I wished for was Aunt Bea.

In the end, though, I knew Mama loved me more than she disliked me. Beyond that, she admired me, and trusted me. She relied on me. This helped me to lay down my shield and sword and feel lucky and good about our relationship.

In the end, it was peace between us.

Chapter Thirty-Five

Decline

They tell you that you'll lose your mind when you grow older.
What they don't tell you is that you won't miss it very much.
—Malcolm Cowley

Mother was lying back in her pearls, a piece of bacon clutched in her left hand. Dixieland jazz played on the CD.

She'd been given morphine and Ativan, as she woke up in the middle of the night and tried to get out of bed, according to Rose, Mama's current favorite hated one.

"Your mother asked for you," Rose told me when I called.

Just yesterday I'd talked with the psychiatric geriatric nurse practitioner, the one in charge of Mama's mental health. She recommended an anti-depressant change: Abilify. Ma had lots of paranoia about stuff, psychosis, the NP said.

"She's got cystitis too, which ain't no picnic," I said. "That can make you crazy all by itself!"

"Yes. And Abilify, in addition to the antibiotic, can take the edge off," she continued as if I hadn't spoken, looking up from her chart under graying bangs.

I realized the kind of psychotherapy they practiced here at Hillcrest was drugs.

"We don't really have the staff for a lot of talk therapy," the NP acknowledged.

"I wish you did," I sighed. "Mama needs that. The chaplain came in once and she loved it. She likes men, especially funny men."

"Yeah," she shrugged. "He can only come about once a month though. They feel they're being poisoned In Mrs. Webb's case, it's also about control, subconscious or unconscious. She's a very self-directed individual, and now she has no control of her situation."

"No shit, Sherlock," I silently seethed. "How would you feel?"

"It's a tantrum. We need to get her behavior stabilized, get the medication in her; then she'll become more compliant and her delusions will disappear."

I bristled.

Beside Mama's bed in large scrawl with a black marker is her current To-Do list, much shorter now:

> *Put phones in chargers*
> *Watch TV*
> *Take Doxipin*
> *Take Abilify*
> *Go to bed.*

I was amazed at what it had come down to.

She was saying to no one, "Old Kay Kyser and his Kollege of Musical Knowledge." Then:

> *Fickle, fickle, fickle.*
> *Love,*
> *What? What? What is fickle.*
> *A pickle.*

Her eyes twinkled.

When I gave her a pony beer from her fridge—to hell with drinking and drugs; she wanted one—she drank it from a half-inch-thick glass, sipping, closing her eyes. "This is the coldest, coldest beer I've ever tasted," she said.

The phone rang. I put it on speaker and handed it to her. It was Corey, my youngest son.

"Hello, Grandmother. I'll do anything you want me to, Grandmother," he said.

In the sweetest voice, she crooned, "You know, I'd like to have a little tiny piece of fee-let mignon. Hmmm—hmmm! And second best I'd like is nothing."

After she hung up, she said to me: "Mainly I want him to check on the lightbulbs at home." (Her usual request of her grandsons.) "But I don't have to have that."

Tom called next and told her he was coming over. To him she said: "I'll certainly do my best to get in my best bib and tucker."

When I arrived later after running a few errands, Rose came in, and I watch her standing over Mama, who was now stark naked. Mama had wet the bed during her nap. I covered her with a gown.

"Marion, I really love you," she said.

But minutes later, "What's the matter with you? Are you crazy?! Do something, Marion! I need to die. Now or never. Now! Call all the people. I don't care if I am naked. Call all the people!" She yanked off her hospital gown.

"It's hot!" she yelled.

I cooled her with an old Southern Comfort fan. She nodded and smiled. "Now, it's definite."

She was seeing something beyond.

I rubbed her back, arms, and body with cream. Soon she would be rid of these devices.

Her moans of anguish turned to moans of pleasure. But she couldn't get comfortable. She was chewing the pink mouth sponges I offered her to bits, particularly with the left molars, gnawing, wanting relief.

Rose, who did her trays, had overreacted and wanted some sympathy. She said Mama was always telling her to shut up, and insisted she didn't want to eat her dinner until eight o'clock.

"Can you stand up?" Rose asked her too loudly. It sounded like a command.

"I can't," Mama refused. She looked like an empty leather glove.

Rose didn't bother to dress her.

"Do we have any clothes out?" I asked.

"No, she never likes what I pick," Rose said, petulant. I felt like hitting her.

Alice entered precisely at that moment.

We could see that Rose wasn't being helpful, so Alice went over to the closet and got Mama's clothes.

As we were dressing her, Mama said, "I've outlived my time. I've lived so long, I'm left behind in another century."

Later I heard her saying, "What good can you do with what has been done to you? You're never powerless."

I wondered who she was talking to—me, or herself? I admired her courage and her struggle to deal with what was happening to her. I was profoundly sad.

Before I left for the night, Mama flagged me over and pointed to the top drawer of her bedside table. I opened it. She pointed to a pad, which I picked up. Out fluttered a piece of paper. Single spaced on two sides was the following verse. I had no idea where Mama got it, but she winked at me as I read it.

I don't want to be old. I don't want to be sick.
I don't want to get tricked by the prurient prick
Of time's sickle, that vulgar device
For the reaping of roses. It's not very nice.
I don't want to be bodily "beated and chopped."
I don't want to be lopped from the limb.
There's an apple uncropped.
I don't want to be stranded without tooth or brain
In some Hillhaven Refuge! I'd count it a pain;
Or yet to be dumped in a lump to some psalmist's refrain.
In my bones in the wind and the rain!
But I do want a present. Compact of my sins—
I'd be helpless without them!—to be born again
At the edge of some high road: or something like this.
Leave the rocks and the brambles: I don't require bliss.
But swaddles would comfort me. Food's not amiss.
And a book. And a song. And a kiss.

I will need just a century: one, maybe two.
If you haven't the time, then a decade will do.
For the loving's unfinished, the work scarce begun.
And there's hardly an instant from sun unto sun
And the dark so importunate! Sprites of the earth,
What I want for my birthday this day is new birth!
As you please. If you don't please, then, dammit, be gone!
If you haven't the leave for the living, move on!
If you can't bless the being, begone!

I kissed her goodnight and wondered who wrote it.
She fixed me with her one good eye.

Chapter Thirty-Six

When All the Parties Are Over

Old wood best to burn, old wine to drink, old friends to trust,
and old authors to read.
—Francis Bacon

My mother's last party was to be a twenty-four-hour birthday present: going back to her home and sleeping in her own bed one more time. How often had Mama begged for this?

The plans were to retrieve her from the nursing home, bring wine and hors d'oeuvres, broil steaks, and celebrate. Kirsten, Tom, Alice, Art, and I would be both hosts and guests. My sister, Carol, was out of town.

Retrieving her was the right word, too, because after all that folderol, when Alice and I got to her room, Mama balked. Dressed to the nines in her wheelchair with all her "beads and feathers" on, not to mention her black seal coat, she cried, "No—o—o! I don't want to go. I'm not ready," over and over again.

But it was too late. We rolled her out against her will, Mama trying to put on the brakes using her tiny gold-chained flats, hollering, and me saying, "No, Mama, we're going! This is what you wanted and everybody's coming!"

Sweet "Ella" helped push her, whispering, "Come on, baby. Come on." She rolled Mama down the long beige hall, past the library and the beauty parlor and the fake fireplace and the stuffed deer to the automatic door and into my car, coaxing her forward like you would a frightened mare.

Alice followed us in her car.

All across town, Mama's lip was stuck out, and she was saying, "I don't want to go—o—o!" I drove fifteen miles an hour through Duke and past the cemetery where her relatives lay.

"What are you doing, Marion? Stop this car."

But my lips were soldered shut.

I'd resolved I would say nothing after my first tries of "It'll be fun, Mama," and "Tom will be there." But even the crown prince was unable to move her. "You've begged for this for months, Ma!"

We finally succumbed to an aggressive silence, me afraid I would swerve to the side of the road if I dared open my mouth.

Mama blinked rapidly, then stared stone-faced out the window, realizing she'd been "had." When we got to her condo, another bout erupted. Alice and I struggled her into her chair and then up the three steps to the front door where I thought we were going to end up in a broken mass on the brick walk because she was so obstreperous, flailing and hollering, and commanding us what to do and what not to do, Alice and I sweating and heaving and struggling to remain calm in the face of what truly was a disaster.

Finally, all four wheels and Mama were inside.

"Stop right here," she yelled in the entrance hall. "Right here. Right now."

We left her—in her fur coat—slumped over in her chair next to the credenza. It was for us a Pyrrhic victory. Yes, we had out-maneuvered her, but at what cost?

In no time, she appeared to be sleeping in the wheelchair. Alice and I slipped off to the kitchen where we could keep an eye on her and wait for the others.

While Mama dozed, I got to know Alice a little better. Connected by her marriage to my first cousin, Tom Raney, who died after they'd been married just five years, we were now connected by Mama—and Alice's tenderhearted, steady care for her. Though Mama often told me she couldn't have done without Alice, she was not an easy beneficiary of anyone's help, particularly anyone she could either boss around or not boss around. Translate: everyone.

While waiting for her to rally, I learned about Alice's great love for Tom, which began when he brought her a plastic rose on their first date.

Tom had been a true "kissin' cousin" to me, even my pretend "date" to various functions as a teenager when I didn't have what it took to get a real one. I described to her all the fun he and I had driving around in his MG with the top down, drinking bourbon and ginger ale in paper cups; how Tom had my back when I was young and imprudent—"hair-brained," Mama would've said. We enjoyed each other back then.

Alice and I looked outside and saw that the sun was over the yard arm. It was clearly time to have a drink. We poured ourselves one and went back out into the hall, Mama was now awake and staring into her living room.

Over her sharp warnings of "Be careful" and "Watch out," we inched her into her pink, white, and sea-green room, exactly as she had left it six months before, the table lamps glowing softly, a tray of cheese and crackers awaiting her on the coffee table, the painting of Mama's Mama, Caro, for whom Carol had been named, smiling down on us above the mantle.

"You're home, Mama," I whispered, feeling sad and triumphant at the same time.

Mama looked doubtful. It took another round of howls and hollers before we could get her out of the wheelchair and into the soft, cushioned club chair next to the sofa, lift her feet up on the needlepoint footstool, and offer her a glass of Chardonnay.

I don't really remember a lot else about that night—not a lot of details anyway. I know Tom and Kirsten came late, Kirsten with flowers from her backyard, Tom with wine. We broiled steaks and made salad and sat on the floor in front of Mama around her coffee table. We drank and tried to make conversation with her; but mainly we ended up talking amongst ourselves, telling stories, while we looked for something that might interest her. She gazed above us at the room through her chalky eyes, perhaps at some long-cherished knickknack, maybe the glass cherry or the peppermint, two hallmark ornamental curiosities we always had to keep the grandkids from touching.

Amidst the clatter of dishes and cutlery, we continued with our tales, Mama frozen in her chair, occasionally deigning to nibble on a Triscuit or pick at a piece of cheese.

Every time we suggested bed, especially taking Mama to bed, she would shake her head vigorously, and say, "No! You all go to bed. I am staying right here!"

The rest of the time, she was just watching or thinking or remembering or saying some irreverent "toodle-oo," waving her fingers at us or at someone else we couldn't see, waving us away.

Occasionally she would slide down in her chair. Someone would rush over to readjust the pillows at her back, and over her protestations, push her up. She allowed Art to rub her neck and shoulders. We carried on at "Mama's party" without her.

About midnight the five of us conferred in the kitchen. What to do next? Tom had to go home. He was bringing his own family the following day for the real party when Carol and John would be returning from their trip to Florida, and all the spouses, past and present, and the grandchildren, and a few neighbors would come over to wish Mama well.

We were dog tired, and decided where we would sleep. Mama wasn't budging. She informed us that she would stay up all night in the club chair. Period.

"You children go to bed!"

Kirsten and Alice made for the upstairs beds. I slept there too, between two luxurious sheets on her white pile rug. Art stayed downstairs, arranged a bed of sofa pillows in front of Mama, at the ready to catch her if she fell out of the chair.

We propped Ebert, the giant black teddy bear Daddy had given her, and the name of her "secret admirer," close by as a nighttime companion.

When I asked my daughter later what she remembered about that last party, she turned up her nose and shrugged.

"She was a bitch. And we were sorry we'd brought her home. That's pretty much what I remember. Until the next morning when she had her resurrection nap."

It was true. She had put a damper on things. And after we had gone to so much trouble honoring her last wish.

But I've never felt sorry we did it. When you're forty-something, it's easy to judge the success or failure of a thing by how it turns out. For me, now at sixty-seven and closer to Mama than ever before, "young-old" as they say, I judge the success or failure of my actions by how true they are to my commitments to myself or others, rather than about how they turn out. Did I do what I promised I would do? Did I come through? Did I take the plunge, regardless of the consequences, and honor my pact? Am I a loyal person, faithful? Did I do my duty?

After all, how we all "turn out" is dead.

It would have been nice to think my mother could gaze on death with some benevolent equanimity, take a long, tender look at her home, her family—and behave! Give us a good time, for God's sakes. Appreciate us. After all, Mama wanted appreciation. And applause. She also wanted not to die, not to be in pain. Everybody wants that.

But that night, applause was not forthcoming, nor was appreciation.

No longer possible to ignore her worsening symptoms, luck had run out. Mama was dying. This would be her last trip home. Before she went "home."

During the night, every now and then I would bolt up wide awake, crawl up off the floor, and tiptoe halfway down the stairs to see what Mama was doing; was she still awake, was she still in the chair, was she still breathing?

Each time, she was just sitting there, the lights on, her eyes open, staring opaquely at whatever it was she was seeing, thinking who knows what; Arthur was snorting and purring in his sleep on the floor. I saw her take a rolled-up cloth napkin in her spindly hand and whack Ebert playfully on his shiny patent-leather nose. Her own ears and eyes long shot, she had no idea I was watching from the top stair, my feet tucked up under my nightgown.

It was a tender scene: Mama—damaged, vulnerable, dying. But she was taking a stand, nonetheless, doing what she wanted to on her last night in her house, to hell with the exhortations of her family, to hell with everybody.

It kind of reminded me of me.

The next morning, we got up early. Aware that Mama had relieved herself, the four of us, one by one, tried to convince her we should help her off to bed and clean her up. Get her ready for her real party. Let her have some sleep before the onslaught.

Again, she refused. We pow-wowed in the kitchen. Enough was enough: We were moving her. There were four of us and one of her. Mama needed attention. At the count of three, we stealthily moved in around her chair and swooped down to pick her up, everyone taking a corner.

"We're going, Mama. We're going."

"Stop it. Stop!" she cried and struck out. "Put me down. Right now!'

But we didn't, and managed to avoid her nippers, too.

She called me a "know-it-all trollop," Art, a "fake Harvard man," and Alice "a ninny."

That last one made me the maddest. Putting people down was nothing new to us, her family. But to the niece who had literally done more for her in the end than any of us! Mama was a wordsmith. She could use words to soothe or incite. She had a "rapier" wit, as she often said of herself. But many times, her wit felt more like a hacksaw.

I couldn't think of another word for her that morning than "arsehole."

As she hurled her defamations, we kept moving Mama toward her bed, rather than dropping her poor little bones on the floor.

Determined, we cleaned her up and got her under the covers, the final indignity. She conked out like a light switched off. I closed the curtains just as the sun was coming up.

Alice went to church. The rest of us flopped down somewhere to catch some shut-eye. At about two in the afternoon, the other family members began to arrive, and I woke Mama up.

Suddenly, she was in an altogether different mood. Propped up in bed, she fluffed her hair, put on a smile, and asked us all to come in, a few at a time.

The granddaughters sat on her bed, gave her cards they had crayoned, and a party hat. The daughters and daughters-in-law circled her like ladies-in-waiting. Tom and Art moved in and out with drinks and finger food. Mama laughed and told jokes. Carol and John and Mary Jo, her long-loved neighbor, came. Mama was a queen summoning her minions, delighted and delightful.

In the kitchen we congratulated ourselves. It was working. Mama was coming through. She had rallied for the little ones. She seemed to be having a good time. I took pictures.

§

Looking back on it now, I can see what may have been going on, why Mama was running so hot and cold.

She'd wanted this so much, had demanded it, orchestrated it, readied herself for it. But then when the time came, she knew this was it: this was her final junket before the grave; her final time in her own house before they zipped her up in the body bag; the final party before the lights went out.

The sun began to sink behind the trees. I reminded Mama that Carol and John would be taking her back soon. Thankfully, they'd agreed to do the "reentry" trip to Hillcrest. Their duty.

"Oh, Marion, I don't want to go back," Mama said, looking up at me imploringly. But there wasn't a lot of fight left.

"I want to do this every month. Promise me, Marion . . ."

And so, I promised.

I still remember all those *promise me*s' and just how many of them I kept or didn't keep.

But it was not to be. Three weeks later, Mama was dead.

Chapter Thirty-Seven

Leaving Us

Death ends a life, not a relationship. —Mitch Albom

Mama died on a Wednesday afternoon in May, her favorite month.

My third child, Corey; her favorite caretaker, Gloria; and I were there when she left. Gloria had been singing "Jesus Loves You" all morning and encouraging Mama, a tenacious hanger-onner, to let go. She was holding Mama's hand when she finally took the plunge.

Earlier when I'd walked in, Mama had smiled at me and mouthed "Hi," then moaned with pleasure as I rubbed some cream I found into her bony spine. For the last two weeks, the only thing Mama said with any intensity was "Up and down and up and down!" as we tried to help her tired and wracked little body find some comfort. In the end, back rubbing was the only solution.

Corey came in an hour later, saying, "Hello, Grandma," holding her hand and finding out how she was doing—from us, not Mama, as she had nearly stopped breathing twice, causing Gloria and I to jump up each time and stand over her waiting for the next inhalation, which finally came after a long moment of hushed stillness.

Corey settled into the recliner, then launched into telling me about a new job offer he might receive, and the intricacies of figuring out what to do with his life now that he was getting married.

Just the day before, Mama had asked for him, saying: "Where is Corey? I bet he's just sitting on his ass!"

"No, he's not, Mama," I told her, always his defender. "No, he's not."

"I bet he is, too!" And then, a few minutes later, she had added, "Tell him to come see me tomorrow. I want to see him." Corey had a palpable calm and grounded energy around Mama, and she gravitated to it.

Somehow, I knew Mama was going that day, but still, it was a surprise when ten minutes after Corey came, two caregivers marched in with their stethoscopes and pulse fingers poised. We arose at once from the chairs, and I held my breath.

"Is she dead?" I asked, putting my hand to her forehead.

"Yes," they nodded. Gloria began to cry. I kept stroking Mama's forehead and saying, "Mama, Mama," not truly believing it was over. Corey stepped outside with his iPhone and began the calls.

There had been talk of washing her body and all kinds of other rituals, but in the end, we just gathered in her room. Those who had really connected with Mama came and paid their respects: Ira Christmas, Keisha, Sheila, "Ella," Dan from admissions, people she had loved and laughed with and taunted and chastised, and who had known enough not to take any of Mama's crap seriously.

After they left, we dismissed the nurses and other helpers, and I looked around the room, happy to be an eternal part of the remaining cast of characters: Carol and John; Art, Tom, Kirsten, Corey; Chris, my first husband, still very much family; Alice, her dedicated niece, the glue that kept it all together for Mama in those last months; and me.

We ate take-out from Whole Foods, drank liquor, told stories, laughed, and cried, Mama still there with us at the party for one last time. I placed her hands just so and put orange Gerbera daisies someone had brought, her new favorite flowers, around her head. I tried to close her eyes and mouth, but that must just work in movies. I tried to fix her hair as well, remembering that hair kept growing after you were dead. Mama was so vain about her hair.

I took pictures of her, too, which caused family members to cry "E-e-wwww!" and "Stop it!" But this was my mama, and I told them I was a reporter like my father, and to can the complaints.

Hours later, almost midnight, a woman came and zipped Mama up in a black leather bag. I still couldn't believe it. Death has a way of being sudden no matter when it comes, no matter how long it takes to get to its unfathomable egress, a crack into that next experience, whatever it is.

Chapter Thirty-Eight

The Day After

Grieve if you must but grieve efficiently.
—Elizabeth Gilbert

The next day was Thursday, my regular day with Mama, so I went shopping.

I knew I would need a suitable black thing to wear when the memorial was scheduled, and I didn't really know what else to do that day. So, in honor of us, I tore around the stores in the mall, buying stuff like a crazy lady, price tag be damned. I also scheduled a haircut for the next day so my ratty mop would at least look a bit tidied up when it mattered. I knew she would approve of my doing anything to make myself look "presentable."

The following Sunday, we laid Mama in the ground at St. Matthew's Episcopal in Hillsborough beside Daddy and all the other dead Webbs way back to the Revolutionary days.

St. Matthew's has a tiny cemetery that twists around trees and is full of shade, a great place for a picnic, just like the ones Mama took us to when we were kids. I remembered balancing on the top of the stone wall that surrounds it, my arms wide, navigating the circumference when I was ten or eleven.

This Sunday, it was hot as we stood around Mama's plot listening to Albert Nelius's lovely Shakespearean tones reading the things from the Prayer Book that made it real, made it final: Mama was dead.

Albert's wife, Sigrid, held his cane and steadied him as he read. I told Albert I wanted to get up with him to talk about Mama one more time. I loved Albert and he *knew* the insides of my mother's heart. He smiled ruefully, and said I'd better hurry while he was still standing. Albert was not well.

After he threw a handful of dirt on the box that held Mama's ashes, I read the Edna St. Vincent Millay poem she'd asked to be read at her burial:

I am not resigned to the shutting away of loving
hearts in the hard ground.
So, it is, and so it will be, for so it has been, time
out of mind.
Into the darkness they go, the wise and the lovely.
Crowned with lilies and laurel they go; but I am
not resigned.
Lovers and thinkers, into the earth with you.
Be one with the dull, the indiscriminate dust.
A fragment of what you felt, of what you knew,
A formula, a phrase remains, but the best is lost.
The answer quick and keen, the honest look, the
laughter, the love,
They are gone. They are gone to feed the roses.
Elegant and curled
is the blossom, fragrant is the blossom, I know. But
I do not approve.
More precious was the light in your eyes than all
the roses in the world.
Down, down, down into the darkness of the grave.
Gently they go, the beautiful, the tender, the kind;
Quietly they go, the intelligent, the witty, the
brave.
I know. But I do not approve.
And I am not resigned.

We don't approve either, Mama, I was thinking.

We shuffled around and said our good-byes, making plans to see each other more often, and soon too—plans we most likely wouldn't keep.

The week that passed felt like two. Or three. So many loose ends to tie up, people to call, cards to be read and answered. These days there was also Facebook and e-mail, instant communication that let me know how much people thought about my mother and how supported I was, though there was no way my responses would be reciprocally expeditious. My life was late nights and little sleep.

Regular life occasionally interceded, more so because all of the things I realized I *had* to do, but now also *could* do, after so many weeks and months of being with Mama, doing for her, worrying about her. I had almost a whole extra day in the week!

Still, it was not settled in my mind that she was really dead. I felt her, especially in the middle of the night and when I woke up in the morning. She was all around me.

I think of my Mama every day, and even though the space her death has created in my life is a welcome one, she's here somewhere and she's right: Maybe now I can finally write, though I sometimes feel at sixes and sevens when I realize I don't really have to call her, don't really have to go over and cheer her up, can no longer hear her biting, funny commentaries, her good advice, too.

My mother has vanished. I have lost my dear, dear friend.

Chapter Thirty-Nine

Where Is She Now?

Sell your cleverness and purchase bewilderment. —Rumi

On the eve of my first post-Mama writing retreat, feeling uncertain, I asked my husband why it was important to write about my mother. After all, everyone has a mother; what was so special about my mama? He said, without hesitation, "What's important about Mena is that she grew—right up until the very end, at age ninety-seven." He rubbed my back in bed.

"How?" I asked over my shoulder.

"Well, for one thing, she opened her heart to a lot of people who had remained outside of it for a long time."

"Who?" I asked, thinking of my brother-in-law whose largess, in my opinion, she had given short shrift for decades. It was a much more complicated story between them, but still, I remembered the last time John had come to see her before she died, Mama opened her eyes and said to him plaintively, "What are we going to do, John?"

Alice and Carol and I quickly left the room to give them the space to do whatever they would do. Later we found out that it was to come clean and make peace with each other.

I admired Mama for that. A lot of people go to their graves holding regrettable resentments and rulings about other people, the tentacles of which can reach far into the future in ruinous ways. But especially because it was hard to think that my mother would choose to die with a hardened heart.

She didn't.

She said her good-byes, thanked Carol and me for being her daughters, and told us she loved us. A lot of my friends didn't get that.

But Art said she did much more than that.

"She opened her heart to me, for one thing, and to Corey, her 'bastard' grandson, born out of wedlock to a daughter she didn't understand. She continued to grow. A lot of people don't do that, Marion. They don't choose to do it. They just close down."

My husband is a long-haired progressive from Indiana, where lineage is less important than it is here in the South. He had ideas he didn't mind saying out loud that provoked and offended Mama. I remembered one ridiculous, but classic, ongoing argument they had about whether his long hair and Jesus's long hair were two different things (as Mama and Carol insisted) or not.

"I think her growing to the very end was good for other people, too—me, for example—but still hard for her," he went on. "Your mother was somewhat of a constitutional feminist, even though she grew up when she did. After your father died, and it was no longer a world of him and her, and she was on her own, she had the freedom—and the necessity—to rethink a lot of issues."

"Like what?" I wanted more.

"Like race, gender, class—the big ones. In the end, she was forced to deal with other people, not only on her terms, but on theirs."

With tenderness, I thought again about The Last Lectures Arthur had single-handedly arranged for Mama at Hillcrest, where for the final time she got to have her say about her dearly beloved Durham and how the city had been nearly a century before.

I thought too about all the people she might have ordinarily shunned, the black people who in those last weeks had ushered Mama about on their arms, walking slowly with her, teasing her gently along the way. Each had been tender and tough with her at the same time, and she had loved them.

"That last year, your mother caught up a little bit in her thinking," my husband continued, "about those bigger issues that are always around us." He paused. "I think having you for a daughter helped."

"How?" I asked, incredulous. "She didn't like how I was."

"Yes, but you took her on. That was important."

I thought about the Stills and Nash song "Teach Your Parents Well." Had I really done that? She certainly had taught me.

One of her last barbs the time we took her home for her birthday, when she hurled insults at all of us for making her sleep in her own bed, was "You're a know-it-all trollop, Marion!"

Trollop. What an old-fashioned word, I remembered thinking, as we hung onto her thrashing little body, the four of us literally carrying her to her bed.

"I took her on, too," Art was saying. "But we really had fun those last years, especially when I went to visit her without you. Then, I wasn't just an appendage. It was just me and her. It was different. We enjoyed each other."

"Tell me about it."

"Oh, we would laugh and tell jokes and then she would ask me things, like what I believed in, and if I just thought she was an old fool."

"What did you say?"

"I said, 'No.' That the fact that she was even asking the question showed she was no fool; that we've all been fools.

"It's easy for us in the Midwest to think Southerners are such racists: the Civil War and slavery and all. But we have our issues with race in the Midwest, too; they're just more hidden. We haven't dealt with race the way people down here have, not really. She liked a good argument." He trailed off. "I respect that."

Art, the inveterate "differences sorter" who even argues with the TV, *would* respect a good argument, I thought.

It was interesting, though, hearing my husband's perspective on Mama, and comforting. We were both seeing her as an individual, divorced from her roles with us, a soul who had come here from somewhere else to birth me and nurture and nettle us both. I was glad he liked her. I liked her too—I, the *know-it-all trollop*, "a woman perceived as sexually promiscuous and disreputable," I read later in the dictionary, though faithfully married to my husband for almost thirty years.

My part in the sixties, my rebellion, my having a child when I wasn't married, messing things up for her with her friends, never really left her.

But it was that bastard child who helped her out of this world, and whom she grew to love and like so deeply. She wanted him there.

I recalled my sister's argument to me as my mother and father's emissary in those days when I was pregnant: that I should get an abortion, that the soul really didn't come in until the third month or some such nonsense, and that she, a right-to-lifer who would absolutely eschew such talk later, had lobbied me so hard for an abortion of that grandchild, the grandchild who took Mama to her last dance.

"What do you think happens to Mama now?" I asked my husband, because just like Mama, I had no idea.

Never one to avoid a meaty topic, he launched right in.

"I think the eternal part, the immaterial part of us, goes on forever, like a light wave," he answered. "There are lots of things that are invisible, but they exist just the same. Scientists have proven that. Mena's just let the cloak go, the rags, and she's out there in the ever-expanding universe. Really smart people think time is a spiral and it's all happening simultaneously."

I sigh. "I can't wrap my head around that, or heaven either."

Life's a mystery, love's complex, and there's no end to it. Someone said that to me once. There is no end to it.

Not even at the end.

Chapter Forty

Flying the Coop

There's always gonna be another mountain
I'm always gonna want to make it move
Always gonna be an uphill battle . . .
Somebody's gonna have to lose
Ain't about how fast I get there
Ain't about what's waiting on the other side.
It's the climb.   —Miley Cyrus

I was writing about Mama full-out now, encouraged by my writing group who agreed I should do it while it was fresh and pressing, as well as by the well-wishes of a lot of folks who sweetly took the time to tell me how much they enjoyed my eulogy at her memorial service, how they hadn't known I could write.

Encouragement was everywhere. There were promises of help from Kelly, the woman who published Mama's last two books. There were so many notes—scribbles, classic "Mena Webb" quotes to get down before I forgot them completely. I was making plans for copies of the video montage at her memorial to go out to friends and family. I felt like a high-level administrator.

I was also having intense fantasies about getting out of Dodge, going while the going was good, flying the coop since Mama had flown it for real. Mama—ethereal now, not just in that cardboard box in the ground, a little of which still resided in a tinier box in my upstairs bedroom waiting for sepulture into the Atlantic. Some of Mama had to go back into Mother Ocean, plain and simple.

Over Memorial Day, my husband and I skipped out to the beach without telling anyone. It was healing there on the aqueous edge of the landmass. I have always gravitated to edges. We made plans to return to our second home in Ecuador in the fall. I found myself late at night scanning Fare Compare for the best prices to all kinds of places. I dreamed of taking Art to Finland, his homeland, or flying to my ancestral home: Scotland. I dreamed of China and Africa. I dreamed about buying an RV and hitting the road for good.

These were daydreams and night dreams. They consumed me. Last night in my sleep, I was already in Ecuador. The sea was blue and shining, the buildings pink and orange. I was with others like me, all from somewhere else, who now chose to spend time on the Pacific coast of Ecuador on this glittering gold and blue day. I woke with my skin feeling bathed in light, every corpuscle loose, unbuttoned, ready to bolt.

Blocked by land and lack of liquid assets, today I decided to bike over to my son's house ten miles away, faithful St. Bernard that I was, bringing him a bit of the hair of the dog in my pannier, three cold pear ales. (He'd Facebooked earlier complaining of a wicked hangover.) It was a destination. A mission! A road trip! To help a member of my family.

This might be a heterodox way of grieving, bike riding and being useful to a family member simultaneously, but it was mine. A two-fer and I could do it. I decided then and there, biking would be my spiritual path.

I pedaled energetically, heading for Dodson's Crossroads, my thighs stinging. It was a long haul, eight miles. By the time I was on Orange Grove Road, I was silently singing the old civil rights song "Step by Step" to spur me on, dry-mouthed, my heart beating wildly on the last hill.

I kept my eyes on the road just beyond the front wheel, no farther, so as not to allow the length of the incline to dissuade me from continuing to pump. Finally, I pushed over the summit for my reward: a two-mile-plus downhill to Corey's turnoff.

All along the down glide, I felt Mama's spirit over me up in the clouds, watching, fully glad that I was enjoying myself, enjoying herself watching me, watching all of us, I imagined. She was free, but she was still choosing to tune in on her babies.

Mama and I talked often about inter-world communication, how we would keep the conversation going. But we never determined just what the "sign" would be: how I would *know* it was she who was giving me the message from the great beyond. (Art recently thought he saw his dead mother in a white snowy owl who landed in front of his desk window, then flew to the treehouse Art built and dropped a feather.)

The wind swirled through my bike helmet. I whizzed past loblolly and cedar, dusty red-clay driveways at high noon, plunging breathlessly onward, releasing the brakes, an eleven-year-old again. I hoped I could stop in time to turn onto Corey's road.

My wheels crunched over the rocks in his driveway. I saw both cars. They were home in their newly purchased bide-a-wee, just starting the Householder stage.

I was going inside no matter what, I told myself. But if I was barging in on their Sunday, I hoped they'd at least mask their irritation. I knocked with my hangover cure in hand. Inside, I heard a lot of running around. Corey opened the door. It was clear: I'd interrupted them.

We sat around their old trunk coffee table, the chitchat awkward. I tried to quickly catch my breath for the ride home, seeing that it needed to be sooner, not later. Still embarrassed and uncertain, I left and pedaled home as fast as I could.

The kids liked having me around, but they were focused on their own lives, mushing on fine without me, thank you very much. I was not necessary, certainly not in the way a daughter is at the end of her mother's life. It was Mama who held me here in Durham, after all, much more than my kids. Caring for her had been exceedingly tiring, but in a way, it had also been nice to be so clearly needed. No ambiguity. No mixed signals.

What would she have done if my sister and I and everyone else hadn't been there for her to wet her lips and squeeze water and soup and Boost and beer into her mouth in those last days? Scratch her back while she moaned, "Up and down," encouraging us. That last day, rubbing cream into her bony shoulders, she had smiled up at me, opened her one good eye, and whimpered in relief. Someone had intuited something to do that would feel good to her, and it had been me.

§

My son called later that night, I thought, at first, to thank me for my gesture.

"Mom," he said at the end, his voice as serious as the grave. I braced myself.

"Please, Mom. Never come over here again on a Sunday morning without calling!"

I was a motherless child. And my children didn't need me. This was a new station for me in life. I was alone on the ice drift.

I searched for the good in the situation.

Though it felt as weird as a mouth full of Novocain, I found it. It was the freedom I was now allowed. I had the freedom to pretty much do whatever I wanted that I could afford and manage by myself.

No one here needed me.

Chapter Forty-One

The Magic of Weymouth

*I have invisible spirit benefactors who believe in me
and who labor alongside me.* —Elizabeth Gilbert

So now it is before me: Six days and nights in December away at
the Weymouth Center for the Arts and Humanities in Southern Pines,
to focus on the Mama book, to focus on Mama.

"Weymouth! Call Sam Ragan, Marion," my sister tells me
excitedly. "Oh, you'll love him, he's such a gentleman, a lovely man, a
newspaper editor. He knew Mother and Daddy well. He could tell you
a lot about Mama, I bet. I love Southern Pines."

§

Leaving the house is a disaster, comings and goings
always hard for my husband and me. The backseat of my car is filled
with boxes and bags and sheets and blankets slung haphazardly
across the seat, a cooler full of food, water bottles, and several bags of
dry goods. I must get there by two o'clock, the acceptance letter reads.
As usual, I have enough stuff with me to run away from home if I want
to, only missing my passport.

I snake through the countryside on two-lane roads and feel my
body and mind unwind as I dip deeper into the sand hills. An hour and
a half later, I am crunching over a gravel lot leading to a lovely,
rambling, white, two-story home with balconies and hip-roofed
dormers, nestled in a garden of azaleas and tulip poplars. The scents
are ambrosial.

Weymouth sits in the middle of a broad, raked winter-grass
lawn circled by firs, hollies, and giant drooping trees. A horse farm lies
to the left. The Weymouth State Park, the old Boyd Woods, acres of
forested horse trails and footpaths, are on the right. Various small
porticos dot the manicured yard.

When I poke my head into the director's office, she says "Oh, your friend Lisa is already upstairs and has your keys. You're the only two here. You'll have the run of the place. Just go 'round back."

Lisa, my writing group pal, is leaning over the fire escape as I trudge in with my first load. "Hey, girl! You made it. Come on up." Her waist-length sandy hair trails over the wrought iron railing like Rapunzel's. She leads me to the Paul Green room, which will be mine for the week.

Curtained around the headboard of my bed is an old-fashioned rose-colored floral drape with matching cloth shades that frame the two windows overlooking the side yard. A love seat is placed against the windows to catch the best light, along with a sizable desk, a chest of drawers, a fireplace, and a large walk-in closet. There's a balcony outside. I click the lights on and off, surprised to find in this old house, they are more than sixty watts, bright enough to write.

I'd envisioned myself crammed into a tiny cell, but I see now that I have more than enough space to hide all my possessions, and multiple vantage points for shifts in perspective. I can fully clear away the detritus of my life and enter the portal of my imagination.

Lisa excitedly shows me around the house. There are so many rooms and nooks and sofas and desks in the writer's residence itself, which is only about an eighth of the mansion. I see I would never have to sit in the same chair twice.

Downstairs, ladies set up for the Christmas party tomorrow in the great room. They are chattering amongst themselves, putting candy canes and candles and Gerbera daisies at each place setting on twelve round tables covered in snowy cloths, white napkins rolled in gold rings.

After Lisa's tour, we settle down in the small writer's kitchen upstairs while I make a sandwich. I'm torn between a nap and a bike ride to both inspect the grounds and limber up my tired bones, another twofer, but decide instead on taking my time to unpack. I explore the Literary Hall of Fame upstairs which we've been told has the best wireless reception. By design, our bedrooms don't.

It takes the rest of the afternoon to unpack. I arrange some pictures of Mama around the room and prop her books on the mantle, the one with her peering out over her glasses looking directly at me. "You're doing it," I hear her saying, smacking her lips with satisfaction.

The James Boyd Library, aka the North Carolina Literary Hall of Fame, is vast, the width of the house. Now it's filled with tables and chairs that are covered with boxes, Christmas baskets, wrapping paper, small artificial trees, ornaments, table decorations, and ribbon. This room obviously doubles as a workspace.

The walls sport full-sized head shots of the North Carolina authors who have been inducted into the Hall of Fame, beginning with Charles Chestnut and Gerald Johnson and ending with Maya Angelou and John Lawson, a man who lived in the early 1700s and wrote *Voyage to Carolina*, along with three present-day authors, the 2012 inductees.

I walk slowly around the room, all these accomplished writers looking down on me and immediately see Mama's teacher and mentor, Manley Wade Wellman, smiling out from a frame. He is sitting on a hay bale in front of a tobacco barn.

I remember Manley, a big, blustery guy, sitting in Mama's living room and holding court with the other members of her writers' group. His picture is just above Inglis Fletcher, the one-time famous historical novelist who bought an old plantation called Blandon outside of Edenton that Mama took me to once, telling me she'd been the "grande ole dame" of North Carolina writers for many decades.

All the North Carolina greats were there: Thomas Wolfe, O' Henry, Paul Green, who I see was a handsome devil, John Hope Franklin, Elizabeth Spencer, Reynolds Price, Lee Smith, and Randall Jarrell, along with many others, plus two pictures of Doris Betts, one young, one old. Mama knew and studied with Doris, her friend.

And there is Mama's dearest playmate and kindred spirit, Fanny Patton—Francis Grey Patton to the world. Mama and Daddy had drinks with Fanny and Louis throughout their adult lives until Fanny died in 2000.

How Mama would have loved to have her mug up in this room. She deserved to be. She was a master in her own right.

In the corner I read that Sam Ragan is also a poet, not only a journalist. There sits a bust of him and all his books. Poetry's hard for me, but I borrow *To The Waters' Edge*, his slimmest volume, to take to my room and read. I see Sam died in 1996. There will be no interview. I remind myself to tell Carol. On the back of the book, I read that he was responsible for Weymouth's salvation. The Sandhills Community

College owned the house but couldn't afford to keep it up. It was slated for demolition. So, Sam bought it.

I am awe-struck in this breathtaking room with the nearness of my mother's spirit saying, "Go, go, do it," in the whispers of the pines outside the windows. It's a happy event that the best internet reception in the house is here, and that I shall have to return in the next six days over and over again to this spirit-filled room.

§

After dinner, Lisa and I take the time to share some personal stories, more than we usually do. I feel that my writer women, even without knowing the details of my life like my other girlfriends might, know me better than anyone, because they see my insides. They hear what I am writing.

Tonight, she and I share some family secrets and resolve to take a trip together in the Westphalia I am intent on buying soon. We clink glasses.

Just before we go to bed, Lisa asks me to walk through the house with her in the dark. "Marion, there are ghosts here. I want to make sure we don't run into one before I retreat to my room." Hers is the Thomas Wolfe Room next door to mine.

"The house is inhabited by strange sounds, voices, cracks, and creaks. Water running. People leave their noises behind, you know," Lisa said. "There was a writer here all by herself once, and she was writing in a chair in the corner of her room, and someone sat down on her lap. It freaked her out so much she left immediately!"

"No shit!"

"Yes, and that is *your* room!"

The rest of the house is unlit. Lisa freezes and whimpers at every corner, holding a flashlight big enough to kill somebody. I tell her I won't go on unless she stops hollering, because it freaks me out. There's no one we can see anyway, so we lock up the writer's residence, and I duck into my room to begin the first long night of rereading what I have so far and chart my course for the next few days.

Before midnight, I fall asleep. I am half way through my review, certain that some pieces about Mama and her life and death are good, some need to be shortened or lengthened, some thrown out altogether. I sleep deeply.

I wake up early and make a cup of coffee. Morning's my best writing time. I am interrupted only once by the sound of women's voices downstairs: the Christmas Party it must be, and then the sweeter, lighter voices of school-aged children singing carols.

Still in my nightgown, I creep to the top of the stairs and sit to listen to a medley of "Jingle Bells," "Rudolph," and "I'm Getting Nuttin' for Christmas." Alongside the applause, I hear the hushed voices of women in the downstairs kitchen. There are so many cookies and cakes within reach at Weymouth that I hasten back to my room to avoid temptation.

§

The next day at lunch, Lisa tells me about John Lawson, one of the 2012 inductees in the NC Writers Hall of Fame. Lawson was a surveyor whom the King of England sent over to America to scout out the scene here, she recounts. He walked from Charleston to Columbia to Charlotte, and then to Hillsborough, turning east toward the Tar River in the dead of winter in 1702. A master of description, he wrote down everything he saw. His was the first substantial account of Indians in the Americas to be sent to the king, the most thorough picture of Native American life—what they ate, did, and thought—ever recorded. He also detailed the flora and the fauna of North Carolina as he followed his Indian guides. In some ways, Lawson used the usual condescending white man's language in his book, Lisa tells me, but his writing also showed a true sensitivity to the Indians, and he admired them. She gives *Voyage to Carolina* for Christmas presents. "It's extremely readable for being three hundred years old. I'll get you one," see tells me. It took Lawson three hundred years to be inducted in the Hall of Fame. Maybe Mama still has a chance!

I don't want to defer my own writing any longer, so I plow on until I finish reading my draft. Then I put on my street clothes at 3 p.m. Delicious. This is exactly the way I want to spend my days.

"Thank you, Mama," I say pulling on a sweater for the bike ride into town. "Thank you, Daddy." I am happy my parents gave me this love of being by myself and telling tales on paper. I am happy they weren't bankers or merchants or all kinds of other perfectly good things to be; that they made their livings with their imaginations, a pencil, and a piece of paper.

I cycle down Broad Street, struck by the pre-Christmas activity that intrudes on this lacuna of space I have provided myself. I am hardly aware of Christmas this year. I think I will make a Christmas tree out of all the old books in my house, books I need to get rid of, stack them up in a narrowing ascension and string lights around them, put a star on top, later offer them as gifts to anyone who wants one. I am a hoarder of good books, bad books, books I might read someday when I am old and housebound. So many excuses I make in order not to get rid of even one.

Southern Pines is full of money. Shops sparkle like beads along both sides of a string that is the railroad track running through its center. Every few hundred feet stands a festively decorated live tree. People on the sidewalk look like my Mama's people in their bright-colored red and blue conservative clothes, fashionable shoes, gold jewelry, and diamonds. The men wear Brooks Brothers suits and tasseled loafers.

I ask directions to the Fresh Market, passing thrift stores along the way, and resolve to reward myself if I get enough writing done tomorrow, return to Fifi's Fine Resale Apparel to see if I can find something wild and baggy and cheap enough for me.

At night I bathe in an antique claw-footed tub, still plowing through a box of Mama's stuff I brought with me. It's such a treasure trove I remain there, reading, until the water grows cold: little snippets of writing that haven't seen the light of day in a long while, assignments from classes she took, a letter from Manley Wade Wellman, one from Fanny Patton, her view of her parents' attitudes toward children, and toward death, musings about growing up in the Victorian age, living in Hope Valley, and what it was like to get old. By ten p.m. I am back in my room, ready again to write.

This is the heaven Mama wanted me to know.

And then I come across this written in Mama's own hand:

The longer I live, the more beautiful plain, ordinary things become.

I look at the lamp on my work desk, the one I had made out of a gallon bottle that once held Canadian Club Whiskey, and it is a remarkably handsome thing . . . the dark brown bottle, solid and sturdy, with its elegant label describing the merits of Hiram Walker and Sons' own brand of spirits and announcing that they supplied, by appointment, three kings and one queen with Canadian Club: Victoria, Edward VII, George V and George VI all had it in their cellars and, presumably, served it with an appreciation for the finer things in life.

Hiram Walker and Sons, Limited . . . that name adds dignity and class to this pine paneled room where I work. I look at the lamp and think: It will be there after I'm dead and gone, and it will please somebody else—I wonder who—who will like the shape of it and the monks' cloth shade and the natural wood base?

And maybe somebody will appreciate the fact that instead of throwing an old empty liquor bottle away, I saw it, in my mind's eye, shedding lovely golden light over me as I type, and with the help of a craftsman, I changed it into an interesting part of my life, something I see and touch every day, something that helps me, something that brings light into my darkness.

I can't help but wonder what old Hiram Walker would think of my lamp, not to mention their majesties: Victoria, Edwards and the two Georges.

I know what *I* think.

I think that without even knowing the lamp was anything but the largest whiskey bottle I had ever seen, I redeemed it — grabbed it on impulse on my way out of Mama's room during one of my trips after she died to collect her writing. I vow that as soon as I get home, I will move it upstairs to my writing room. I will benefit from knowing how Mama felt about this lamp. It will illuminate my late-night writing until the day one of my own creative children can claim it for their own after I die. The beauty of things well loved.

My time here at Weymouth is a vault to the life I was meant to live.

Chapter Forty-Two

Getting Old

Death finishes nothing. Death begins the harvest—the harvest of pain, of administration, of clerical work. And the gradual transformation of a difficult parent into a demi-saint. Scratch demi. Parents get nobler and nobler after they die. They also get funnier and more endearing.
They come to deserve your desperate love.
—Erica Jong

Last night, Art and I watched a video his surgeon had given him about hip operations, a presage to his in a few weeks. While intending to be upbeat and reassuring, the video was sobering. Art finally realized that no, he will not be back in the saddle in three weeks' time. And I was busy planning everything I wanted and needed to do beforehand, because nothing much else but caring for him would be happening afterwards. Already I was getting up earlier to write and do my ablutions. Art happily let me "practice" doing all the dishes.

My own hip operations had started years ago, brought on by a bike spill and a cracked femoral head followed by necrosis—bone death. A year later I got a new ball-joint.

I told myself mine was just the result of an untimely accident, but watching Arthur hobble around, as well as seeing my drooping neck, new "freckles" and "laugh lines" appearing every day out of nowhere, there was no denying it. I was getting old. Even my once age-proof, girl-like legs had traded their beauty for puckering skin and baggy knees.

Of course, it was "young-old," I soothed myself. Plenty of time left to do all the things I wanted to do. Even with the dreaded diagnosis of macular degeneration two months ago, the same thing Mama had, I could see fine with glasses now. And to prove it, I did indeed buy an old Westphalia, a well-kept pop-up Volkswagen van, and pressed the timeline of my longed-for life on the road forward. Ah, traveling, seeing new things, meeting new people, recapturing my youth, or at least some of the freedom of my youth. It beckoned me more vigorously now.

"Taking care of the ole body simply has to be fit into the schedule, Marion," I said to myself out loud. "Otherwise, you'll just collapse like a mushroom returning to the earth. Get up! Hup: one, two, three."

I thought of Trotsky's quote that "Old age is the most unexpected thing that can happen to a person."

§

Just yesterday at my granddaughter's Tumble Gym birthday party, my son Tom kindly pointed me and my clunky shoes to a cubby on the top. "So, you don't have to bend down so low, Ma."

"Keep it up," I smiled at him, relieved he was even aware of such things.

I remembered Mama on the subject one Thursday just before she fell.

"Getting old is boring to the young, even the middle-aged, who still think they're young. No one but other old people want to spend a second on it," she'd said. "They are still sucking in their stomachs, ignoring the dappling of their skin, buying new outfits and expensive exercise machines, reading *Men's Fitness* on the toilet, playing pick-up basketball, and eating all the pork they can stuff in their faces."

It was true. Today, my thirty-something son was sky diving. He wrote his father a "secret" e-mail telling him what to do in case of his untimely demise, and a casual "I love you all." Death seemed so far away to him.

For sure, life is meant to be lived, and taking risks is an important part of living. *Nothing ventured, nothing gained* had been my motto all my life. So, jump, my son, I thought to myself, wishing it were me he had written.

Still, I noticed I was paying more attention to where I stepped these days. My mother had a friend who died after a three-inch fall off a simple curb. *Look before you leap* had merit too.

Last night in bed, as my husband was snoozing to my right, I was wide awake. (I wasn't sleeping as much as I used to; something to do with the Long Sleep, maybe?) I was listening on my computer to Thich Nhat Hanh in a discourse he called *Meditating on the Body*.

"No one gets out of this life alive," the Buddha taught. "The way to get out of the world of birth and death is to meditate on your body and see the four elements: water, air, earth, heat, that are also outside of you. Here, you touch the world of no birth and no death; you touch the kingdom of God.

"When you look into your body this way, you also see your ancestors. They continue with you into the future in every cell. … Our ancestors expect us to live our lives in a way that can help them continue to be nourished and loved, even continue to be liberated. They didn't get it all done when they were here either. And they're not really gone. So, say to them, 'You are my ancestors, and I accept you as you are.' Thinking this way will free us from thinking we are a separate self. Because we're not."

I resolved that today when I walked mindfully, I would walk for my mother. I would walk for my father.

During our "bed time"—more important these days because in three weeks' time, my husband will not be able to sit up, turn ten degrees without help, and will be wearing white compression stockings to prevent thrombosis—I am brought into the present by Arthur's gentle ministrations. Still, my thoughts returned to the aging process. What do I really know? I ask myself, staring above his shoulder out the windows into the gray blanket of clouds that swaddle the day.

I'm periodically able to light in the present, like now with Arthur. Thank God for sex and hugging, for bodily intimacies of every kind, even going to the bathroom, things that stop the thinking process. The here and now.

I reached out for my husband.

But again, my eyes returned to the sky.

"This doesn't look like such a great day for a jump," I mumbled.

Art raised his head. "Nope."

"Sure would rather he jump on a sunny day."

"Yep."

"That's gotta be scary. Going through those clouds."

"Oh, they won't be jumping through those clouds," he said.

"I wouldn't be so sure. They have to get high enough for the chute to open."

I remember descending through clouds like this, only about 1000 feet up, over many an airport.

"I bet they will fly above the clouds," I protested. "It'll be hard not to see where you're going."

My husband didn't argue.

My son was at the age where he thought he knew a lot. The two older children were beginning to suspect they didn't know too much. And I *knew* there was not much I knew anymore, as well as how big the gap was, anyway, between knowing and being.

I was free-falling. Through the clouds. Not sure where I might end up. The frailty of the human condition.

§

I remembered Mama in her last days, clinging to life but losing weight, little interest in eating.

I'd better learn to love drinking like she did, I told myself, so I can at least get a hit of the "sauce" with my pink mouth sponges, a last mind-altering escape from the serious business of dying. Is it serious? Or is it just "me" dissolving into the bigger me along with everybody else who's dead?

I imagine myself slipping away, unable to see, aware of how little I have to offer anybody anymore, my few remaining verbal skills dissipating, trying to smile, clutching the hands of visitors.

Will I even have visitors? I was unable to imagine my children willingly taking time out of their busy lives for some old dying person. Even their mother. Maybe, especially, their mother. I felt essential to my grandchildren's lives, but often peripheral to my children's. Would they make me feel guilty? Or give me their allotted thirty minutes and then run out shouting, "Time's up!"

Still, this getting old shit somehow empowered me to be whatever I wanted, too. Now. If I was gonna kick out of here pretty soon, I wanted to do some stuff. I no longer had to be afraid of failing, afraid of what other people thought about me.

Mama had said it one day: "I couldn't conceive of ever being like Papa and Mama. I felt sorry for them. They worked and worried and never seemed to be having any fun. Mama even fretted over meals, what she was going to have, and then when it was on the table, she talked about whether it was cooked right or not. Not long after supper, they said they were tired and went to bed. Poor things. They were old, but I'd never be that way."

"It kinda sneaks up on you, doesn't it?" I agreed.

"Even when you and Carol used to ask me how I felt, and I'd say, 'Not too well' or 'Oh, I guess I'm all right . . . just tired,' and you'd get this look on your faces—the same blank expression I'm sure Papa and Mama witnessed on mine. I could have told you that I don't really feel old inside, in my spirit—that I feel exactly the way I've always felt *inside*. It's just my body that's tired and getting old. But that look of incomprehension would still be there, because there's no way to bridge the gap. Not then. You thought your skin would never get soft and wrinkled, and that your slim little waists would never thicken. You'd never feel sad because life was flying by and you hadn't had time to do everything you wanted to."

"Well, that stage is long past," I said, patting my belly.

She continued as if I hadn't spoken. "Youth blinds you, and it's a good thing. We need blinders at times. I wish I had some now. You let feeling take over and possess you. Even sadness, being miserable, is good when you're young. Sorrow has a kind of beauty; it's all of a piece, and you are in it, instead of it being in you."

"Yeah . . ."

"But later on, you try to temper all that emotion because it's uncomfortable if it's too strong. Better to be lukewarm than to burn with too bright a flame. You'd rather be comfortable. It's a little like being in a harness. You feel the traces on either side, and they keep you in the middle of the road where it's safe, away from the ditches and the deep embankments—the wide, open, scary stretches that could lead anywhere."

I was only partially following.

"Sometimes, I wonder how I got on this safe, straight road to death. When did I cross the invisible line between young and old? At what moment, exactly, did I discover that strong feeling was bad on my heart and my blood pressure, that peace of mind was the be-all and end-all of living? When did I decide that cooking the meat just right was all-important? It seems like when you leave youth behind, you should at least know it. There ought to be a requiem of some kind. A demarcation. When you care more about cooking the meat just right than you care about how many people are starving all over the world or how a black man feels when somebody calls him Nigger, you at least ought to know when you changed."

§

Nonetheless, I remembered looking forward to the time when I was a little old lady ever since I was quite young. I could see the freedom in it. I pictured myself in a shapeless dress with a knot of hair at the nape of my neck, happy, saying anything I wanted to say without approbation.

But I could no longer wait 'til I was *ready*. I had to be ready now. The world was still my oyster for just a little while longer.

Before I finally went back to sleep, I recalled the Five Remembrances of the Buddha.

> *I am of the nature to grow old. . .. to have ill health*
> *. . . not to escape death.*
> *All that is dear to me, and everyone I love, is of the*
> *nature to change. There is no way to escape being*
> *separated from them.*
> *My actions are my only true belongings. I cannot*
> *escape the consequences of my actions.*
> *My actions are the ground upon which I stand.*

So, what I did with each day was all important. My actions had ripples. In fact, if Thich was right, I might still be holding my ancestors up, just as they were holding me. The ripples might go all the way up to heaven. I felt the thinness of the veil that separated me from Mama.

When I woke up the next morning, I was no longer thinking about the other side. I was thinking about the road, the open, scary stretches that could lead me anywhere. Delicious. I felt like running away from home. My blood was rushing. In my mind, I was already gone, gone, gone.

Arthur was still asleep. I slipped out of bed and dressed quickly for an early morning walk. Outside the day was cold and bright. I saw my breath in front of my face. I inhaled deeply and set out.

"Do you feel it, Mama?" I asked.

"Today, I am walking mindfully: for you, Mama, for us. I'll be with you in the ether before you know it, as you are here in me.

"I am already there."

Chapter Forty-Three

Into the Deep

Something unknown is doing we don't know what.
—Sir Arthur Eddington

The day before we scattered my mother's ashes in the Atlantic Ocean was a mix of sun and clouds, not hot, not cold; the mood inside our cottage variable: the granddaughters squabbling, arguments ensuing about what the children would be fed for breakfast.

My son was on his iPad, fixated on property values, the housing slump, and his lifelong dream of owning a house at Topsail. My daughter was restless about her job, her child, her life. Only unflappable Jack, the boy born with equanimity, seemed to rise above it all, playing with this and that toy, smiling amiably, finding ways to entertain himself.

My husband had returned to the Triangle for work. I was left alone with my books and my writing, which I hadn't touched in my all-consuming Oma role, plus a little of Mama's ashes.

"There's only one more day to do it," I told myself and her, staring at the tiny, unadorned box on my bedside table, the one I'd been given as a keepsake after the rest of her went into the ground at St. Matthew's. It had long been a promise, both to her and to myself, that we would return Ma to Mother Ocean when the time came. And the time was now.

I called a number from a billboard in Surf City to rent a boat for noon the next day.

"It'll just take about an hour," I suggested.

"Yes. A hundred dollars or whatever you can give," they told me.

"We're doing it tomorrow," I announced to the kids. To the grandkids, it was just a boat ride.

They looked up, bored, inaudibly groaning, as if to say, "Oh, here goes our Mama with her crazy notions," and returned quickly to whatever they'd been doing.

I would not be neglecting Mama in death, I thought, just as I had tried not to neglect her in life, especially during those last years that stretched into a decade because she had the "longevity gene," and then the last six months at Hillcrest where she was bereft because the end was closer and she had not managed to avoid the dreaded nursing home.

The burden of caring for her was also a joy. It gave a purpose to my days. It was what good people did, and I would be a good person, I told myself. It was what I would have wanted. This would be my last official act.

§

The day of the scattering rose cold and rainy. Before the others were awake, I peered out the window at the empty sky, and knew if I wasn't resolved, I would be driving back on I-40 with Mother's cremains in the passenger seat. Cap'n Edwards told me they could go rain or shine, as they had a large enclosed cabin and room for all of us inside, so I sat before my computer and looked up things to say on www.ashes-to-the-deep. I wanted something short and secular, because nobody but me would probably be standing out in the rain deep-sixing Mama. My little assemblage was "spiritual but not religious," and the grandkids didn't need to know what was going on. There was worry it would freak them out, though I clearly remembered knowing such things as a small child, and both my granddaughters had talked straight with me, out of the earshot of their parents, about Mimi dying.

Julie was curious about where she had gone. Mena Claire, Mama's namesake, already a budding scientist, was immediately interested in telling me that Mama was now just bones and she wanted to see them, though what was in the box more closely resembled kitty litter.

I went upstairs and started preparing the picnic for the boat, frying bacon for the BLTs, deviling eggs. I'd bought a key lime pie at the Gift Box earlier, and stuffed paper plates and cups and utensils in a bag, smiling at the others as they came up the stairs. The grandkids were oblivious, but my children looked at me as if I had lost my mind. There were many comments sprinkled throughout the morning about the crappy weather and the advisability of the whole endeavor that I steadfastly ignored, telling them what Cap'n Edwards had told me, and assuring them it would be "fine." We were to meet the Topsail Belle behind the Breezeway Motel on the sound at noon. They returned to their doings and devices, depressed.

I snuck downstairs and walked outside to feel the rain, finding it steady but light and not too cold. "A mere mist," I told myself. Surely, we can handle a mist for Mama. There would be no more beach trips this year, not with this many family members in tow, and Mama would have wanted some kind of private good-bye, though she, too, would've probably thought that unloading her in the Atlantic on a day like this was "some fool thing Marion thought up." This was true. Sheer cussedness.

"Right to the end, Mama," I said to myself. "I may as well stay in character."

As the families gathered in their cars, I alone in front with my bright bravado and the others traveling behind me, the sun came out. Just briefly, but it did. It was an omen, I thought, honking happily and pointing up to the sky for the others, whose dirges I could almost feel through the steel skin of my Prius. Then the rain, ever so slightly, began again.

When our entourage pulled up to the pier at the end of Channel Boulevard, the clouds parted once again (sign #2) allowing our little party, all bundled up in hats and raincoats, to embark without incident, the "grands" skipping happily down the ramp for their promised boat ride. My children feigned smiles: "Let's do this thing!" We all got on the boat to hearty welcomes from Pete, the first mate, who would be our guide and protector while the captain manned the boat.

We put the kids in life vests. Jack ran around on the back deck exploring, with his father grabbing for him and calling "Jack, Jack" every second. The little girls settled more cautiously on the interior seats, side by side holding hands, their mothers clucking over them. I went to the makeshift table and began to assemble the sandwiches, handing everyone a deviled egg to curb their hunger before the boat launched.

The Belle started up and the Cap'n throttled us forward, while Tom sat on the cooler in the stern, admonishing Jack. Then Tom's smile grew brighter as he chatted amiably with Pete, someone other than his mother to deal with.

I don't remember much of it, except going in and out of the cabin, finding it was raining again, the first mate talking on and on, and everyone eating. Tom was being "the man" and no one was crying. We motored slowly along the waterway.

The water grew choppier as we neared the ocean, and then choppier still. We all hung on and chatted and listened as the engine roared louder and louder. The seas up ahead looked darker and darker. Waves whapped against the sides of the boat. The Cap'n's visage was severe.

The first mate continued to talk. This relaxed us. Finally, the Cap'n shouted, "We're almost to the Atlantic!" I looked out the windshield of the cabin, and saw a squally, uneven mess where the ocean met the sound. I heard the motor groaning to get over the waves. Fifteen feet on the other side, he hollered, "Now!"

I took Mama in her little box out to the stern on the port side where the boat tilted out of the water about a foot, and there was another break in the rain (Sign #3). Tom came with me. I reached in my pocket for the sticky notes I often used to capture Mama's colorful language. This morning, I'd copied on them what I was going to say:

> We commit the earthly remains of
> Wilhelmena Katherine Fuller Webb
> To the deep.
> "Ashes to ashes, dust to dust.
> From water all life arises,
>
> Mother of waters, father of rain,
> You have taken back your own.
> As a stream flows into the river,
> As a river flows into the sea,
> May her spirit flow
> To the waters of healing,
> To the waters of rebirth."

It was by Anonymous, which I thought just right. The boat lurched and the engine was bellyaching. I fumbled with the box and barely got it open. I tilted it slightly sideways when an angry gale took Mama out and blew her back in my face.

Then she was gone.

"Bye, Mama," was all I got out. "Bye."

Later, when I told this story to Cookie, a friend of my sister's, and described how I should have been on the other side of the boat and paid attention to how the wind was blowing—that Mama's ashes flew back in my face, challenging me, uncooperative, violating me literally with her bones in my mouth—she laughed and said, "I've heard that from other people. It happens a lot with burials at sea."

What I heard from Mama was, "Your problem is you never admit when you are wrong, Marion."

"Off the same bolt of cloth as you, Mama," I said back to her.

"Flying in the face of logic and common sense," she clicked her tongue, "taking those little children, and poor Tom, out onto a boat in weather like that to do that fool thing!"

But what I also heard in the wind at my back on our return to shore was:

"Bye, bye, baby," and several times her deep, unfeigned gratitude saying:

"Thank you, Marion. Thank you."

Afterword

"Whickery as a Nanny Shad"
by Tom Krueger

I'm whickery like a nanny shad
I'm not feeling too good. I'm not feeling too bad
If I seem a little seldom
Well, I guess I'm a tad whickery
Like a nanny shad.

My automobile wasn't feeling too good
So, I asked Mr. Melvin to look under the hood
After nine hundred dollars and a pain in the rear
Mr. Melvin proclaimed that the problem was clear.
He said, "It's whickery like a nanny shad.
It's not feeling too good. It's not feeling too bad.
A new alternator might help it a tad.
It's just whickery, like a nanny shad."

Well, I saw my physician just the other day
'cause I had a suspicion that I had a malaise.
I said, "Please dear doctor, don't you pull out the rug."
He said, "Don't worry, honey, all you need is a hug.
You're just whickery, like a nanny shad.
You're not feeling too good. You're not feeling too bad.
It's not the epizootics or the East Asian rag.
You're just whickery, like a nanny shad."

I suppose my disposal done give up the ghost.
My toaster is coastin'—won't toast me no toast.
My damn dishwasher is in need of repair

And my freezer is frozen, won't freeze me no air.
I guess they're whickery, like a nanny shad.
They ain't feeling too good. They ain't feeling too bad.
Well, my kettle won't settle
'Cause it's feeling a tad whickery, like a nanny shad.

Well, I cast me a ballot for the democracy
'Cause I had it up to here with the hypocrisy.
When the tallies were totaled and the winner declared,
I could see that the country was in a state of despair.
It's just whickery like a nanny shad.
It's not feeling too good. It's not feeling too bad.
If you're hanging onto hope like a dangling chad,
You're just whickery, like a nanny shad
If you're feeling more than "foin" it's just a frivolous fad.
We're all whickery, whickery, whickery,
Like a nanny shad.

Bibliography

Wilhelmena Katherine Fuller Webb's books

The Curious Wine (out of print)

Jule Carr: General Without an Army

Out of My Mind (out of print)

The Way We Were: Remembering Durham

Marion Webb OMalley's books

Dealing with Differences: A Training Manual for Young People and Adults in Interpersonal Relations. Diversity and Multicultural Education (out of print)

Shopping with Mama: Write 'Til the End

Two Dates A Week: Rekindling the Spark with Art Scherer

NOTE: Marion has some copies of each book listed as out of print. If you would like a copy, please email her at marionwomalley@gmail.com

Acknowledgments

I gratefully acknowledge my supporters, especially my writing-group pals: Becky Bostian. Lisa Neal, Donna Gulick, Virginia Chambers, Sharon Rothspan Kurtzman, Laurie King Billman, and others who are now far flung.

To all the folks at the Weymouth Center for the Arts and Humanities, my refuge on so many writing retreats, and to my fellow scribblers there: Christina Askounis, Pat Reviere-Seel, Krista Bremer, Melissa Seligman, Kelly Mustian, Dana Wynne Lindquist, Dina Greenberg, Dawn Reno Langley, and again Lisa Neal, who stimulated and supported me.

To my editors extraordinaire: Liz Brown, Dina Greenberg, Becky Bostian, Kirsten Krueger, Dawn Reno Langley (who also became my writing coach), my writing group gals again, and my sweet husband, Art Scherer, who has been my writing champion from the word "go." Each of them made my writing better with their encouragement and their careful eyes and ears.

To Juanita Wrenn at Wrennworks, who executed this stunning cover design, and to Betsy Lash, and, again, Juanita for assisting and designing the photo insert.

To my three kids, Tom and Kirsten Krueger and Corey OMalley, who I'm quite sure have their own versions of events, as well as of their Granny and Mama. Thank you, Tom, for the song: "Whickery as a Nanny Shad." All of these kids have amazing writing chops of their own. Let's keep the thing going!

To my grandchildren, Jack and Julie, Mena (Mama's namesake), and Maeve and Harrison. They give so much joy and meaning to my life. Someday soon I hope you will read about your grandmother and great grandmother.

To my sister, Carol, who lived this life with me, and was a lifelong ally, as well as a formidable counterpoint.

And to all the friends and family of my Mama: Mena Fuller Webb, who urged me to finish the book and told me they couldn't wait to read it.

Finally, I acknowledge Mama, who hovers over now, nagging me to get this damn book out!

Progeny

Jack Henry Krueger, Harrison Rae OMalley,
Julia Kate Krueger, Mena Claire LaVelle,
Katherine Maeve OMalley - all three girls
with one of Mama's names

About the Author

Marion OMalley was born into a family where both of her parents wrote for fun and profit. Growing of age in the sixties in the South, her interests in diversity and nonviolent communication led to a thirty-year career in peace education. She started the NC Center for Peace Education in 1984, served on the board of Educators for Social Responsibility, and received the country's first National Grassroots Citizen Peacemaker Award.

Marion has published in *The Sun* as well as several international magazines. She wrote a quarterly newsletter, *PeaceTalks* for seventeen years, and co-authored *Dealing with Differences: A Training Manual for Young People and Adults in Intergroup Relations, Diversity and Multicultural Education.* She and her husband, Art Scherer, recently collaborated on the Amazon bestseller, *Two Dates A Week: Rekindling the Spark.* Marion lives in the woods and is currently writing full time. She has two novels in progress.

Shopping With Mama: Write 'Til the End is her first memoir, in which she humorously describes how she utilized her peacemaking skills with her diametrically opposite mother, author Mena Webb, for more than a decade.

Made in the USA
Columbia, SC
17 July 2022

63601546R00171